Something to Hide

Something to Hide

The Life of Sheila Wingfield, Viscountess Powerscourt

Penny Perrick

THE LILLIPUT PRESS
DUBLIN

First published 2007 by
The Lilliput Press
62–63 Sitric Road, Arbour Hill
Dublin 7, Ireland
www.lilliputpress.ie

ISBN 978 1 84351 093 2

A CIP record for this title is available
from The British Library.

1 3 5 7 9 10 8 6 4 2

Set in 11.5 on 14.2 pt Granjon
Printed in England by MPG Books, Bodmin, Cornwall

Contents

Acknowledgments // vii
Introduction // ix

1. Secrets and Lies // 3
2. Departures // 16
3. A Masquerade // 27
4. Married to the Descendancy // 35
5. Burning with Ambition // 46
6. Mrs Wingfield and Mr Yeats // 58
7. On a Pink Beach // 69
8. In Golden Fetters // 79
9. Bad Behaviour // 88
10. An Evasive Autobiography // 96
11. Ways of Escape // 107
12. The Unrelenting Day // 115
13. Writing on the Wall // 123
14. Ireland's in the Way // 133
15. La Contessa // 142
16. An Unreliable Memoir // 156
17. A Poetic Revival // 167
18. A Frightened Creature // 175
19. Miss Wingfield Gets Her Way // 184
20. Last Things // 192
21. Afterwards // 200

A Selection of Sheila Wingfield's Poetry // 205
Notes // 221
Sources and Select Bibliography // 227
Index // 231

ACKNOWLEDGMENTS

It would have been difficult, if not impossible, to have written this book without the help of two of Sheila Wingfield's children: Grania and Guy, who answered questions for months on end, showered me with letters and photographs and generously allowed me to disrupt their lives. David Pryce-Jones, Sheila's literary executor and Peter Hetherington and Philip Prettejohn, Sheila's financial advisers, allowed me access to her papers. Sheila's granddaughters, Miranda Markes, Atalanta Pollock and Georgina Wallace; her godchildren, Deirdre Pegg and Guy Beddington; her former daughter-in-law, Wendy Watson; David Wingfield and Jocelyn Wingfield, the family archivist, all gave me invaluable help.

I would also like to thank the following. In England: Jean Archibald, Isobel Armstrong, Neil Astley, Colin Bardgett, Charlotte Berry, Richard Bland, Elizabeth Bonython, Lord Brabazon of Tara, Major A. Brady, John Byrne, Roy Clements, the late Alan Clodd, William Corke, Jacqueline Cowdrey, Naomi Cream, Malcolm C. Davis, Tania Earnshaw, Mick Felton, R.F. Foster, Jessica Gardner, Charlie Gladstone, Victoria Glendinning, Philip Goodman, John Gross, Angela Gustafsson, His Honour Judge Christopher Hordern QC, Frank A.L. James, John Jones, John Kelly, Peter Kemp, Caroline Kenward, Francis King CBE, Ian A. Laker, Antonia Leak, Hermione Lee, Mark Le Fanu, Christopher Maclehose, Eileen Marston, Derwent May, Nicholas R. Mays, Martha Mehta, Robin Morgan, Robin Newell, Sir John Nutting, Caroline Oates, Terence Pepper, the late Kathleen Raine, Deryn Rees-Jones, George Regal, Simon Rendall, Bruno Rotti, Basil and Linda Samuels, John Saumerez-Smith, Miranda Seymour, Christopher Sheppard, the Society of Authors,

Stephen Stuart-Smith, Mrs James Teacher, Steven Tomlinson, Catherine Wilbery.

In Ireland: the staff of the National Library of Ireland, in particular Tom Desmond. Also: Christopher Ashe, Turtle Bunbury, Alex Davis, Margaret Dunne, Antony Farrell, Alex Findlater, Desmond FitzGerald, Anne Fogarty, the Rev. Andrew Grimason, Joan Kavanagh, Marie Kennedy, Joan McBreen, Joy McCormack, Elizabeth, Countess of Meath, Stanley Monkhouse, the Earl of Mount Charles, Richard Murphy, Robert Nye, Robert O'Byrne, Raymond Refausse, Tim and Mairead Robinson, the Earl of Roden, K.C. Rohan, Sarah Slazenger, the Rev. Chancellor A.E. Stokes, Caroline Sweeney.

In the USA: the angelic archivists: Elizabeth L. Garver at the Harry Ransom Humanities Research Center, University of Texas at Austin; Gina L.B. Minks at the Department of Special Collections, McFarlin Library, The University of Tulsa; Mr and Mrs William C. Cawley.

Particular thanks are due to my editor Fiona Dunne, to Kate Fraser for typing the manuscript and to Gerard Hill for the index.

PERMISSIONS

The author gratefully acknowledges permission from the following sources to reprint material in their control: The Enitharmon Press for permission to publish Sheila Wingfield's poetry; the Estate of Sheila Wingfield; the University of Exeter for the A.L. Rowse Papers; the Rebecca West Papers, Department of Special Collections, McFarlin Library, the University of Tulsa; *Letters on Poetry from W.B. Yeats* (1986) by permission of Oxford University Press; Harry Ransom Humanities Research Center at the University of Texas at Austin, for letters to Lady Ottoline Morrell.

The author has made every effort to contact the owners of copyrighted material. So that changes can be made in later printings, omissions or errors should be called to the attention of The Lilliput Press, 62–63 Sitric Road, Arbour Hill, Dublin 7, Ireland.

AUTHOR'S NOTE

Unless otherwise stated, direct quotations attributed to Sheila Wingfield are taken from her three memoirs, *Real People* (1952), *Sun Too Fast* (1974), written as Sheila Powerscourt and *Ladder to the Loft* (1987).

INTRODUCTION

Hardly anyone, nowadays, has heard of Sheila Wingfield (1906–1992) or read her poetry. She was once famous as the wife of Viscount Powerscourt, owner of one of the grandest estates in Ireland. As a poet, her work was praised by W.B. Yeats and James Stephens, among others, but is now largely forgotten. I hadn't heard of her either until I bought a glass bowl in a Connemara junk shop, whose owner wrapped my purchase in an old copy of the *Sunday Independent*. A short poem in the crumpled paper caught my eye because I saw in it my own name, Penelope. It was called 'Odysseus Dying':

> I think Odysseus, as he dies, forgets
> Which was Calypso, which Penelope,
> Only remembering the wind that sets
> Off Mimas, and how endlessly
> His eyes were stung with brine;
> Argos a puppy, leaping happily;
> And his old Father digging round a vine.

I liked the instant intimacy of that 'I think ...' and then the reasonable but original conclusion that to a dying man, even a hero, the memory of women in his life dissolves into a mishmash. Those short lines shimmer with an inventive undeludedness, and, like all the best poetry, are both accessible and mysterious. Sheila Wingfield's poems, I discovered, often referred to Homeric characters but she treated them as though they were ordinary people with whom she was quite well-acquainted. This is perhaps how she thought of them, for she was a lonely girl who taught herself

Greek; she knew more about Odysseus and Hector and Helen than the people she lived among. She believed that reading was 'much better than making a new friend – it is living extra lives'.

'Odysseus Dying' had appeared in the *Sunday Independent* as part of an interview which the ageing Viscountess Powerscourt had given to the RTÉ producer Anne Roper some years before Sheila's death in 1992. It was republished to coincide with the opening of Powerscourt to the public in 1997 and was accompanied by photographs of the mansion and its grounds and of the young Sheila, a serious beauty. The story which she had told Anne Roper in 1987 was about her struggle to be a poet despite every discouragement from her husband, Pat Wingfield. Pat was the story's villain; according to his wife he was an illiterate philistine who, in the early days of their marriage in 1932, after sampling a literary salon, extracted from Sheila a promise never to mix with such 'literary scum' again. This promise, she insisted, condemned her to a life of literary isolation and, after Pat inherited Powerscourt at the end of the Second World War, to the lofty duties of an aristocratic chatelaine, so that she was able to write only between the hours of 3 and 7 am. She sounded like a fascinating, if garrulous, woman but also, if 'Odysseus Dying' was typical of her work, a very fine poet.

The fact that she had been a highly unusual mistress of Powerscourt also had something to do with my decision to write a biography of this intriguing woman. I had always been fascinated by the Irish Big House, both through its fiction – Elizabeth Bowen, Somerville and Ross – and through visiting the actual buildings. The first thing I discovered was that nearly all of Sheila's babbling disclosures to Anne Roper were figments of her imagination. Not for nothing was Sheila Wingfield the great-great-niece of Mary Elizabeth Braddon (1837–1915), creator of the Victorian 'sensation novel'. In her correspondence throughout her life, Sheila consistently reinvented her past. These inventions came late in her career, after Pat's death, after which she could say what she liked about him. When she first began to publish poetry, her marriage to Pat wasn't perceived as an obstacle to her being a poet. Rather, it allowed her to be the darling of both the gossip columns and the literary journals and to be a glamorous aristocrat as well as a gifted poet, as can be seen in this unconsciously condescending item printed under the heading, 'Hon. M. Wingfield's Poetess Wife', from the Dublin *Evening Mail* of 18 October 1938:

A London firm announces early publication of a volume of poetry by Sheila Beddington, [sic] young wife of the Hon. Mervyn Wingfield son and heir of Viscount Powerscourt. The poetess is the mother of two children.

Being remarkably photogenic, she was catnip to the Irish newspapers, which proceeded to fill their pages with photographs of the smouldering beauty, exquisitely turned out on the hunting field, or snuggled into expensive furs. 'Miss Beddington is very good-looking', they commented, on announcing her engagement. Her fashionable and extensive wardrobe suggested that the good-looking Miss Beddington was also extremely rich. At some stage prior to the publication of her first book, Sheila decided not to write under her maiden name and it was as Sheila Wingfield, the 'poetess wife' that she brought out *Poems*, a month after the *Evening Mail's* report. The book, whose flyleaf carried praise from Walter de la Mare, James Stephens and W.B. Yeats, was well received. The novelist and critic Hugh Walpole wrote in his *Daily Express* column that 'this costs only three and sixpence, and one day this slim volume may be precious indeed on your shelves'. A mistaken prediction. Although Sheila Wingfield went on to write seven more collections of poetry and was regarded by the poet Kathleen Raine as a leading poet of her generation, her work has been 'lost in an all-enveloping obscurity', as the contemporary academic, Anne Fogarty of University College, Dublin, an admirer of Sheila's poetry, has noted.

I wanted to find out why Sheila Wingfield's poetry has been so forgotten and, as my researches carried me further into her elaborate concealments, I also wanted to discover what it was that she refused to remember. For here was a woman who gave everyone the slip, who reinvented her ancestry and wrote three sparkling, anecdotal memoirs. These told you a lot about the people she knew and almost nothing about herself. John Betjeman, in his genial preface to the first of these evasive books, *Real People* (1952), called it 'a new kind of autobiography, a selfless one'. It would have been hard for Sheila to have written any other kind, since her sense of self was unreliable. An addiction to deception was ingrained in early childhood and she seemed to find it almost impossible to live her life, only to play it, as though it were a role that she had written for herself. Thus it was inevitable that she became a writer, a profession which the poet Simon Armitage calls 'a form of disappearance'. Sheila, tending to go to extremes, took her vanishing act too far, which may be one of the reasons why her poetry is, again in Anne Fogarty's words, 'obdurately irretrievable'.

As well as striving always to conceal her Jewish ancestry, Sheila tried hard to conceal other addictions, to drug-taking and alcohol. The drugs and booze were to muffle pain, caused by a mysterious illness that remained undiagnosed throughout her life and by the mental anguish that was the price she paid for the grim game of bluff played with herself and others. There never seemed to be a time when she could be open about who she was, or what she wanted to be. She had determined to be a poet from the age of six, but reading was discouraged during her childhood. This led to the first of her many deceptions: sneaky visits to the bookcases in her parents' gloomy London house; she claimed that her 'fear of being discovered only intensified this secret pleasure'. From then on, concealment became second nature, almost as much as her later addiction to pain-killers and regular glasses of vodka. Even when she became a published poet, she learnt not to advertise the fact too freely for she had to be careful not to seem scarily intellectual to the Powerscourts' Big House set.

It wasn't true that Pat forbade her to mix with other writers, but he was baffled by his wife's bookishness. Ascendancy aristocrats of his day were devoted to the outdoors, their farms, horses and what was left of their estates. Edith Wharton, who came from a similarly upper-class milieu on the other side of the Atlantic, summarized the situation in her autobiography, *A Backward Glance* (1934): 'My literary success puzzled and embarrassed my old friends far more than it impressed them, and in my family it created a kind of constraint which increased with the years.' At least Mrs Wharton didn't suffer from the disadvantage of a title. Edward John Moreton Drax Plunkett, (18th Baron Dunsay) a generation older than Sheila and a playwright whom W.B. Yeats described as a man of genius, was familiar with the distrust shown towards Anglo-Irish aristocrats who took up the pen. He wrote, 'The greatest barrier over which my dreams have had to climb appears to have been the belief that titled dilettantes trying to write, in order to take the bread out of the mouths of honest men, should be discouraged by every man of independent spirit.' In Sheila's case, early publicity as a novelty – 'poetess wife' – added to her struggle for serious recognition. Disapproval was probably a major cause of the undiagnosable pain she suffered whenever a book was nearing completion. On the eve of publication of her first book of poems, her illness was thought to be neurotic. She wrote miserably to her friend, Lady Ottoline Morrell, '[They] can find no hideous, hidden secrets or worries – except they think I pay more attention than I should to writing poetry and not enough to my children.' The children grew up, the pain reappeared with each new manuscript and Sheila resorted to drugs and, finally, exile from her family.

Her literary ambition wasn't the only reason why Sheila worried that she was looked on as an outlandish choice of bride for the future Lord Powerscourt. Although she was impeccably Anglo-Irish on her mother's side, her father, Claude Beddington, was Jewish. Claude, unlike his pious father, wasn't a practising Jew and regarded himself as an Englishman through and through. In other people's eyes, however, he was Jewish, an uncomfortable thing to be in his lifetime. A. Alvarez, reviewing Todd M. Endelman's book, *The Jews in Britain* in *The New York Review of Books* (16 December 2004), argued that no matter how many centuries Jews have lived in England and no matter how assimilated they have become, a sense of 'outsiderness' remains and that 'the only solution is disguise and impersonation ... In England, where appearances matter a great deal, social embarrassment and anti-Semitism are always entwined ... Being Jewish was a social gaffe'. Sheila struggled to downplay or conceal this aspect of her background and saw the only solution to her situation as 'disguise and impersonation'.

It was when I realized the extent of the disguise she wore that Sheila began to come alive for me. I am Jewish myself and sometimes I've kept quiet about it, to save other people, as well as myself, embarrassment. And every time I've done this, the feelings of lonely apartness have been overwhelming. So I sympathized with Sheila, who spent her grown-up life hiding who she was. Everyone I met who had known her described her, sometimes with affection, as 'a difficult woman' but if she gave other people a hard time, she gave herself a harder one. She felt compelled to reinvent not only herself but her ancestors, insisting that Claude's family, pillars of the Anglo-Jewish establishment, had belonged to the Church of England for centuries. In a note to one of her poems, 'Origins', she owns up to one long-ago, sixteenth-century Jewish forebear. In Sheila's old age, when her younger son, Guy, wondered whether the Beddingtons might be Jewish, Sheila denied it. In mitigation, she wrote these letters during the rise of German neo-Nazism in the 1980s to a son who often travelled in that country. Michael Holroyd wrote in his mysterious and lovely memoir, *Mosaic* (2004): 'The lies we tell ourselves and others, the half-truths that through repetition we almost come to believe, the very fantasies that follow us like our own shadows, become part of our actual lives.' Sheila had (almost) come to believe the fantasy that the Beddingtons were Church of England, so she was genuinely outraged and profoundly shaken by Guy's innocent inquiries.

She never denied that her hybrid Anglo-Irish ancestry conferred a certain 'outsiderness' but, according to her, this duality lay in a confused nationality from which the Jewishness was expunged. 'English father, Irish mother, an upbringing divided between two countries – what a difficult combination to define,' she wrote midway in her career, when her 1954 collection of poems, *A Kite's Dinner: Poems 1938–54*, had been made a Poetry Book Society Choice, foreseeing, correctly, that reviewers would find her hard to categorize. She compounded the identity problem of a poet raised in England, but with a possessive love of Ireland, when she later left Ireland, the inspiration of her best poems, for the perpetual dullness of a Swiss lakeside, gaining the dubious label of 'exilic marginality', as the late Edward Said has called it.

She had never really known her place; her parents had seen to that. Claude Beddington and Ethel Mulock had been determined not to let their identities be confined by their backgrounds: clannish Anglo-Judaism in Claude's case, the provincial dullness of the Bog of Allen in Ethel's. Marrying each other – for they were unlikely partners – was part of their rebellion. They may have escaped entrapment but provided Sheila with an emotionally chaotic childhood. Tormented by Ethel's toxic mothering, she was left with a damaged, self-sabotaging psyche. Inclined to be unsettled, she was grateful, at least at first, for the restrictions and duties incumbent on her as Viscountess Powerscourt. Playing such a role allowed her to go into hiding. When, following Powerscourt tradition, she became the chief commissioner of the Irish Girl Guides and designed a glittering, flamboyant uniform for herself, she wasn't showing off, only sheltering behind the flashy braid and buttons. As she got older, she took to wearing extremely unflattering wigs. 'She looked as though she was constructed out of something else,' was Isobel Armstrong's first impression of the ageing poetess when, as a young academic, she met Sheila for the first time.

Like many insecure people, Sheila found it impossible to be spontaneous or self-forgetful, or to allow her children to be. 'What will people think of *me*?' she screamed, whenever they tried to cross some small boundary. She so hated being caught in a state of unpreparedness that, when a favourite granddaughter called on her unexpectedly at her London hotel, Sheila wouldn't come down to meet her. Being with other people was like being an actor who was never off stage. No wonder that she often took flight: to a London nursing home, to a seaside hotel in winter or to her own cosseting bedroom, where, claiming illness, she could uninterruptedly read and write. Being a poet was the greatest escape of all, because, through her poems, she could run away from herself, poetry being, as another poet, Nick Laird has put it, 'a walk through someone else'.

Sheila felt constantly disapproved of, but she inspired great affection in many quarters. People responded to that appealing mixture of frailty, grit and shining intelligence. There was something attractive, if exasperating, about this clever woman who went about her life the wrong way, pulled by conflicting desires. She was serious about becoming a poet and, perversely, equally serious about being a successful Lady Powerscourt, somehow failing to see that supervising the restoration of Powerscourt's seventy bedrooms seemed at odds with being a poet who longed for 'a sweater and an attic', as she put it. In her poem, 'Brigid', a wistful tribute to the saint who was 'once/Protector of poets', Sheila ends with the line, 'Lady, I bow to your diversity.' Only saints, perhaps, can cope successfully with the kind of multi-tasking that Sheila attempted. Her life was full of mistakes, as she acknowledged in poetry which, over time, became increasingly regretful, although never whining or self-pitying. There was something brave about her refusal to stop writing when it would have made her life so much easier had she done so. As Stevie Smith put it in her poem, 'Mrs Arbuthnot', 'Nobody writes or wishes to/Who is one with their desire.'

Sheila Wingfield's poems are so sure-footed, so pleasurable to read, that although obscurity is a state which threatens many poets, alive or dead, it is surprising that in her case it has been so completely all-enveloping. Somehow, she has missed out on the current interest in Irish women poets who, after years of neglect, have been rediscovered. *The White Page/An Bhileog Bhán: Twentieth-Century Irish Women Poets* (1999), showcases the work of 113 poets, Irish-born or 'of Irish ancestry and non-nationals resident and writing in Ireland for long periods', criteria which Sheila's work adequately meets but which, in this roomy anthology, has been ignored. Similarly, in Volume V of *The Field Day Anthology of Irish Writing* (2002), stuffily subtitled 'Irish Women's Writing and Traditions', Sheila has again gone missing. Not only is she absent from the list of fifty-nine contemporary women poets, but there are no extracts from her three memoirs, although they provide beautifully written and diverting accounts of life inside and outside the Big House in Ireland. She fares better in standard works of reference – *The Dictionary of Irish Literature*, *The Oxford Companion to Irish Literature* – but their entries comment as much on the fact that her poetry has been overlooked, as on the poetry itself. 'Her work has probably not received the acclaim it deserves,' and 'this underrated poet' are their apologetic conclusions.

Maybe the 'tiresome combination', as Sheila described it, of being both, and not quite, Irish and/or English has something to do with this neglect, or perhaps it demonstrates the prejudice she feared against her wealth and title. She may have been left out in the cold because she doesn't properly fit the label 'female poet', in the sense that she is so thoroughly unconfessional. Her poetry is never a nervy exploration of herself. Deryn Rees-Jones, the editor of a recent anthology, *Modern Women Poets*, although anxious not to present women poets as pathological cases, does argue for their collective 'unstable selfhood' and their 'anxieties about their self-presentation and poetic determination'. Five of Sheila Wingfield's poems were chosen for this anthology although she doesn't fit the usual profile. She was an objectivist, which, as her admirer G.S. (George) Fraser wrote in the preface to one of her collections, *Her Storms,* 'is something rather unusual in women poets', whom we might expect to be poetic introverts, preoccupied with their womanhood. Sheila described her poetic outlook as quite otherwise: 'What is personally felt must be fused with what is being, and has been, felt by others [underlined]. But always in terms of the factual. Nothing woolly or disembodied will do.' Nothing plaintive either; she kept her whining for her correspondence. Although she was insecure in every other aspect of her life, her poetry is sturdy and robust. Germaine Greer predicted that the objectivist woman poet would not have an easy time of it. In *Slip-shod Sibyls: Recognition, Rejection and the Woman Poet* (1995), she wrote that such poets 'because they fail to flay themselves alive, [they] will be called minor and forgotten … Until such a time as we come to prefer our poets of all sexes with the skin on.'

Like T.S. Eliot, Sheila used poetry as an escape from personality. When she wrote, she was all eyes, in the middle of a love affair with perception. She viewed the world as separate from herself, with its own shapes and colours, and turned it into what Seamus Heaney calls 'holdable words'. You can see this most of all in her poems about Ireland, the country she loved and calamitously, in a fit of petulance, left. Here is the beginning of 'Any Weekday in a Small Irish Town':

A rusty, nagging morning.
By the pub's
Front door, now shut ...

If I ever had to leave Ireland, poems like this would recreate it perfectly for me.

I can't tell how far I have come to know Sheila Wingfield or succeeded in portraying her. Biography is, after all, only a way of telling, while a life is a way of being. I think that she was an extraordinary woman and a poet who is in urgent need of rediscovery. I wanted to do right by her and yet I was always aware that she would have seen any biography as hugely intrusive. It was probably to discourage nosiness by future biographers that she destroyed her manuscripts and letters and why her archive in Ireland's National Library is disappointingly meagre. When her daughter, Grania, drew attention to a box of photographs in her mother's Swiss apartment, every picture of Pat had been removed by the next morning. Sheila didn't want her life examined, because she saw it only as a role she played. What she lived was her poetry.

Something to Hide

1. SECRETS AND LIES

'My father did not care for books.'
Sheila Wingfield, *Real People*

The last thing that Claude Beddington wanted was for his daughter to become a poet. His wife, Ethel, had put him off bookish women; she was always boasting of her accomplishments – 'I talk four languages equally well, including my own' – and holding salons in the drawing room of their dark London house, at 26 Seymour Street. Here she dazzled her admirers, who sat on fusty, velvet-covered sixteenth-century Italian chairs and sofas, beneath portraits of their hostess by John Singer Sargent and Philip Laszlo de Lombos. Claude favoured a more robust decor: elephant-foot wastepaper baskets and rhino-hide table tops, mementoes of his expeditions in Africa, before he made the mistake of marrying Ethel. Three years after the couple became legally separated in 1926, when Sheila was twenty, Ethel wrote a giddily self-referential memoir, *All That I Have Met*, in which she claimed to have 'more ink than blood in my veins'. This possibly hardened Claude's resolve to stop his daughter becoming a poet, which was what she most wanted to be. He made sure that she was kept so busy keeping house for him, acting as his hostess at dinner parties, going to dances and accompanying him on country-house weekends, that she wouldn't have time to read a poem, let alone write one. 'My father did not care for books and disapproved of high-brows and wished to steer me away from all that,' Sheila recalled sadly. She once urged Claude to read Donne's poetry: 'He handed me

3

back the book without a word. Never was literature, after that, mentioned again.'

Sheila learnt not to mention books but she went on reading them, one a day, or rather night, after her compulsory socializing. Being forbidden to read was nothing new: throughout her childhood, the bookcases at Seymour Street had been kept locked. But, as a little girl, she had managed to get her hands on 'a huge old *Chamber's Cyclopaedia of English Literature*', which she defiantly read: 'My fear of being discovered only intensified this secret pleasure.' The novelist Jonathan Franzen has observed that 'The first lesson reading teaches is how to be alone.' Reading made Seymour Street bearable, so that Sheila would write later: 'Those long stretches of solitude in childhood have made it impossible ever to feel lonely or bored.' She was determined to be a poet, although she wasn't quite sure yet what a poet was. The *Cyclopaedia* belonged to Ethel; Claude owned only a multi-volume, forever unread, *Life of Disraeli*, and it's strange that his wife, who listed reading and writing in her *Who's Who* entry, under 'Recreations', kept her bookcases locked. She was an unkind and spiteful mother and probably wanted to deny Sheila the pleasure of reading. Ethel's torment of her daughter knew no bounds. She sent her to children's parties wearing drab serge frocks and surgical boots, which she didn't need, and left her in the care of unbalanced governesses because she was too mean to pay the wages of good ones.

Claude, on the other hand, loved his daughter and his reasons for stopping her reading were more complicated. He was afraid that if she appeared to be too clever, too intellectual or, in any way, too eyebrow-raisingly 'different', she would not be accepted in the hunting, shooting, pleasure-seeking English society that Claude himself, in spite of his distinguished military record and superb sportsmanship, must sometimes have felt that he belonged to only by the skin of his teeth. For the fact was that Lt Colonel Claude Beddington, of the Westmorland and Cumberland Yeomanry, had been born Claude Moses, into a Jewish family of City merchants. They all changed their name to Beddington in 1868, the year of Claude's birth. Beddington was the name of a village in Surrey and perhaps it was chosen because it sounded so reassuringly English. This en masse change of name prompted the rhyme: 'Moses, Beddington, Beddington, Moses/Changed their name but not their noses', which was chanted in the City streets. When one newly-renamed stockbroker arrived for work, he found a banner hung across the main hall of the

Stock Exchange with the greeting, 'And the Lord said unto Moses – Good morning Mr Beddington'.

The Moses family had lived in London since the middle of the eighteenth century, arriving from Colmar in Alsace, their wealth already established. They were philanthropists, who built synagogues and served on the boards of hospitals, orphan asylums and as Justices of the Peace. Claude's father, Alfred H. Beddington, né Moses, was a founder, with other family members, of the Central Synagogue in London. He also served on the committee of Jews' College, the Jewish Middle Class School for Girls and the Jewish Association for the Diffusion of Religious Knowledge. By the time Claude was growing up, the Beddingtons were settled in large houses in Marylebone and Mayfair, well-placed for attending fashionable synagogues and for carriage rides in Hyde Park. They became anglicized enough to hunt, shoot and fish and acquire or rent country estates, but still clung to their Jewish heritage to some degree; their male children, including Claude, were sent to Polack's House, at Clifton College, a Bristol public school. Polack's had been founded in 1878, so that Jewish boys could go to a public school while maintaining their religious observances and traditions. It was 'a ghetto within a ghetto', as another past pupil has described Polack's House. He thought it an uncomfortable place, its pupils self-consciously separate from the rest of the school.

Claude, though, was highly acceptable throughout Clifton, because he was an exceptional sportsman and a member of the team which won the inter-school Ashburton Shield for shooting in 1885. He went on to Cambridge, grew a handlebar moustache and gained a First in Law. At this stage, he might have been expected to marry into 'the Cousinhood', other rich, public-spirited Anglo-Jewish families: Henriques and Montagues and Sebag-Montefiores, those pillars of society who are treated entertainingly and irreverently in Stephen Brooks' gossipy book *The Club* (1989). Instead, Claude became an explorer in West Africa. He took a doctor and a geologist with him and brought home kudu heads, ivory tusks and an undiscovered type of pygmy buffalo which he gave to the Natural History Museum in London, which named it after him: *Bos cafferi Beddingtoni*. He also brought back a boy from the Gold Coast, and his sister, to be butler-valet and lady's maid at Kirtling Towers, the Tudor house near Newmarket that Claude was then leasing. At the outbreak of the Boer War in 1899, Claude, aged thirty-one, joined the Westmorland and Cumberland

Yeomanry. In South Africa, he was put on the staff of the commander-in-chief, Lord Roberts, who, coincidentally, was a close friend of the Mulocks and had known Ethel since she was a baby. It's possible that he even introduced her to her future husband.

Badly wounded during the war, Claude was awarded the Queen's medal with three clasps, and, although he went on to serve in two further wars and win other medals, this was the one he treasured most. The Boer War saw a vicious outbreak of anti-Semitism in England; it was referred to as the 'Jew war in the Transvaal', and was supposedly organized by international Jewish financiers whose aim was to seize South African gold. A TUC resolution in September 1900 condemned the war as designed to 'secure the goldfields of South Africa for cosmopolitan Jews, most of whom had no patriotism and no country'. Claude, a patriotic Englishman prepared to die for England, must have been horrified. He began to see his Jewishness as a shameful secret and dissociated himself from his father's way of life which was centred on the synagogue and committee work on behalf of Anglo-Jewry. He turned his back on the eligible young women of 'the Cousinhood' and then, in a final break with his past, on 16 October 1900, when he was thirty-two, he married the 21-year-old Frances Ethel Mulock, from the Bog of Allen in the Irish midlands.

Ethel was ravishingly beautiful, a fearless rider to hounds, and thoroughly nasty. When they were children, she told her sister Enid, whose blue eyes were faultless, that she had a squint not visible in a mirror. Her parents noticed her chilly personality and how it became even colder after her return from the Dresden Conservatoire, where she had studied music. Her mother said, 'There was a definite moment when she came back from Dresden as if made of stone. There was no God. And she would hate men as long as she lived.' Ethel must have hated the Bog of Allen even more than she hated men, since she married the first young man, who happened to be Claude Beddington, offering to take her away from it. The Bog of Allen in Offaly, then King's County, is a region often described as rather lacking in outstanding scenic features, apart from the heathery Slieve Bloom Mountains. Ethel was born in 1879, the year that Michael Davitt's Land League was founded, followed by the introduction of the boycott and the withholding of rents. The first of Gladstone's Land Acts, which secured fixity of tenure and fair rents for the Irish tenantry, was passed two years later. The period following Parnell's death in 1891 saw an emphasis on cultural autonomy instead of political independence.

The 1890s was the decade of Gaelic revivalism, a flowering of Anglo-Irish literature and the foundation of the Irish Literary Theatre. But all this intellectual excitement took place in Dublin, seventy difficult miles away.

Although she liked to play the wild Irish colleen in London drawing rooms, Ethel had not actually spent much of her youth in the Irish midlands. Her father, Francis (Frank) Berry Mulock, served in the Indian Civil Service and Ethel was brought up by a duenna, Mary Holden, 'Auntie', who had seen service with three generations of Ethel's mother's family, as well as by a series of governesses in various European countries. The name Mulock was originally Mullock or Mellick, possibly derived from an Irish word meaning 'bog', and Ethel's family had lived around the Bog of Allen for generations. They weren't rich by Ascendancy standards; Ethel's father and uncles had been educated in Italy to save money before they went on to Trinity College, Dublin. Her father prospered in the Indian Civil Service, becoming Commissioner for the Central Provinces. He spoke exquisite Italian and read Dante every morning of his life, but was happy enough to spend his well-pensioned retirement at Bellair, County Offaly, the nineteenth-century villa built by the architect Richard Morrison (1767–1849), a former pupil of the great James Gandon.

Morrison, in partnership with his son, William Vitruvius Morrison, made his name with modest establishments, which combined simplicity and elegance and were compact and comfortable. He had built Bellair in 1807 on the site of a small, tumbledown castle. The two-storey villa had a semi-circular, pillared porch and recessed doors and sash windows with unevenly-blown thin panes. There was a concave surround over the front door and a flight of white stone steps. Framed by the plum-blue Slieve Bloom Mountains and ringed by beech trees, a farmyard and medieval ruins, Bellair was an appealing estate. It had once been called Bally Ard, meaning settlement-on-a-hill, until an eighteenth-century Mulock anglicized it to 'Bellair'. Frank Mulock's older brother William, who had lived at Bellair before leaving it to Frank, had cleared the fields of stones and put up solid farm buildings, and Frank continued with the improvements – a stained glass head of Dante let into a window; peacocks in the garden. Ethel was not impressed.

The Mulocks had literary connections. One of Ethel's distant cousins was Dinah Mulock (1826–1887), author of the best-selling *John Halifax, Gentleman* and the wife of George Lillie Craik, a partner in the publishing house of Macmillan. She wrote a prolific amount of improving literature of which the American *Illustrated Christian Weekly* wrote disparagingly: 'We believe the mother who wishes to guard her daughter against the sensational novel of the day will find in Miss Mulock's fiction a useful means to aid her in the accomplishment of her design.' Ethel's aunt, Hester Mulock, married Alfred Austin, who became Poet Laureate in 1896 and was the composer of a ludicrous couplet,

> They went across the veldt
> As hard as they could pelt

which appeared in a poem about the Jameson Raid. 'Mr Alfred Austin has a clearly defined talent, the limits of which are by this time clearly recognized,' *The Daily Telegraph* reported dryly. On her mother's side, Ethel was related to another best-selling and prolific author, M.E. Braddon (1837–1915), the 'Queen of the Circulating Libraries', who wrote more than eighty novels, most famously *Lady Audley's Secret* (1862). Mary Elizabeth Braddon is regarded as the founder of the sensation novel 'as written by women for women'. She had many admirers, including Henry James, who applauded the lack of sentiment in her writing. This lack was not surprising. Braddon had endured much hardship, living with her publisher, John Maxwell, for many years before being able to marry him when his first wife died. In her memoir, Ethel described Mary Braddon, 'the Aunt', as a kindly, dignified and very respectable figure, celebrated for the lunch parties which she and her husband gave at their Georgian house in Richmond. There is no mention of the Aunt's scandalous past. These ancestral authoresses gave weight to Ethel's claim that she had more ink than blood in her veins, although what blood she did claim was blue-tinged – unverifiably, the Mulocks were supposedly descended from Niall of the Nine Hostages, King of Ireland in 371 AD. Ethel's paternal grandmother, Frances Berry, counted Edward I and Charlemagne among her ancestors.

There were literary connections on the Beddington side of the family too. Ada Leverson (1862–1933), and her sister, Violet Schiff (1875–1962), were Claude's first cousins. Ada was Oscar Wilde's solicitous 'Sphinx', literary hostess and the author of some elegantly witty novels, which enjoyed a belated vogue during the 1960s when they were republished by Virago. Colin MacInnes praised Leverson, in a foreward to the 1962 Virago edition of *The Little Ottleys,* as 'the classic author of the comedy of manners'. Claude would certainly not have boasted about his relationship to a friend of Oscar Wilde; deeply and purposely conventional, in spite of his eccentricities, it's quite likely that he never mentioned it. Violet was equally scandalous. Her husband, Sydney (1885–1944), who wrote novels under the pen-name Stephen Hudson, was a renowned patron of the arts and, like his wife, an avid cultivator of leading figures of the modernist movement. *A Night at the Majestic*, Richard Davenport-Hines's recently published account of a dinner party for the Ballets Russes hosted by the Schiffs in Paris in 1922, the only occasion at which Joyce, Proust, Picasso, Diaghilev and Stravinksky were all in the same room, has returned the Schiffs to the limelight.

It's understandable why Ethel and Claude were attracted to each other at first. Beautiful and slender with black hair and big, dark eyes, Ethel loved hunting as much as Claude did. The fox-hunt provided an excellent marriage-market for Victorian women. Caroline Blackwood has noted that, riding side-saddle in their fetching hunting jackets, female huntresses, in every sense, delighted 'in a new-found sexual power in which they could attract the opposite sex even when their faces were bleeding from bramble scratches and spattered in mud'. Especially at that time, because added to the attraction of fearless heroine was that of damsel-in-distress. Irresistible. Ethel's Irishness was also in her favour because, as the Irish-American Hazel Lavery, wife of the painter John Lavery, put it, it was 'positively chic' to be an Irishwoman in London society. Hazel Lavery went a bit over-the-top in this role: she cultivated an Irish accent, began to celebrate her birthday on St Patrick's Day and later appeared against an Irish landscape in a portrait by her husband, which formed the central motif of the first banknotes of the Irish Free State. Ethel never rose to that level of celebrity but she wore Celtic-inspired evening dresses, favoured decorative touches of harps and shamrocks and entertained her guests by playing Irish folk music. These daughter-of-Erin shenanigans, like so much about Ethel, were bogus. The Mulocks were Anglo-Irish Protestants who served the Empire in the armed forces and the colonial services. Their position in Ireland was ambivalent, and would become more so. Ethel didn't go in for soul-searching but Claude, Anglo-Jewish, would have noticed in this Anglo-Irish girl an 'outsider-ness' that matched his own.

Claude was as dashing as Ethel. The regiment he commanded was, in his daughter's words, 'carefree, casual, unabashed' – precisely the effect that Claude himself tried to give. The beginnings of the Yeomanry in 1819 were not glamorous, but by Claude's time, it had become fabulously showy. Its horses' equipment included false tails, possibly for a smarter parade presence. Claude had a hand in designing the officers' full-dress uniform, in Sheila's words, 'reminiscent of both a Death's-Head Hussar and the work of Fabergé'. How could one fail to impress in a heavily gold-frogged tunic, fur-bordered jacket ornamented with silver, dark breeches with gold stripes, Hessian boots with silver knots and a busby foaming with osprey plumes? Claude and Ethel each saw the other as a ticket to freedom. Claude wanted to escape from the oppressive decency and slightly foreign clannishness of the Beddingtons, while Ethel needed a larger stage than the unexciting Bog of Allen to display her beauty and accomplishments. The death of Claude's father, the religiously observant Alfred Henry, in January 1900, made it easier for Claude to marry a Gentile.

Before his marriage, Claude had been living in London with his widowed mother and older brother, Herbert, at 8 Cornwall Terrace, and the atmosphere there before his wedding must have been quietly reproachful. The Mulocks, however, had no objections to the match. Not only did they want Ethel gone but they were very fond of Claude, as he was of them. Irish Grandpa and Grandma, as Sheila would call them, were altogether warmer-hearted and more accepting than his own constricting family. The marriage took place at the Marylebone Register Office, Ethel's father and Claude's brother Herbert standing as witnesses. Ethel might have been expected to marry in a flurry of bridesmaids and rose petals in the church at Liss, near her family home at Bellair, where her mother chose and played the Sunday morning hymn, but the Boer War still had two years to run and, in wartime, hasty civil marriages were excusable. The honeymoon was spent aboard the 2nd Duke of Westminster's yacht, the playboy Duke 'Bendor' being a friend of Claude's. The bride was seasick for most of it: 'about as wretched a beginning as can be envisaged for an already doomed marriage', her daughter decided.

It didn't seem doomed at the start. The young, attractive couple were perfectly positioned to take their place in Edwardian society. The English aristocracy has never had much trouble welcoming rich newcomers, and this was particularly true at the beginning of the last century, when social values were beginning to oust moral ones. There was a feeling that the country was owed some fun as the stultifying reign of the widow of Windsor drew to its stately close, and Claude and Ethel helped provide it for their social circle. The beautiful bride, who looked good on a horse or seated at the piano, had an interesting connection too: one of her Mulock aunts, Nina, the wife of Arthur Kennard, a rich ironmaster, was rumoured to be a mistress of the Prince of Wales. Claude and Ethel's fizzy personalities suited the liberating, colourful times, that last, carefree holiday before the darkness of the First World War. The newly-wed Beddingtons accepted English society for what it was: good-humoured and ill-educated, devoted to outdoor pursuits and suspicious of bookishness. This would cause no end of trouble for their daughter.

Sheila, born on 23 May 1906, was the couple's second child; their first, a son, Guy, was four years older. Claude was now a Major and the family was living at Milford-on-Sea, a little town halfway between Lymington and Christchurch, favoured spots for sailing. They also retained the lease of Kirtling Towers in 'that country of wide open spaces where horses are horses', as Ethel indisputably described Newmarket. As well as the horses, there was game shooting: pheasants, partridges and hares. One gets the impression of a rich, leisured family with a taste for outdoor pursuits, although Claude must have spent some time in London. In 1902, he set up Abdulla & Co. Ltd, Cigarette and Tobacco Manufacturers, importers and exporters with offices in the City. Ethel wanted a London salon; that had been the whole point of her escape from the Bog of Allen. So, after a period in Northamptonshire, riding with the Pytchley Hounds, Claude sold his horses and became a full-time City merchant, that typical Beddington occupation. He bought 26 Seymour Street, behind Marble Arch, close to other Beddingtons, although no one seemed to be on visiting terms. Claude's relations would have found Ethel's Italianate drawing-room with 'its collections of caricatures and photographs of Famous Persons (mostly singers) all devotedly signed', in Ethel's words, a bit on the showy side. And they would have been embarrassed by Claude's Gentile wife, who boasted of her Irish ancestry, while she played Cecil Sharpe's arrangement of the 'Londonderry Air', insisting, 'Here is a wonderful thing my sister discovered in an Irish cottage.' With her Greek chignon and long, pleated gold dress, Ethel was living proof that, once again, Claude had gone too far. Claude himself never set foot in the drawing-room. His daughter later thought that 'perhaps he had given up being anywhere near her [Ethel] as far as this was possible while living in the same house'.

Ethel and Sheila provide conflicting accounts of the latter's childhood. In Sheila's second memoir (*Sun Too Fast*) – the first to mention her mother, long dead by then – Ethel is a wicked witch with 'black hair, dark eyes, a thin body and a mind surging with hate for her parents [Irish Grandma and Grandpa] as well as for husband and children'. That black hair, Ethel boasted, was brushed daily with Macassar oil and washed only once a year. Sheila thought that it smelled disgusting. Maybe it did, but in some quarters Ethel was thought to be the most beautiful woman in London. She certainly doesn't look witch-like on a Christmas card, sent out by the Beddingtons some years before the Great War. In it, pretty Ethel's two children are pressed fetchingly against her skirts; Sheila, angel-faced with cascading ringlets, Guy in a sailor-suit. Sheila wasn't having any of this; she insisted, in spite of photographic evidence to the contrary that, 'I know I was a plain child and horribly dressed.' According to Sheila, her childhood was all hateful tapioca pudding and worse chastisements.

Ethel stuck to the Christmas card version, in which she oozes maternal sheltering. In her memoir, she congratulates herself for not forcing a small son, afraid of water, to swim, and for supervising the nursery food: 'I made out elaborate lists for the kitchen of each child's favourite and abhorred dishes ... every delicacy was pressed upon them.' When the children were ill, 'their time in bed was made as comfortable and amusing as my ingenuity could devise'. You begin to doubt these accounts of tender mothering when she describes a seaside holiday with her three children in Brittany in 1921, shared with Queen Marie of Romania and the Grand Duchess Cyril of Russia, and their children. Ethel boasts that no nursery governess was employed, so 'We all met on the common ground of motherhood, and could compare notes in the evening as to which child had splashed us in its bath, or tried to drown itself in the sea or overeaten itself at the patisserie, etc.' In 1921, Guy was nineteen, Sheila fifteen and Niall, the youngest, nine: all of them rather old for bathtime frolics. Ethel contrasts her maternal tenderness with the harshness of her own upbringing at the hands of 'Auntie'. That duenna, a Scots Presbyterian, had a mission to save her charge from vanity. 'She would say: "Did you notice how those two young men stared at you in church today? That was because they were so horrified with your ugly face."' Perhaps that's why Ethel hung portraits of herself on the walls of her Seymour Street salon and, in her memoir, never missed a chance to recall a compliment paid to her looks.

Apart from her secret reading, Claude was the bright spot in Sheila's sombre childhood. When he was at Seymour Street, he trailed a breezy atmosphere of gaiety and jokes. He and Guy made Sheila apple-pie beds while Sheila had her bath, her 'heart thudding from steam and soaping and anticipation', wondering what she would find among the bedclothes. Once it was a chest of drawers, another time, 'no bed at all, only four brass knobs laid on the linoleum where its corners should have been'. She stopped being afraid of the dark after Claude had taken her hand tightly and led her into a dark room saying, 'Isn't this cosy? I do like the dark, it's so warm and nice.' Guy, too, lightened her life. Sheila lived for his school holidays when the two of them made up plays for their puppet theatre and Guy entertained her with conjuring tricks. But Claude had his office; Guy was at boarding school. For most of the time, Seymour Street meant loneliness and Ethel's cruelty. A weekly respite from both was the outing to Oxford Street with a kindly housemaid who would buy the little girl a bag of caramels with her own money, Sheila's pocket money of a penny having been confiscated by Ethel's Italian lady's maid, for 'leaving my bedroom slippers in the wrong place or brushing my teeth sideways'. This was the London childhood; the Irish one was much happier.

Sheila's Irish holidays were spent in two places: Ower House, near Loch Corrib in Galway and Bellair, the house of her Mulock grandparents in Offaly. Claude rented Ower House while he looked for a site to build a house of his own nearby. Sheila was a small girl when she first stayed there, too small to get on her bicycle except by dropping onto the saddle from a branch of a low-branched tree, but old enough, once she was astride it, to explore disused churchyards and fields of wild flowers. Bellair was even more beloved. The Georgian house had 'an atmosphere of uncritical and overflowing love', so unlike Seymour Street. And as for Irish Grandma: 'abounding love – this was the feeling that embraced you when you were in her arms, or in her house, or anywhere near her'. Guy, too, loved Bellair and his grandparents. He would get into bed with his grandmother in the mornings and have *The Jungle Book* read to him. Once, on the day he had to leave, he hid in the hay barn and nearly suffocated because he couldn't bear to go back to England. All this is recounted in *Real People*, written when Ethel was still alive. One wonders how she felt, reading of the deep affection between her parents and her children; it had, after all, been Irish Grandma who had abandoned her to the sadistic Auntie.

The three children were at Ower House in the care of a governess during the summer of 1914, miserable because Claude was away fighting, along with thirty-seven other Beddingtons who all distinguished themselves on the battlefield. He came back on leave, the very picture of a military hero, with a bandage around his head, before rejoining his regiment. In this war, he was in command of a battalion which took 450 horses to Flanders, to be kept in reserve near the front. The Yeomanry suffered great losses and, in 1917, Claude was wounded again and sent home; he was then forty-nine. The small, bronze, oak leaf he was awarded signified 'Mentioned in Despatches'. Towards the end of the war, the Yeomanry was dehorsed and given bicycles. With their horses picketed in mud, the cumbersome, stately, cavalry regiments had shown that they were unfitted for modern warfare.

Meanwhile, Ethel was doing her bit for the war effort. Persuaded by her admirers, possibly without difficulty, not to ruin her hands scrubbing hospital floors or making bandages, she put her musical talents to use, starting off by playing the piano to wounded officers, but soon graduating to organizing entertainments to raise funds for war charities. Through this, she came into contact with various society ladies and, even more gratifyingly, became friendly with the actors and musicians who took part in her entertainments – Ivor Novello, Noel Coward and Mrs Patrick Campbell among them. This was, finally, the life – to be part of London's grand bohemia, a long way from the Bog of Allen. She continued to hold her Seymour Street salons, occasions of torment for Sheila, who was eight at the outbreak of war. During these musical tea-parties, Ethel made Sheila sit on a stool and forbade her to move. Then, when the cake-stand was brought in, Ethel would publicly scold the girl for not proffering it and tell her guests that Sheila needed 'waiting-on hand and foot'.

In her first memoir, Sheila called Claude 'The Acceptable Parent', and devoted several admiring chapters to him. However, he did some pretty unacceptable things while his daughter was growing up, not only leaving her to his wife's untender mercies but keeping her away from his own Jewish family, whose older members had not become as anglicized as Claude himself. When she was old enough to go visiting on her own, Sheila did visit the widowed 'Grandma Bel', Claude's mother, at 8 Cornwall Terrace, a dark London house, which frightened her as much as her portly, ugly grandmother. In *Real People*, she tells an anecdote about a Beddington great-uncle who read his newspaper in his carriage outside his house, explaining, 'I am taking the air without fatigue,' but does not seem to have met him. She also wonders, 'Why did I not see more of ravishing great-aunt Zillah?' but doesn't seem to know why, or pretends that she doesn't.

This great-aunt, née Simon, was married to Claude's uncle, Samuel Henry Moses, later Beddington, and was the mother of Ada Leverson and Violet Schiff. In her rare appearances in Sheila's memoirs – Ada and Violet are never mentioned – Zillah Beddington is presented as a deliciously indulged beauty. However, she was more interesting than that: a very musical woman with a piano on every floor of her London house. She formed friendships with some of the best musicians of the era, including Léon Delafosse, a protégé of hers who was one of the models for Proust's fictional character, Charlie Morel. The Acceptable Parent handed down the denial of his origins to his daughter, who later handed this same denial down to her children. By that time, she was styling herself 'Viscountess Powerscourt of Ireland', and preferred to stress her Mulock connections.

Claude and Ethel, hardly on speaking terms, left Sheila to grow up in an unconsidered way so that she never knew what was going on, or why, only that she felt alienated, never quite at home. Her upbringing at the hands of two warring parents made her feel split into halves that didn't make a whole. To know who you are, you need a place to come from. Sheila had two places, England and Ireland, neither of which she quite came from. Throughout her childhood, the ground was always shifting beneath her feet, denying her that rootedness which defines identity. Her sense of self was continually in crisis although she never acknowledged this, perhaps didn't even realize it, as, in her adult life, she stitched herself into a dazzling variety of patterns: sportswoman, celebrity, aristocratic chatelaine and, almost surreptitiously, poet and woman of letters. A sense of apartness, of something disconnected, certainly gave her poetry its elliptical originality, but played havoc with her life.

2. DEPARTURES

'All I wanted was a sweater and an attic and to teach myself to write.'
Letter from Sheila Wingfield to Robert Nye, 14 April 1978

Claude and Ethel's marriage came to an end, in the form of a legal separation in 1925, but there had been no real family life at Seymour Street for years before that. Claude spent more and more time in Ireland, planning the garden for what he hoped would be a rebuilt Ballycurrin House, at the edge of Loch Corrib in the west of Ireland. Ballycurrin was where, before the Great War, Claude had planned to build a house and create a garden with fruit orchards. He had already dug the foundations and planted nectarines, filberts, walnuts, cherries, mulberries and peaches. During the Irish Civil War (1922–23), the new Free State government appropriated the land, fruit trees and all. The house was never built. Back in London, Claude, like many another rich, unhappily married English gentleman, consoled himself with a series of mistresses. A ballroom dancer was succeeded by a manicurist, discreetly housed by Claude in a house in St John's Wood.

These dalliances faded into the background when his son Guy, then at Cambridge, was found to have TB of the lungs. He had contracted the disease while at Eton but it wasn't diagnosed until Cambridge's cold, misty fenlands aggravated the symptoms. Claude's time was now taken up with trying to save his son's life. Tuberculosis, then often more romantically called consumption, was the killer disease of the nineteenth and early twentieth centuries. Fresh, bracing air was thought to be the remedy and sufferers were sent to remote sanitoria for months, sometimes years, to endure a regime of gusty breezes and rest. Sometimes, they were put out in the snow, which would pile up on their blankets, or would be left outside for hours with sandbags strapped to their chests, supposedly to strengthen their lungs. TB became properly treatable from 1948 with the discovery of streptomycin, a form of penicillin, more than twenty years too late for Guy, who put up with years of primitive and painful treatment with debonair courage. Ultimately, his suffering proved in vain. He died aged twenty-three in 1925.

The end of her marriage, the death of her eldest son. Neither is mentioned in Ethel's memoir, that relentlessly upbeat and often fictitious chronicle. Ethel continued in her career as theatrical impresario long after the armistice. She put on charity entertainments, sometimes in stately homes. In 1921, she noted, 'The directors of the Carl Rosa Opera begged me to interest myself, in every respect save financially, in their autumn season at Covent Garden.' A perfect excuse for her to throw parties at which guests were persuaded to book boxes and stalls beforehand. As a friend of the famous, she gave her children a taste of the bright lights: 'The children's great joy was that George Robey should come to nursery-luncheon.' Then more joy was reported as the violinist Albert Sammons came to 'nursery tea', right after his recital at the Queen's Hall, and played the children's toy violin. Some doubt is cast on this event, however, by the fact that Ethel gives the date of this impromptu performance as 14 October 1926, by which time Guy was dead, Sheila was twenty, Niall was fourteen and Ethel had ceased all contact with her husband and two surviving children.

Because of the messy situation in Seymour Street, Sheila was sent away to school. In 1918, she became a pupil at Roedean, a private school for girls on the South Downs in Sussex. Its dark bulk, set in forty acres of downland between the gaudy town of Brighton and the immaculately pretty village of Rottingdean, looked like a cross between an ancestral home and a lunatic asylum. The school had been established in 1885, by three sisters, Penelope, Millicent and Dorothy Lawrence who, like the founders of the Girls' Public Day School Trust, Dorothea Beale of Cheltenham Ladies' College and Frances Mary Buss of the North London Collegiate School, helped put an end to the reign of the governess and her flimsy educational methods during the latter half of the nineteenth century. These new girls' schools modelled themselves on the English public schools which many of their pupils' brothers attended: the syllabus was aimed at university entrance, the aim of their playing fields was to foster house and team spirit and there was a prefectorial system to bolster discipline. Educational equality took its time. In 1938, when Virginia Woolf published her essay 'Three Guineas' on the subject of female education, she found that there were seventeen Cambridge colleges for men but only two for women, both poorly endowed.

Sheila preferred boarding school to living at home, in spite of having to play 'strange games on a field next to a steely sea'. At Roedean, all she had to do was learn what the rules were and abide by them, knowing that they would not change according to someone's tyrannous whim: 'Artificial as the code and outlook imposed on you appeared to be, yet the framework, if bizarre, was rigid in itself, and once you had learnt that the co-ordinates were keenness and exams, you could find your way about anywhere on the chart without getting lost.' The uniform at the time was a dark, short-sleeved serge dress worn over a white, long-sleeved blouse, black stockings and a round-crowned, narrow-brimmed hat, much like the one that Ronald Searle designed for his St Trinians' belles. The regime was Spartan: chilly lino, 'lung-tearing games on top of suet puddings' and chilblains. She described the now ancient Misses Lawrence as 'noble ruins' and the school itself as being completely outside real life: 'It was possible to feel neither happy nor unhappy here, but merely a temporary lodger in some peculiar place governed by strange laws.'

In her memoir *Growing Up Into Revolution* (1949), a former Roedean pupil, Margaret Cole, disparaged the school's academic standards and claimed that its high fees appealed more to its 'bourgeois clients' than its scholarship. This is not borne out by the 1924 Speech Day report which lists three Girton scholarships and several other university places, as well as one awarded by the Royal College of Arts. Sheila features prominently in the report of that year, her last at Roedean. Her poem, 'Names', is published in it, the last verse a foretaste of her objectivist style:

> And there, the dream is fled;
> And leaves me,
> Cold
> In open-eyed reality.

In the school concert, she played the violin in Bach's 'Andante' from *Concerto in D minor* and in Pugnani-Kreisler's *Prelude and Allegro* and conducted the school orchestra in Schubert's *March in D*. She also gained distinctions in French and Drawing in the School Certificate examination. Sheila always claimed that when she was fifteen, she passed the entrance examination to Cambridge, although the school's records don't show this. When her housemistress heard that Sheila was to go to a French finishing school, 'she was as horrified as if it had been planned to send me on the streets'.

This finishing school was a 'small, dilapidated chateau', in a suburb of Paris and Sheila felt that the only reason she had been sent there was 'to learn what underclothes to wear and how to put up my hair'. She begged to be taken away but was made to stay; by then her parents had other things on their minds. It's ironic, however, that Ethel refused to let her daughter go to university, since she herself appreciated the value of an Oxbridge education. Her will is scattered with bequests to Oxford and Cambridge to provide a 'Mrs Claude Beddington Prize', usually in modern languages. Perhaps, with their handsome, clever son slowly dying and their marriage falling apart, they couldn't face another extraordinary event – and for Sheila to go to university would have been regarded as peculiar in the Beddingtons' social circle. They were looking to her to restore the family's conventionality by becoming the sort of good-looking, mindless girl preferred by upper-class Englishmen. The Paris finishing-school wasn't in the same class of ordeal as the freezing sanatoria which Guy had to endure, but it was an ordeal nonetheless. Having to put up with a life they hated made Guy and Sheila closer than ever in the little time they had left.

In February 1922, Guy wrote cheerily to Sheila, then at Roedean, from a fresh-air-cure hut in the New Forest: 'The doctors always tell me off like anything for letter-writing and tell me I ought to understudy a cabbage … I can now play the ukulele in any key, upside down or underwater.' By November of that year he was in a nursing home in Bournemouth, a seaside resort on the south coast thickly planted with pine trees, thought to purify the air. He wrote to Sheila to congratulate her on being made a prefect and to chastise her for her poor taste in popular novelists: 'By the way, how you can read Ethel M. Dell without getting a bilious attack is beyond my comprehension. You'll be reading Ella Wheeler Wilcox next.' He added, 'I've been in bed eleven months today, which seems quite enough, but I'm afraid it will take another six for me even to begin to think of beginning to get up.'

Ethel's reaction to Guy's illness was horrifying. She blamed him for having an incurable illness and claimed that TB 'comes from dissipation', because Guy had twice played the drums in a jazz band. One evening, at the dinner-table, she remarked that 'All consumptives are liars.' At this, Sheila left the room 'and never spoke to my mother again, although we were to be under the same roof for some years to come'. This is recounted in *Sun Too Fast*, but her vow never to speak to Ethel again is contradicted a few pages later in the same book when Sheila writes that, at the age of nineteen, she asked Ethel to explain the facts of life to her. Ethel's reply was to ask her 'ferociously' if she was going to have a baby and then 'brusquely' hand her an unenlightening booklet on the birds and the bees. It was Claude who, 'horrified at my ignorance', enlightened her.

The Bournemouth nursing home, where Guy had been forcibly bedridden for almost a year, produced no improvement, so Claude bought a house in Italy, the Villa Yolanda at Ospedaletti, on the Italian Riviera. It was a place bathed by the southern sun and protected from the north winds by sheltering mountains. When Claude could not be there with Guy, he relied on daily postcards which recorded the boy's sputum count and temperature. Ospedaletti got its name, meaning 'little hospital', on account of the reputed healing powers of its sulphur pool. But sulphur could not cure TB. Meanwhile, miserable in Paris, Sheila took charge of her own education. She stopped going to the useless lessons offered by the finishing school and went to art classes instead. To the end of her life, she kept a folder of drawings which she had completed in 1921–26, including some life studies from her Paris classes. They are lively but not outstanding. She now taught herself Greek from a primer and began her years' long habit of reading a book a day. She discovered a favourite bookshop and Guy, lonely in Italy, wrote to her plaintively, 'Do ask your young man in the bookshop to send me books occasionally ... I suppose you've read *Le Martyre de L'Obèse* – I loved it.' She sent him 'a *Contes Drolatiques* with Gustave Doré illustrations ... the best present I have ever given anyone', and bought for herself Fustel de Coulange's *La Cité Antique* and a novel by Colette which she couldn't understand. She was starting to acquire an angry tenacity which she referred to as 'chance of character'. It made finishing school bearable because she simply ignored the restrictions that it tried to impose on her.

Sheila was back in London in 1925 when Guy, at the age of twenty-three, died in Munich. He had been taken there, to Professor Sauerbruch's clinic, for one more painful operation. The Professor had already treated him in Italy, cutting out sections of his ribs under a local anaesthetic, which gave Guy the grim opportunity 'to smell my own bones grilling'. In Munich, he died of a haemorrhage which might have happened at any time. Sheila doesn't explain why the family were in London while Guy was having his last operation. Instead she recreates the dramatic scene in Seymour Street following Guy's death. She and Ethel had eaten their 'usual silent dinner'. Ethel is wearing her customary dinner-gown of dark red velvet with a fur-edged décolleté, which showed off her white breasts. Claude asks, 'Will you come to Munich for the funeral?' Sheila continues that her mother 'looked down, found a tiny footstool and put her feet on it. "I am unwell," she said, without raising her eyes.'

There is only one oblique reference to Guy's illness in Ethel's memoir. She writes that Maud Ashley, beloved daughter of the financier Sir Ernest Cassels, died of TB. 'Money – what did money matter? – was spent like water on every imaginable alleviation; every whim was indulged; every luxury was provided; but she grew steadily worse, until in 1911 the blow fell.' She has transferred Claude's attentions to Guy onto Cassels and his daughter. Then, she adds, 'Dr Felkin [then Head Physician of the sanatorium in the New Forest] said to me in 1922: "It is easier for a camel to go through the eye of a needle than for a rich patient to be cured of TB." ' There is no mention that her own son, during that year, was one of these 'rich patients'. As always, when writing about her life, Ethel is determinedly cheery. Personal tragedy was unmentionable, sometimes, it seems, even to herself. Perhaps this explains her dismissal of her sick son and her furious refusal to mourn. But what a strange thing for Dr Felkin to say, if indeed he was quoted correctly. Poor patients had even less chance of recovery.

Ethel didn't attend the memorial service which Claude held at their house for Guy's friends. Instead, she put a huge card on the hall table which read, 'To the Servants. There is a memorial service at 3 pm in the Colonel's study. No refreshments need to be served.' Ethel often communicated through written cards. On the night of the service for Guy, Sheila found one beside her plate which read, 'I am the seagull that soars in the pure blue sky. You are the offal below.' Ethel's great-nephew, Sir John Nutting, told me that he remembered a large card in Ethel's Grosvenor Square flat in the 1950s, which named his father, Anthony Nutting, as her next of kin. When Anthony Nutting got divorced, his name was savagely crossed out and the name of his ex-wife substituted.

To Sheila, Guy was 'a sun-god ... the young Apollo who had charmed such a wide circle of friends'. He was certainly very good-looking; a photograph of him at Bellair, reproduced in *Real People*, shows a young man with the high, pale forehead and sensual features of a matinee idol. In this first memoir, Sheila wrote that her brother, already bedridden, invented a ship-to-shore wireless system which he patented in his own name and that Gugliemo Marconi, 'as soon as Guy died', used the patent, giving its inventor no credit, to cause Italian ships in the bay of Naples to light up at a signal from the shore. Like her account of the silent feud with Ethel, this is questionable. Marconi had himself filed a patent relating to the transmission of radio waves in 1896. His company, Marconi International Marine Communication, had established reliable communication with ships over 2000 miles away as early as 1902 and messages from *Titanic's* Marconi wireless summoned help to the ship, saving many lives. By 1925, the year that Guy died, Marconi had returned to Italy and joined the fascists. It's hard to see why he would have needed Guy Beddington's patent and this incident highlights Sheila's tendency to re-invent the past. What cannot be doubted is that Sheila adored her brother when he was alive and worshipped his memory after he died. Having described him with passionate admiration in her first memoir, she repeats much of the same material in her second, admitting 'Perhaps I never shall be through with Guy.' He was her ally against Ethel, he guided her reading, he was the one she loved the best and went on loving the best, the ideal against whom all other young men were measured. This made for a difficult relationship with her own sons, who fell some way short of being sun-gods.

The Beddington marriage ended with a legal separation the year after Guy's death. Claude bought Ethel Arkwright Lodge, 'my dream house up on the Hampstead Heights', as she described it. A newly-designed bookplate pictures her new sitting room. It looks charming with its parquet floor, log fire and Irish harp and low, built-in bookshelves placed within easy reach of a cushioned, high-backed chair. Hampstead had literary and family associations for Ethel; her distant cousin, Dinah Mulock Craik, had lived nearby at Wildwood Cottage in North End. Claude paid his wife £6000 a year tax-free and gave her a Rolls-Royce, chauffeur and lady's maid. But according to her daughter, that recognizably unreliable narrator, Ethel claimed extreme poverty and left bus tickets in visiting-card trays. She communicated with her family – including her mother and sister – via an occasional frosty postcard, such as: 'Anyone who sees fit to associate with my husband will never be received by me. E.B.'

The only reference to Ethel's departure in *Real People* requires a bit of guesswork. 'It was at this time that a cloud of unhappiness which had overshadowed our lives lifted and as my father and my younger brother and I moved to 33 Grosvenor Street, we stepped into a fresh landscape.' Later, Sheila gave 'the cloud of unhappiness' the name of Ethel. 'My mother was reduced to the sickening memory of a Grimms' tale witch,' she wrote in *Sun Too Fast*, but the 'fresh landscape' had its shadow side for now she had to act as hostess for a demanding father. This obligation led to what she called 'a comedy of deceit', but wasn't always funny. She loved 33 Grosvenor Street; it had belonged to an American heiress who, on marrying an Austrian nobleman, became Princess Hatzfeld. The back drawing room was Sheila's own. It had panelled walls of light-coloured oak taken from a French boudoir and a view of a pretty mews, Three Kings Yard. It was only half a mile away from Seymour Street but in a far more elegant world, at the very heart of Mayfair. This was always Sheila's favourite part of London. When she lived in Ireland and, later, Switzerland, on her visits to England she always stayed at Claridge's, the luxurious hotel in Brook Street, on the far side of Three Kings Yard. She was entirely happy reading and writing in her panelled boudoir and trying to meet similarly-minded intellectuals, such as the young woman whose sitting-room 'had cushions on its floor and low bookshelves filled with a whole *terra incognita* of literature.' But Claude had other ideas. He gave his daughter a generous dress allowance and expected her to be permanently on show in his own literature-despising world.

The French finishing school had reported that 'Sheila has a great appearance of willingness,' correctly implying that the appearance was deceptive. In Grosvenor Street, she complied with Claude's wishes, and, at the same time, defied them. She attended the luncheon parties, dinner parties and balls and saw to 'the detailed running of the large staff, which in itself felt like talking a strange language in a remote country'. She discomfited her dancing partners by asking them their opinion of Schopenhauer. She accepted the dress allowance but 'squandered' it in the bookshops of the Charing Cross Road. When she was expected to have new dresses for Ascot, she sold back the books or patronized a very inexpensive dressmaker, 'Miss Florence', who lived off the Edgware Road. Claude had a sharp eye for dress and used to say, 'If a woman comes into a room and people say, "What a beautiful woman," the dress is a success.' Sheila had dark, rather intense good looks and the kind of fluid slenderness that was fashionable in the 1920s, the age of the flat-chested flapper. She could usually carry off Miss Florence's creations, with only the occasional rebuke for reallocating her dress allowance. Claude loved his daughter and looked after her until the end of his life but his love came at a price: Sheila had to be the right kind of daughter because Ethel had been the wrong kind of wife. And the right kind of daughter was an obedient one.

In between her social duties, Sheila attended T. Frederic (Fred) Wilson's lectures at the Victoria and Albert museum. In *Real People*, she devoted a whole chapter to this gifted Irishman who knew everything about the applied arts, painting, sculpture, myth, religion and philosophy. He was also a cordon bleu and, for a time, a war correspondent. None of these attainments supplied him with a pension and he died in poverty, a few years after the Second World War, in a house in 'one of the grimier side streets of West Ealing'. At Wilson's lectures and at concerts she met people who shared her interests, but she was as disconcerting in their world as she was among the debs' delights who claimed her evenings. Her pampered life of servants and chauffeured cars went strangely with her bluestocking ways. '... although I imagined that I knew what world I wanted, I never knew what world I was in'. She didn't really belong in either.

At least with one man, first encountered during that deceitful time when she was in her early twenties, she always seemed to know where she was. Colonel J.T.C. (Ivon) Moore-Brabazon, was already in his forties and long married to his wife Hilda, (née Crabbe) when he was introduced to Sheila at a dinner party at the Café de Paris. The following summer, probably in 1930, Sheila, a novice at sailing, was crewing for him on his Redwing on the Isle of Wight. After one perilous trip, Ivon said, 'You're the bravest girl I know. I thought it certain we'd drown. I can't get over your bravery.' Her courage was due to ignorance; she had thought that the waterlogged boat with mainsail spread flat on the sea was a common experience. Learning otherwise, she bought a handbook on elementary sailing and hired a sailboat on the lake at Regent's Park to improve her skills. Sheila wrote about Ivon in *Sun Too Fast*, which was published ten years after he died in 1964, aged eighty. She listed his many achievements, which included: first English aviator to hold the certificate granted to pilots by the Royal Aero Club in 1910; head of Aerial Photography in the First World War; Minister of Transport and then of Aircraft Production in the Second; president of the Royal Institution, 1948–63; the man after whom the Bristol Brabazon airliner was named and who made witty speeches in the House of Lords after he became the first Lord Brabazon of Tara in 1942. She wrote of his sportsmanship, salmon fishing, hunting, motor-racing and golfing as well as his sailing and various experiments, such as adding two rotary blades to the cut-down mast of his Redwing to increase speed – 'This autogyro I refused to crew in. Decapitation seemed certain.'

Sheila and Ivon rode, hunted and played golf but not all their shared activities were outdoor ones. Ivon introduced Sheila to the astronomer and physicist, Sir Arthur Eddington, over creamed haddock on toast at the Embassy Club in Bond Street. 'The Prince of Wales often took a woman companion there; and [the] band played softly and seductively,' Sheila wrote, so you wonder whether she, too, was being softly seduced. In 1929, she had begun corresponding with J.W. Dunne, author of *An Experiment in Time* (1927) and Ivon encouraged her to write an article for the magazine *Armchair Science*, discussing Dunne's theory of a four-dimensional space-time continuum. Her article 'Can You Remember the Future?' was published in the magazine's April 1932 issue, and she was paid three guineas. In the article, she wrote about the importance of attending to one's dreams, a subject that never stopped fascinating her. In her portrait of Ivon Brabazon, Sheila mentioned the games of postal chess which she played with him for years, after she became Lady Powerscourt, but not the ardent letters which he wrote to her during the Second World War and for some years afterwards. Neither does she say how she managed to escape Claude's chaperones – 'his rules about my own sexual behaviour were puritanical' – so that she could eat creamed haddock in a nightclub with another woman's husband. Claude, in spite of the manicurist in St John's Wood, his exotic man-servant and his amusing eccentricities, expected his daughter to be a model of decorum. It's extraordinary, and rather admirable, that Sheila was able to outwit her all-controlling papa, but, by then, although only in her twenties, she'd become almost addicted to having secrets. Her relationship with Ivon established another covert pattern in her life: close friendships with rich, protective, older men; usually married, idiosyncratic and powerful; men, in fact, who were rather like her own father.

In 1929, at the age of twenty-three, Sheila already held strong views on cultural institutions and she wasn't afraid to express them. She didn't keep a copy of a letter she wrote to the British Museum in January of that year, but the Museum's rather tongue-in-cheek reply gives some idea of her forwardness and hints at her lifelong addiction to letter-writing:

> Madam,
> I am much obliged to you for the suggestions contained in your letter of Jan 21st. I feel some doubt as to the suitability of stage lighting for the permanent illumination of a museum gallery; but if the new room for the Parthenon marbles comes into existence, your suggestions will be taken into account before a decision is arrived at as to the method of decoration.

Suggesting ideas for museum lighting when she should have been choosing hats or luncheon menus was as much a part of Sheila's comedy of deceit as dinner dates with Ivon Brabazon. But the major deception remained her reading. The intense secret pleasure of the pigtailed book-worm, half-thrilled, half-terrified that she might be discovered with a book in her hand, became more intense, and more pleasurable, once the pigtailed little girl became a young woman. In her inaugural lecture, 'Reading in Bed', given at Oxford in 1999, Hermione Lee traced the history of women's 'illicit' reading and demonstrated that, for many centuries, 'women's secret reading has been thought – probably rightly – to be a dangerous habit'. Even in 1992, female contributors to an anthology called *The Pleasure of Reading'*, cited by Lee, remembered 'a settled hostility to the reading girl'. Claude wasn't alone in his antagonism towards female bookishness. He just went further than most in his determination to squash any sign of intellectual tendencies in his daughter, because he couldn't bear the thought that she might turn out like his wife.

3. A MASQUERADE

'Acting a triple role to please my father ... wife surrogate in the form of
hostess and housekeeper ... fashionable daughter ... substitute son.'
Sheila Powerscourt, *Sun Too Fast*

Claude, unconsciously, tried to turn Sheila into the girl that Ethel
Mulock had been when he'd first fallen in love with her, when she
loved hunting and shooting and the race track and gave no hint that what
she really wanted was to preside over a highbrow London salon. So Sheila
had to go along with Claude's game plan, which meant putting in hours
of practice at clay pigeon shooting and the 'monotony of those prescribed
activities which were termed pleasure'. There was nothing she could do
about it: 'To revolt would have hurt my father unspeakably and, besides,
what would I then have turned to? I was inexperienced, untrained; more-
over the stuff of revolt was not in me.' It was Claude himself who, by not
letting her go to university and by discouraging her from reading, made
sure that she stayed inexperienced and untrained. He would have agreed
with Robert Southey's advice to the young Charlotte Brontë, who had sent
him some poems. 'Literature,' Southey told her, 'cannot be the business of
a woman's life. The more she is engaged in her proper duties, the less
leisure she will have for it, even as an accomplishment and recreation.'

Sheila detested her mother for being a spoilt and petulant hothouse
orchid, who constantly pained her husband by rejecting the sporting life
that he loved. She recalled how once, after a fall, she saw Ethel 'walk in
with mud on her riding-habit skirt, a black eye, and her face a white mask

of tragedy that such things could be'. This, according to Sheila, 'put an end to the countryside' for Ethel. Ethel didn't see herself this way at all. In her own memoir, she wrote that she attended shooting parties as late as 1914, the year she stayed at Somerhill, the Jacobean home of the d'Avigdor Goldsmids, in Kent. These were distinguished members of 'the Cousinhood', those Anglo-Jewish families of wealth and influence who were active in public life. It's possible that Sheila went with her, because she remained friends with this family all her life. Ethel wrote enthusiastically about Newmarket – admittedly, as much for the pleasure of meeting titled acquaintances as for the racing – and reels off the names of stable-owners, their winning horses and bets won and lost.

Ethel loved horses almost as much as she loved aristocrats and wrote wittily about her favourite horse, Old Times, who let her children climb up his legs and whose hoof she had mounted on a plaque after his death. She described one serious fall she had in 1913, when out with the Pytchley Hounds. Her horse put its foot into a hole, threw her but, luckily, didn't roll on her. According to the American gentleman who picked her up, 'She was black in the face, nearly asphyxiated by the mud in her nostrils … her nose was bleeding … well, ye know, ordinarily she's a very pretty woman, but on that occasion she looked positively plain!' It's typical of Ethel to brag of compliments to her beauty and it's possible that this whole incident was as much a product of her imagination as playing at nursemaids with Queen Marie of Romania. There's something in the way she writes about hunting and horses, however, that rings true. It's hard to imagine her daunted by one tumble into a rabbit hole; she's all pluck and swagger. Ethel went to extraordinary lengths to avoid acknowledging distress, her refusal to attend her sons' funerals being the most extreme example. She would never have worn 'the white mask of tragedy'.

Sheila couldn't bear to follow in Ethel's footsteps. If Claude insisted that his daughter hunted and rode, she had to convince herself that her mother had always hated being on horseback. When she wrote about Ethel abandoning country life, it was also to show that Ethel had never loved Claude or bothered to please him, whereas Sheila did both, however high the cost to her emotional and physical well-being. Sheila writes painfully and modestly about her hunting days, with never a reference to Lord Lonsdale of Barley Thorpe or any other aristocratic host. You would not guess from her nervous descriptions of putting on her hunting clothes – the boots that 'for vanity's sake must be tight to a fraction of a millimetre

yet for comfort's sake not tight enough to pinch' and the 'snowy accura-
cies' of the tie which she addressed 'with trembling fingers' – that the end
result was exquisite. Ivon Brabazon in a wartime letter to Sheila, wrote
yearningly, 'Was there ever anyone who looked better on a horse? Was
there ever anyone braver than your wonderfull [sic] self when you turned
out with the Quorn in swallowtails?' Not being Ethel, Sheila did not
parade this compliment in print. According to her daughter, Grania Langrishe, Sheila was exceptionally clumsy, 'always dropping things and
crashing gears'. She wasn't exaggerating about those 'trembling fingers';
the perfection which Ivon so admired had been achieved at a price.

Ethel's descriptions of hunting sparkle with eager gaiety but her
daughter's reek of anxiety and fear: 'a wait that felt like a yawn in
expectancy of danger', and she presents herself as a forlorn novice, 'left in
dwindling company to realize, sickly, that everyone else had gone off on
the right track and that you were miles behind, with hours of dogged
road-work or inspired cross-country improvisation needed to find hounds
again if you were lucky …'. During all those tense periods of waiting for
something to happen, Sheila developed a scrutinizing habit. She notices,
for example, that the day has been, in turn, thirty colours and lists them in
three columns, starting with 'lichenous' and ending with 'clay' by way of
'cindered' and 'madder'. One of her first published poems (from 'The
Journey', *Poems,* 1938) is all damp, wintry outdoors:

> Where winter oaks have always stood,
> A pheasant slide into a wood;
> I mark the hushed and bleak appeal
> Of the long pastureland, and feel
> The snow-sky like a pigeon's breast
> Hold me entranced and repossessed.

She was always to write about the countryside, even years after she had
given up country pursuits.

Sheila was Claude's hostess at Glendye, the grouse moor in Kincardineshire, rented from Sir Albert Gladstone, for ten years. Glendye was ten
miles square and 'with some twenty or thirty lines of butts so that you
never shot over the same line twice in a season'. The hours of clay-pigeon
shooting paid off. She 'got the knack and rejoiced his [Claude's] heart.'
Her own heart was not rejoiced. 'Evening after evening, I came back
[from the butts] with aching arms and aching legs and an aching head and

aching back, exhausted and rained through, or just exhausted.' Reading far into the night didn't improve her energy levels but, her duties as surrogate wife and surrogate son over for the day, she battled on with her self-taught Greek, the austere ordeals recounted by Homer no doubt helping her maintain a hard resolve. She wasn't the only young woman of her time who, denied the chance of going to university, had to console herself with a self-guided, wide-ranging education, but how lonely it must have been living like that, never meeting anyone at all like herself. And mustn't it have seemed odd to all those hunting, shooting and fishing acquaintances of Claude's that he made his daughter work so hard, so that she had to be a crack shot by day – and a much too competitive one – and a fashion plate in the evenings?

Such a strange sort of daughter too, out of her social depth at any hour. The trouble was that Claude didn't really know the rules; he'd grown up with a different set of customs, handed down from his father and father's father and featuring a paternal heavy-handedness. Sheila's willingness to submit to her father's control is perhaps more complex than she claims. Like her dead brother, Guy, Claude is someone with whom she would never be through. He takes up three chapters in her first memoir and his story threads its way through the second. In a radio broadcast in 1952, called 'A Parent', Sheila returns to Claude again: his courage, intelligence and sound common sense. She sums him up as 'a warm, human contradictory person whom I think of as the best parent in the world'. Never a mention that his love for her was autocratic and over-protective, with an element of exploitation.

The hosts and hostesses of the weekend house parties attended by Lt Col and Miss Beddington, as described in *Real People*, are never named. Sheila is so withholding that everything she writes is overlaid with mystery. Whose was the house in Dorset where 'guests are said to have piled coats on their beds, then their bedroom rugs and carpets and finally the pictures off the walls, in attempts to get warm'? Who was the 73-year-old host who drinks 'a bottle of hock for breakfast, half a bottle of brandy at lunch and a wide and deep assortment of wines at dinner, every day for fifty years', and is still straight-backed and boyishly energetic? His smoking-room contains a bath, surrounded by a trellis made of stuffed snakes. In such eccentric surroundings, Sheila and Claude's arrival with their Ceylonese manservant, Namo Kallasagaram, would not have seemed unduly bizarre. But Miss Beddington was a bit out of the ordinary: too determined to excel at hunting and shooting, too serious on the dance floor. Those dancing partners whom she embarrassed with her philosophical enquiries were mostly wealthy so had no need to woo Claude's bluestocking daughter. They probably changed partners at the first opportunity.

And there was another reason why Miss Beddington, in spite of her beauty and wealth, was not altogether a catch. In his sequence of novels, *A Dance to the Music of Time*, Anthony Powell draws a perceptive portrait of a well-connected young Jewish woman, Rosie Manash. Her first appearance is as a 'lively, gleaming little Jewess', who, during a strained pre-ball dinner party given by the aristocratic Walpole-Wilsons, carefully mentions that she has had an audience with the Pope. Nevertheless, Powell notes that she looked 'quite out of place in this setting'. Rosie is one of the most sympathetic characters in Powell's story; she is shrewd, intelligent and attractive and marries two presentable men, but that initial impression of difference is never quite dispelled. There were several Jews in Edward VII's inner circle: Rothschilds and Sassoons and the aforementioned Sir Ernest Cassel. They were part of upper-class English life, which, in the period between the death of Queen Victoria and the Great War, was languorous and non-judgmental. By the 1920s, when Sheila was 'coming out', much had changed. In *Anti-Semitism: The Longest Hatred*, Robert S. Wistrich writes of an 'elusively polite anti-Semitism that tinged much of British life between the wars'. A loss of continuity in society could be blamed on Jews, that cosmopolitan and free-thinking tribe. In his 1919 poem 'Burbank with a Baedeker: Bleistein with a Cigar', T.S. Eliot wrote: 'The rats are underneath the piles./The Jew is underneath the lot.'

During Sheila's 'grand-scale visits', as she described them, she met with 'a high standard of consideration and good manners'. The people she mixed with on grouse moor and hunting field had probably never heard of T.S. Eliot and had been brought up to mask social dislike with politeness. Sheila presented an acceptable picture in her 'effectively simple dresses', and the London dinner parties and magnificent entertaining at Glendye eased her way, at least on the surface. But that decorous surface was thin and brittle. In 1945, a year when one would have supposed a certain sympathy towards Jews, Harold Nicolson wrote in his diary, 'Although I loathe anti-Semitism, I do dislike Jews,' a view that was not unusual among members of his class. The uneasiness of her position in English society had a lot to do with Sheila's determined evasiveness in both her life and work and her horror of being exposed as less than fault-less. Her children thought her ridiculously self-obsessed but they had never had to go through those motions of playing in a masquerade, never quite sure of who you were or whom other people expected you to be, always a little undefined. Sheila regarded, or pretended to regard, Claude's Jewish roots as buried in the distant past. Her complicated relationship with her Jewish ancestry will be discussed later, in light of her reaction to queries from her son Guy about their family history. The only identity problem she ever admitted to, with rueful pride, was the English/Irish one. As a published poet, she thought that reviewers might have a problem, with it: 'This duality was often a puzzle to myself.' The puzzle of her Jewishness was never admitted.

She found occasional refuge from Claude at Quenby, the Leicester-shire home of her aunt, Enid Nutting. Enid was the antithesis of Ethel, her elder sister. Ethel was slender and dark, Enid 'inclined to plumpness, her squarish, Mulock jaw, her most golden of fair hair, blue eyes and radiant complexion', joyfully described by her niece. Enid 'embodied durable affection. This had enfolded me with a truly comforting and maternal love. Unselfish, undemanding, sustained devotion.' As a girl, Enid had been a talented violinist, winning the Gold Medal at the Dublin Festival of Music before going on to study in Brussels. She then married Lt Col Sir Harold Nutting, the owner of Quenby, a large Elizabethan manor house, and Master of the Quorn. A diabetic who was also a keen huntsman, Sir Harold injected himself through his breeches when it was impractical to dismount. His wife disliked horses and preferred indoor comforts; in winter she stayed in bed with her tapestry work and small dogs. She refused to go near her husband's stableful of horses and ignored guests who reproached her for her lack of heartiness. It was when staying at Quenby, freed from Claude's zealous chaperoning, that Sheila could ride with Ivon Brabazon 'across a country of large enclosures, fit for gal-loping between the tall, strong quickthorn hedges that kept bullocks from breaking through', and leave him smitten by the sight of her in swallow-tails. But even that possibility didn't make her any keener to hunt. Setting out for a meet, she is reminded of the mournful verse: 'Farewell house, and farewell home/Shees for the Moores and Martyrdome', and wrote, 'Terrible bright eyes of a bird found in the heather wounded instead of dead, excited eyes of young retrievers, abstracted eyes of horses – these haunted me in turn.' Not the words of an enthusiast.

3. A Masquerade

At the age of twenty-five, in spite of her constant, if unwilling, attendance on the hunting-field and in the ballroom, Sheila was still unmarried. She belonged to a social class where a successful girl was one who was engaged to be married by the end of her first season; Sheila and Claude, neither of them comfortable with failure, knew this. At some stage, as the years of Sheila's spinsterhood passed by, an Anglo-Irish husband must have been considered. Both father and daughter loved Ireland. Claude's happiest times had been spent planting fruit trees in the garden at Ballycurrin, and although he was never to have a home of his own in Ireland, he made frequent visits. His elder brother, Herbert, lived in County Cork, and Claude who, as one might expect, had 'precision and patience with a dry fly', fished there. He was also warmly welcomed by his Mulock parents-in-law at Bellair, the house where his children had spent blissful childhood holidays. Although Sheila stressed her duality – 'Bally Ard in my bones and full of love for England', Bally Ard had, one feels, first claim. It's there in her 1949 poem, 'Ireland': 'This is the country/That has no desolation, no empty feel'. And Dublin was 'The only city that has lodged/Sadly in my bones' (from 'A Melancholy Love' in *Her Storms*, 1977).

The events of the 1920s, the Troubles followed by the setting up of the Irish Free State and then the Civil War (1922–23), didn't daunt those members of the Ascendancy class who remained in Ireland. The social season continued as several Big Houses were burnt by rebels and the occasional owner shot dead. There was a widespread desire that the country should settle down. So on went the hunting and balls, the Spring Show and the Horse Show, the racing at Punchestown and Fairyhouse, the polo tournaments and luncheon parties at the Viceregal Lodge, hosted now by obliging Irish Governor Generals. Sheila went to Ireland as often as she could; it was where she was loved and at her most loving. The Anglo-Irish weren't as judgmental as their English counterparts, or so she felt. When the 4th Marquess of Headfort married a Gaiety Girl, Rosie Boot, in 1901, he was shunned in England but never in Ireland, where his wife, in spite of her former career and her Catholicism, was welcomed. Brendan Behan dismissed the Anglo-Irishman as 'a Protestant on a horse', but he was more interesting than that, determinedly rooted while his world swirled about in change.

Ascendancy families were, for the most part, poor, stripped of their land by more than two decades of Land Acts and having no compensating industrial or commercial shareholdings. This was an advantage: a down-at-heel aristocrat, heir to a magnificent but increasingly decrepit Big House, might welcome Claude's daughter if she brought Claude's money with her. And as for Claude's daughter herself, did she notice that these Ascendancy families had any failings? Few of them appreciated a reading girl, as perhaps their eighteenth-century ancestors might have done. In 1899, Standish O'Grady, the Anglo-Irish editor of *The Kilkenny Moderator*, had fought a losing battle to persuade Ascendancy leaders to 'reshape themselves in a heroic mould', castigating them in editorials: 'God save us all! You read nothing and know nothing.'

J.M. Synge noted this cultural slippage in his essay 'A Landlord's Garden in County Wicklow', published in *The Manchester Guardian* in 1907: '... they [Irish landlords] do not equal their forefathers, and where men used to collect fine editions of *Don Quixote* and Molière, in Spanish and French, and luxuriantly bound copies of Juvenal and Persius and Cicero, nothing is read now but Longfellow and Hall Caine and Miss Corelli'. Almost a century later, in her perceptive essay on the Big House, Lorna Reynolds wrote, 'To be an intellectual in such a society is to be considered, if not a freak, something extraordinarily rare.' Someone with a less divided self than Sheila's might have thought that leaving Claude for such a milieu meant leaping from the frying-pan into the fire, but Sheila was always ready to sacrifice the reading girl inside herself, and then complain bitterly at having made the sacrifice. In the spring of 1932, in the mist and mud of an Irish point-to-point, she met the Honourable Mervyn Patrick Wingfield, heir to Viscount Powerscourt and as perfect a specimen of a Protestant on a horse as it was possible to be.

4. MARRIED TO THE DESCENDANCY

'Romantic love is a device every bit as curious and elaborate as the millions upon millions of other disguises used by nature for perpetuation.'
Sheila Powerscourt, *Sun Too Fast*

'The Anglo-Irish Ascendancy of the end of the nineteenth century and the beginning of the twentieth century was an enormous confidence trick shored up by faithful servants and good horsemanship.'
Gifford Lewis, *Somerville and Ross: The World of the Irish RM*

Mervyn Patrick 'Pat' Wingfield was an attractive young man, tall and fair, with a moustache that made him look a bit like the film-star Douglas Fairbanks Senior. He was charming and friendly with an easy-going lack of introspection. He had what the Ulster poet, Louis Mac-Neice, has called the 'obsolete bravado' of his class. In Pat's case, the bravado looked very much like courage, as did the adaptability that was to see him through every change of circumstance: his family's declining fortunes, a series of dead-end jobs, years as a prisoner of war and, finally, the sale of Powerscourt, his ancestral estate in Enniskerry, County Wicklow, owned by the Wingfields since the time of Elizabeth I, and to which Pat had devoted his life. Pat was born in 1905, to a life of great privilege and with every expectation of continuing the lifestyle led by previous generations of Wingfields: that of benevolent landlord to a grateful and loyal tenantry. This in spite of the fact that the preceding century had seen the political and economic power of the landed gentry in Ireland seep away. R.F. Foster estimates that 'political deference probably lapsed beyond control in the 1870s', while a landlord in Down who sold his lands in 1874 declared that 'an Irish estate is like a sponge and an Irish landlord is never so rich as when he is rid of his property'. Pat's father, the 8th Lord Powerscourt, (hereafter referred to as Mervyn), did not believe that the Ascendancy was redundant. In his own eyes, and in the eyes of many of his tenants, he was an essential and useful member of society. He had no intention of selling his estate to become a homesick nobody somewhere else.

Pat, as was the Wingfield custom, was sent to Eton but was expelled after accusing a master of lying. He resumed his education at another public school, Fettes, in Edinburgh, before going on to the Royal Military College, Sandhurst. He then joined the Irish Guards, the regiment of which his father had been a founding member when it was formed in 1900. By the time Pat came of age, in 1926, Mervyn could no longer afford the regimental mess bills and living expenses and Pat had to transfer to the less exclusive 8th Hussars, where he became a lieutenant. Ascendancy life became bleaker during the 1920s; the Land Commission, first established in 1881, was reconstituted in 1923, with a new Land Act, by the new Free State government. The Commission compulsorily purchased and redistributed property held by Ascendancy landlords, the Powerscourts among them, so that in less than ten years, 450,000 acres were distributed to 24,000 families. There had been a series of Land Acts since 1870 but previous legislation had offered some advantages to landlords, in the form of compensation, often recklessly spent. Returning the land to the people was seen as 'reversing Cromwell's policy', and helped to ensure peace and stability in post-Civil-War Ireland. The price paid was the loss of some of the country's historic houses, whose owners, deprived of the surrounding estates, could no longer afford to maintain them. Even before the 1923 Land Act, however, the Big House had been threatened. Between 1921 and 1923, almost 200 Big Houses were burnt down.

It was characteristic of the Wingfields to carry on regardless and difficulties were forgotten at Pat's coming-of-age celebrations, held at Powerscourt on 22 August 1926, to which 500 guests were invited. The proceedings started with a dinner for the outdoor staff and refreshments were provided throughout the day. When darkness came, an elaborate fireworks display lit up the sky. *The Irish Times* reported in its account of Pat's birthday party that 'Whatever changes may have taken place elsewhere in the relations between the landlord and tenant, there [has] been no change in the relations between the people of the County Wicklow and the house of Wingfield.' The Powerscourts had a reputation for being good landlords. Like his ancestors, Mervyn had been an improving land-lord, modernizing his tenants' homes and building new ones. The Pow-erscourt tenants had continued to pay rent through the rebellious 1920s and, although, on three occasions during the Troubles, intimation was given that Powerscourt was to be burnt, the house was spared, supposedly because of Mervyn's popularity. Mervyn gave a speech on this occasion which illustrated how he viewed his position as landlord as well as an assumption that nothing could ever really rock the foundations of his class:

> I trust that whatever laws are passed in the future to regulate our positions, our heart strings, tying us together as friends, may prove themselves so strong that we can always afford to laugh at those who tamper with what used to be the Powerscourt estate.

But the government had taken away his land and not compensated him for improving living conditions on the estate. He had begun to see himself as a poor man, whose underqualified son was going to have to find a job.

Once the party was over, Pat went out to work. In his early twenties, he was employed by the government of Northern Ireland to boost army recruitment. Then he went to the Sudan, to a job on a cotton plantation, where he learnt Senussi, a language that was to play a fateful part in his war service some years later. The plantation failed and, in the autumn of 1932, now aged twenty-seven, Pat joined the British section of the Pales-tine police as a constable. His lowly employment was newsworthy – 'Peer's Heir as P.C.' was the headline in *The Daily Mail*, above an article that quoted a gloomy Mervyn explaining, 'Jobs are difficult to find nowa-days and there was nothing else for my son to do.' Learning how to manage the Powerscourt estate was not an option. In the six years that had passed since that lavish coming-of-age party, it had become increasingly likely that there would not be an estate for Pat to inherit.

From 1932 on, the Ascendancy slipped further into the Descendancy. On 12 March that year, Eamon de Valera's Fianna Fáil party, elected on a platform of agrarian reform and distribution, defeated W.T. Cosgrave's government and immediately increased income tax and withheld the land annuities due to Britain under the terms of the 1921 Anglo-Irish Treaty. This led to retaliatory trade legislation and the start of the economic war. Ascendancy landowners such as Mervyn weren't the only people to feel the pinch, but de Valera's 'social justice' policies certainly made their position in the country uncertain. In that same year, grants were withdrawn from Ascendancy strongholds such as the Royal Dublin Society (RDS), founded in 1731 to promote agriculture and scientific research, just as Mervyn was elected the society's president. The future of the horse-breeding industry, mostly Ascendancy-run, was thus also put in doubt. In June, the Catholic triumphalism of the Eucharistic Congress so sickened Æ (the writer George William Russell) that he sold his Dublin home and moved to England. In its account of the huge open-air Mass held in the Phoenix Park and attended by nearly a million people, *The Irish Times* conveyed Protestant unease at the spectacle. The Congress was a gleeful demonstration of how Fianna Fáil, excommunicated in its former guise for its part in the Civil War, had become the well-behaved servant of the Church. It also made clear that non-Catholics in Ireland had been relegated to what the poet Patrick Kavanagh would call in an article he wrote for *The Standard* in 1943, 'lookers-on', people who were not 'part of the national consciousness'. In a speech in July 1932, British prime minister, Ramsay MacDonald, described de Valera as 'a fool put into a china shop in hobnail boots and with liberty to smash'. Mervyn was more circumspect. He told the Royal Dublin Society:

> Should the voice of the people declare that they no longer wish for our services, which in every case are unremunerative, then we will go, possibly with broken hearts, but with no feeling of resentment and leaving behind us our earnest good wishes for a prosperous and more peaceable Ireland.

Six years before, he had made a speech to his former tenants, stating his devotion to his house and 40,000 acres. Now, he put the estate up for sale. This, like his son's lack of prospects, made newspaper headlines – 'Famous castle to be sold. Taxation too heavy for Lord Powerscourt'.

Looking at the history of the Wingfields during their long tenure at Powerscourt, it is understandable why thoughts of leaving the estate would be heartbreaking. Richard Wingfield (*c.* 1550–1634), the first Viscount Powerscourt, born in Suffolk, displayed the charm and the zeal for public service that marked out his descendants. Having defeated the wild Wicklow rebels, the O'Tooles and the O'Byrnes, he was asked by Elizabeth I what he would like by way of a reward and replied oilily, 'The scarf which Your Majesty wears is sufficient reward for me.' His smarm brought him large amounts of land, including Powerscourt, once held by the de la Poers, and, in 1618, a viscountcy. He died childless as did the Wingfield for whom the title was recreated in 1642. In 1743, the title was revived for the third time for another Richard Wingfield (1697–1751), 'a civil, well bred man', according to a contemporary. This Richard's out-standing achievement was to build, between 1629 and 1743, a magnificent house which incorporated the thick-walled tower where his rougher ancestors had lived. The tower had been a necessary fortress but, by the early eighteenth century, the Anglo-Irish felt as secure in Ireland as they would ever be, quite forgetting, in Elizabeth Bowen's words, that they were 'imposed on a seized land'. They could afford, in every sense of the word, houses that were sophisticated and cosmopolitan. The new house and its owner were the subjects of a gushing poem by an anonymous admirer of the cultured Viscount:

> Eden springs where late you found a Waste
> Sketch'd in your House, the candid heart we view,
> Its Grace, Strength, Order all reflecting you.

The architect of all this grace, strength and order was Richard Cassels (*c.* 1690–1751), who later simplified his name to Castle. He was 'the German architect with first-hand experience of the exuberant classicism of Central Europe' and the creator of much of Georgian Ireland: the Rotunda Hospital and Leinster House in Dublin and the country houses Russbor-ough, Carlton and Westport. 'The beauty of Irish Georgian architecture is that it is never pretty,' R.F. Foster has observed, and Powerscourt is a case in point. Built of grey Wicklow granite from the Glencree quarries, glinting against the backdrop of the Sugarloaf mountain, its three-storey centre block has a tower surmounted by a copper cupola at each end and is joined by single-storey links to two-storey wings in the Palladian manner. The first-floor 'Saloon', or ballroom, was, according to Mark Bence-Jones, 'the grandest country-house interior in Ireland'. Eighty feet long and forty feet wide, it had fluted marble columns, a high, gilt-encrusted ceiling and a richly-patterned walnut parquetry floor.

What it didn't have, until the nineteenth century, was a fireplace, leading to the conjecture that the house may have been intended as a villa for summer entertaining. During wet Irish winters, eighteenth-century Wingfields were supposedly elsewhere, this being the golden era of the Grand Tour. Cassels began work on the gardens which successive gener-ations of Wingfields went on to elaborate. The unadorned grass terraces were transformed, in the 1840s, into a magnificent Italian garden by the Scottish architect Daniel Robertson, who added broad flights of steps with inlaid paving, statues and fountains. Nearby, the 398-foot-high waterfall – the highest in Great Britain and Ireland – tumbles down wooded hill-sides. All this, and the great wrought-iron gates and serpentine beech avenue ensured inclusion in Peter Coats' book *Great Gardens of the Western World* (1953) since it was, Coats wrote, 'probably the last garden of its size and quality ever to have been created'.

The Wingfields were extravagant. The Lord Powerscourt (1729–64) known as the 'French Lord' because of a long lingering at the court of Louis XV, brought back from his Grand Tour in the early 1750s many paintings, including two seascapes by Claude Joseph Vernet. He also built a townhouse in South William Street in Dublin, now a multi-level shop-ping centre. Elegant and glamorous, he was thought to be looking for an heiress to fund his spending but became ill, dying at thirty-five. In the nineteenth century, incumbent Viscounts unpacked the French bronzes, Italian marbles, gates from Vienna and Russian ornaments acquired by a consumptive predecessor and lavishly added to the beauty of house and garden. This was the era of Daniel Robertson, who, during the Famine years, provided a hundred men with employment, supervising the new landscaping from a wheelbarrow in which he was carried about drinking a bottle of sherry, stopping work when the bottle was empty.

The 7th Viscount (1844–1904), author, in 1903, of a published *Description and History of Powerscourt*, intended, since he was childless, to spend the entire Wingfield fortune before a despised brother inherited. How-ever, after sixteen years of marriage, he suddenly fathered five children, of whom the eldest was Mervyn. Fatherhood didn't cramp the 7th Viscount's style: he built a new wing, a new dining-room and ran up large debts. Mervyn himself continued to enhance the gardens. With his wife, Sybil, he created a Japanese garden reclaimed from the bog and built a tower to house an impressive collection of cannon, which he had begun to acquire and catalogue in 1907. Not everyone was impressed by the Wingfield flamboyance. Mrs Elizabeth Smith of Baltiboys, a modest estate in nearby Blessington, visited Powerscourt in 1849 and complained, 'I don't myself like this style of architecture, too formal, nor can I endure these palaces with their stiff gravel terraces amid the natural beauties of trees, fields and ocean,' but, of course, subduing nature's wildness was the whole point of Victorian landscaping.

In spite of their spendthrift habits, the Wingfields had a strong sense of duty. The 4th Viscount (1762–1808) was one of only five Irish peers who voted against the Act of Union in 1801, and, although suffering from gout, got out of bed and kicked downstairs the government agent who came to try and bribe him with an Earldom to support the Act. He was so proud of having shown the agent the door that he had the words, 'You are not going to bribe me' inscribed on the frame of his portrait. He feared, correctly, that the Act of Union would set Ireland on the slippery slope towards Catholic emancipation, the disestablishment of the Church of Ireland and land reform. In other words, it would sideline dutiful grandees such as himself. His son, Mervyn's father, was president of the Royal Dublin Society in the 1890s and Mervyn himself, uncomfortably adrift in the new Free State, also worked on behalf of the society. He was, for a few years, a Free State senator, one of the few peers elected to the Senate by W.T. Cosgrave. He was also the chief commissioner of the Boy Scouts in the Irish Free State. There was, supposedly, a curse on the Powerscourts, which decreed 'that no holder of the title should ever see his heir'. This proved to be alarmist but there were more than a few early deaths: the second Viscount died at thirty-four, the fifth at thirty-two and the sixth at twenty-nine. Mervyn inherited the title in 1904, aged twenty-five, a year after his marriage, from his father who had inherited it at the age of eight.

Elizabeth Bowen described Irish estates as 'something between a raison d'être and a predicament'. You get a sense of this in a letter from Lady Diana Manners to her future husband, Duff Cooper, written in September 1917 on a visit to Ireland:

> I went over to a place called Powerscourt. I was much impressed by the beauty. An ancestor who discovered Italy with the rest of them in the eighteenth century stocked his garden with great marble Nikes and fauns and tender Ganymedes and Tritons blowing fountains a hundred feet high against the higher mountains. I was struck too by the pathos of Lady Powerscourt, a frail pale woman who lives in strictest poverty in the gaunt house stark alone. About thirty-five, an enthusiast of life as I might be, she is facing with only faint misgivings this coming impossible winter with two servants and no petrol.

Mervyn's wife Sybil, Lady Powerscourt, the former Sybil Pleydell-Bouverie, was indeed facing grim times. Her husband, having survived the Gallipoli campaign of 1915, was still in battle, serving as a captain in the Irish Guards and there was a temporary servant shortage. But this 'strictest poverty' was seen through Lady Diana's pampered eyes. She was the youngest daughter of the 8th Duke of Rutland, who owned a house in Mayfair as well as Belvoir Castle in Leicestershire, and was far grander than the Powerscourts. Sybil Powerscourt, photographed a year before Lady Diana's visit, looks remarkably in the pink, riding side-saddle on her way to the hunt. Poverty-stricken by Lady Diana's standards, the Power-scourts managed to rub along pretty well until the 1920s, when the Irish Free State was founded. Mervyn found himself unable to maintain his son in the Irish Guards or keep him idling at home and, a decade later, felt obliged to put his estate up for sale. If the Wingfields were to remain at Powerscourt, something needed to be done. In the very nick of time, on a misty spring day in 1932, Pat Wingfield met Sheila Beddington.

They must have got to know each other during that summer and autumn but there doesn't seem to have been a whirlwind romance since, in September, Pat was despatched to Palestine because 'there was nothing else for my son to do'. His job in the police force was more boring than dangerous, his log books are a stultifying record of cases of petty larceny and rowdy local skirmishes.

There had been vicious riots in Jerusalem in 1929, which left 250 Arabs and Jews dead, but by the time Pat arrived an edgy peace pre-vailed. Isolated and lonely, he can't have found much to do in the evenings. He was a sociable man; nearly everyone thought him good company, just as nearly everyone found Sheila a bit difficult. Maybe he sighed over a copy of the portrait of Sheila which Sir John Lavery had painted the year before. Lavery was now the most fashionable of artists. His portrait of Sheila is insipid and overposed, a bit cloying. The sitter is very beautiful, dark-eyed with drawn-back hair and wearing a simple blue dress. But the way she's seated stiffly on an Empire chair, holding up a spring of freesia, makes her look as if she's agreed to the sitting against her will. Still, to Pat, lonely and homesick, she must have looked like the girl of his dreams, more exquisite than the big-boned Anglo-Irish girls he had grown up with and who, now of slender means, like him, could not be considered marriage material. Sheila, on the other hand, could be an exit visa from this lacklustre stint of foreign service, and besides, this girl, although brought up in London and alarmingly chic, was not just a lan-guid fashion plate. She was an excellent shot and a brilliant rider-to-hounds, the perfect mate for a sportsman. This cynical tone is mine not Pat's. I think that he and Sheila were then genuinely in love, with a strong, mutual physical attraction. The problem was that as time went by, they stopped liking each other.

They got engaged in November. There is an unverifiable story that, after the engagement was announced, Mervyn dashed into the Kildare Street Club in Dublin and announced, 'He's done it; she's Jewish but she's rich.' Not that the acquisition of a rich daughter-in-law seemed to change his pessimistic attitude, at least not at first. On 2 December, Mervyn was elected president of the Royal Dublin Society and made a widely-reported speech, in which he said, 'Life becomes increasingly difficult almost daily and lowering clouds surround us on all sides.' On 17 December, the day after Pat and Sheila's wedding, he again threatened, in another speech, 'I may have to resign and leave the country I have loved and lived in for so long.' The Beddington fortune soon chased those lowering clouds away. Like everything that the Powerscourts did, Pat's engagement was all over the newspapers. The *Evening Herald* commented that 'the bride-to-be comes of a well-known Irish family on her mother's side. Miss Beddington, who is very good-looking, is an excellent shot, and is equally at home in the hunting field or sailing a yacht. Her mother, Mrs Claude Beddington, is one of the keenest patrons of the opera'. No mention of the bride's father, whose family had been deliberately kept in the shadows.

Powerscourt tradition demanded a big Ascendancy wedding at St Patrick's Cathedral but the circumstances of the bride's parents were too awkward. Families like the Powerscourts did not go in for legal separations, which they regarded as uncivilized. Sybil and Mervyn's own marriage was not perfect; they both had affairs and their younger son, Brian, Sybil's favourite, who died when he was seventeen, was rumoured to be the result of her adulterous passion. They stayed together as a duty, because that was the done thing and because it was in the interest of Powerscourt that they both worked dedicatedly together to maintain the estate. They were spared what would have been the ordeal of a conventional wedding with unconventional in-laws because Claude organized a registry office wedding for his daughter in Jerusalem, far away from the attentive Irish press, with only himself, Sybil and Niall in attendance. Sheila made a ravishing bride, sleek and elegant in a narrow, white dress and a wide, white bandeau in her hair. She found the whole thing wonderfully romantic, even when viewed from a more disillusioned viewpoint in 1952:

A dreamlike glimpse from the train of a string of camels silhouetted against a pistachio dawn; from the vague and international hotel, to the glittering

cold outside of Jerusalem in December; and from a simple marriage gone
through in a trance, to the reality of my husband's strong hand holding mine.

Pat and Sheila's long honeymoon was sunlit. When they lunched at a village
inn near Claude's Italian villa, 'on an omelette, good local Chianti, cheese
and fruit', they were given as a present a local wine that was 'aromatic,
golden: the delicious taste is unwritable'. Love had made Sheila voluptuous.

The young Wingfields' return was to an Ireland which George Moore
described as 'as narrow as a pig's back' and which even Hazel Lavery, long
a champion of Irish independence, was soon to abandon. 'As for hoping,
I haven't any hope left; it makes me so anxious the way even God seems
to [be] fighting for that old de V,' she wrote crossly to Thomas Bodkin,
director of the National Gallery of Ireland, at the beginning of 1938. The
newly-weds' arrival at Powerscourt was ceremonial: they were met by 300
estate workers and then drawn along the mile-long beech avenue in an
open carriage, escorted by a guard of honour of Girl Guides. In the newspaper photographs showing the arrival at the front entrance of the house,
Pat and Mervyn, both moustached and wearing plus fours, tower over
Sheila who, in a fur-collared tweed suit, cloche hat and white gloves, a
clutch bag under her arm, looks overdressed and slightly out of place. Pat
made a speech in which he stressed his duty towards the erstwhile tenantry and assured his audience that his wife would come to love Powerscourt 'as everyone did'. Mervyn, in his speech, said he hoped 'that I may
be permitted to end my days in their [the tenantry's] society'. He spoke of
the time when Pat would come to live among them and of his confidence
that his new daughter-in-law 'would not shirk her responsibilities, and
that she would emulate those ladies, her predecessors, who had given their
hearts and hands to the heirs of Powerscourt and who had nobly fulfilled
the charges that had been entrusted to them'. Only a few months ago,
Mervyn had warned that he might have to leave the country; now it
seemed that the Powerscourts were there to stay.

On this ceremonial and highly-charged occasion, Sheila didn't look
like a vulgar upstart and probably didn't feel like one. By now, the Beddingtons weren't far behind the Powerscourts in aristocratic accou-
trements, which included their own crest and motto (*Ex Fide Fortis:* From
faith, courage), although, admittedly, these had been granted within
Claude's own lifetime. Yet, there's a difference between the too-chic bride
and her husband and father-in-law, who are dressed with just the right

degree of shabbiness. These tall, lanky men perfectly illustrated Rosamund Lehmann's description of upper-class casualness in her 1953 novel, *The Echoing Grove*: 'their ease of mind and body, decorating bored leisure with a flourish'. Sheila would never have that ease of mind. She didn't like Mervyn going on about her future duties and responsibilities – since the age of twenty she had had more than enough of both – but she could ignore her father-in-law's demands for the moment. She and Pat were going to live in England, where Claude had found Pat a job in a printing company. Sheila would not have to emulate all those worthy Lady Powerscourts, at least not yet.

Sybil, brought up in Wiltshire, had had to take on the burden of Powerscourt right from the beginning of her marriage. Since then, her life had been that of an inadequately funded Lady Bountiful. During the First World War, she worked for the Emergency Help Committee of the Order of St John and the British Red Cross Society. Later, she became president of the County Wicklow Branch of the Queen's Jubilee Nurses and vice-president of the Soldiers', Sailors' and Airmen's Help Society. Her most public position was chief commissioner of the Girl Guides of Ireland; she and Mervyn dedicated part of the demesne to the Scouts and Guides. Sybil's favourite hobby was needlework. In *Real People*, Sheila wrote a warm, witty chapter on 'A Father-in-Law', but ignored his dutiful and diligent wife. Sheila was tickled by Mervyn's eccentricities: the way he filed his dentures on a lathe and his obsession with drains – 'for, on the substance, girth and lay-out of drainpipes he had profound and sombre knowledge' – but Sybil was too serious to be eccentric. It appears that she and Sheila didn't get on; Sybil probably thought that Pat had been bought by the Beddingtons, who would turn his head by introducing him to the high life in London, which she regarded as unsavoury. She had never had much time for her first-born son, exasperated by his expulsion from Eton and his failed African venture. In a rare moment of emotion, in 1925, when her younger son, Brian, died very suddenly, having caught pneumonia from falling into a cold river, she had screamed at Pat, 'I wish it had been you.' But except for Sybil, everyone was delighted with Pat and Sheila's marriage; Mervyn and Claude as well as the young Wingfields themselves had all got what they wanted, or what they thought they wanted.

5. BURNING WITH AMBITION

'She's *too* keen to publish and be reviewed but that may be naiveté.'
Signe Toksvig on Sheila Wingfield in her diary entry, 25 April 1937

'This burning and hidden ambition of mine.'
Letter from Sheila Wingfield to Ottoline Morrell, 26 October 1937

As Pat's wife, Sheila had more freedom than she had ever had as Claude's daughter. Now she could do whatever she wanted and what she wanted now was to get to know other writers. After only a few months of living near Hyde Park, in the heart of Beddington territory, she and Pat moved to a rented Tudor farmhouse, Stonepitts, near Sevenoaks in Kent. The house was close to Somerhill, home of the d'Avigdor Goldsmids, long-time friends of the Beddingtons. But its closeness to Somerhill wasn't the only reason why Sheila wanted to live in this part of Kent. It appealed to her because it was the setting for Virginia Woolf's *Orlando*, published in 1928. The book's hero/heroine is based on the writer Vita Sackville-West. Her childhood home, Knole, a vast house that was almost its own world, is a leading character. Sheila admired the book's protagonist, sassy and androgynous, liberated from the restraints of time and gender; its premise that each individual has, potentially, many selves, and the copious descriptions of swanky cross-dressing in top hats, ruffs and swirling cloaks. A photograph of Sheila in her own top hat and the admired swallowtails at a meet of the Quorn Foxhounds in 1933, shows a young woman who might have stepped out of the pages of *Orlando*:

boyish, svelte and romantic. Slim-hipped, even in old age, Sheila wore trousers whenever she could; she was delighted on one occasion to be mistaken for Pat's brother while on honeymoon.

Finally out of Claude's reach, and as determined to be a poet as she had always been, she began to mix in literary circles on both sides of the Irish Sea. Sometime before her marriage, she had befriended Bethel Solomons, Master of the Rotunda Hospital in Dublin since 1920 and the first Jew to hold that post. In his autobiography, Solomons wrote of Sheila, 'She was modest about the possibility of achieving anything with her poetry and I gave her all the encouragement in my power, for I was thrilled by their quality, when she first showed her verse to me.' He was well placed to help her; his sister, Estella, an artist, was married to Seumas O'Sullivan (the pen name of James Sullivan Starkey) a poet and the editor of *The Dublin Magazine*. Solomons was a friend of James Stephens and the dedicatee of his first novel, *The Charwoman's Daughter*, and of W.B. Yeats, who had leased the top two floors of the Solomons' house, 42 Fitzwilliam Square, in the late 1920s. A highly cultured life was lived at Number 42 and, when not working or visiting Dublin's literary salons, Bethel Solomons could be seen pouring out sherry for the actors of the Gate Theatre, who sometimes rehearsed in the garden that lay between the theatre and the Rotunda. By the late 1930s, however, Sheila was starting to see herself as troublingly alone in the literary world. In 1938, the year that saw the publication of her first poetry collection, her cousin Violet Schiff was a close enough friend to be able to write concernedly, 'I wish you were not so sure of inevitable isolation.'

Parenthood was, inevitably, a major distraction from writing. Pat and Sheila's first child, Grania, was born in Claude's Grosvenor Street house with Irish Grandma, her maid and a pet monkey, who refused to be parted from the maid, in attendance. Claude withdrew to a nearby hotel during the confinement. When Irish Grandma informed Ethel of the birth and suggested a visit to Hampstead, she was sent the standard postcard: 'Anyone who sees fit to associate with my husband will never be received by me. E.B.' How galling for Ethel that said husband was now hobnobbing with one of the grandest Ascendancy families and that her daughter would, one day, be Viscountess Powerscourt. Perhaps now, estranged from her entire family, Ethel reflected on the consequences of the night of Guy's remembrance service, when she had put that card beside the plate of her grieving daughter. While her grandmother was staying with her, Sheila broached the subject of Ethel. She said that she would have understood her mother better 'if she'd been human enough to have a succession of lovers'. Irish Grandma replied, 'My dear child, to have a lover means to give.'

On 6 January 1935, in Switzerland, Sheila's younger brother, Niall, skied into the path of an oncoming train and was killed. He was twenty-one. For the second time, Ethel refused to attend a son's funeral, claiming another engagement. A sorrowing Claude told Sheila that he was still treating Ethel in his will as if she had been the best wife in the world – 'After all, she is the mother of my children.' But ultimately he left Ethel nothing, so either Sheila, not for the first time, was sentimentalising her father in retrospect, or Claude changed his mind. On 3 September that year, Sheila gave birth to her first son, Mervyn. In accordance with tradition, a canon was fired to proclaim the birth of a Powerscourt heir. The baby was christened at Enniskerry church; the event drew droves of press photographers. In their pictures, the baby's parents are as glamorous as movie stars: Pat dapper in a double-breasted suit, Sheila wearing a dark, lace-collared dress and a small hat tipped over one eye.

Even with two small children, Pat and Sheila spent lots of time alone together. 'We had only been married three years and did not quite know what to say to each other,' Sheila wrote bashfully in *Real People*, of a sailing experience when she and Pat got into difficulties near Dover harbour on their 21-foot-long dinghy, *Odile II*. They had bought the boat because it 'was as good a way as any of maintaining an overdraft, while living in her for a fortnight was a better holiday than most'. They must have been very much in love to spend that amount of time together on such a small boat. Two years later, in 1937, they holidayed even more primitively in the Outer Hebrides, setting lobster pots and digging potatoes since there was nothing else to eat. 'Slept in our clothes as we would be getting up in them anyway, and were ecstatically happy,' Sheila reported. In between these idyllic holidays, she and Pat went on two cruises on Claude's newly-built Brixham trawler, *Cachelot*. This was a much more luxurious affair than *Odile II*, with five white-carpeted cabins, a dining-room with mahogany panelling and a crew of nine, including a doctor and Namo, who, by this time, had served the Beddingtons for thirty-five years. When Guy had died, Claude, with 'his strong need for change and the solace of moving about quickly', had taken his two surviving children on a motor tour of Europe. Now, after losing his second son, he sailed his new gaff-rigged ketch on a six-month Mediterranean cruise, travelling as far as Cyprus before returning to Brixham, in Devon, via Gibraltar. It was a getaway on a grand scale. That December, Pat and Sheila, leaving their two small children behind, joined the yacht at Suez, with, according to Claude, 'four portmanteaux, three bulging sacks, a hat box and eleven brown paper parcels', even though Sheila had promised that they had 'only a suitcase each and my handbag, Daddy'. They spent their time fishing, putting into lively ports, entertaining and being entertained.

Claude was more adventurous the following year, sailing *Cachelot* down the West African coast as far as the Cameroons. Once again, Pat and Sheila left their children to spend Christmas without them. They joined the yacht at Dakar in December, returning home in the third week of January, while Claude sailed back at a more leisurely pace, reaching Brixham on 16 March. His account of these two winter journeys were published in *We Sailed from Brixham* (1938), a sparkling book in which Claude not only describes the cruises, the crew and the wide variety of people he encountered, but gives his views on governing Africa, race relations in the middle East, nightclubs, trade, food and more. Many of the book's excellent photographs were taken by Sheila, including one of Pat, delightedly fishing. A photograph of Sheila is as still as a studio portrait. Wearing a beautifully-fitted safari shirt, she is lovely, immaculate and, as usual, unsmiling. It would appear, since he was able to take such long holidays, that Pat no longer had a full-time job, unless it was being constantly on call for his father-in-law. Not that he saw this as a hardship; as well as being of the appropriate sex, Pat was more temperamentally suited to the role of Claude's surrogate son than Sheila had been, having no wish to read poetry. He was the perfect companion for Claude's old age, sports-loving, sociable, with an uncomplicated view of life that Claude approved of. Sheila was pleased with the photographs she took during the *Cachelot* cruises and reproduced many of them in *Real People*, including one entitled, 'Gambia River: Crocodiles aboard *Cachelot*'. Her descriptions of the journeys are gently ironic and she is less inclined to romanticize than her father, noting that a young missionary suffered 'the twin tortures of heat-rash and acne', and that, due to her incompetence, the group missed the chance of seeing elephants.

Reproaches over the missed elephants notwithstanding, this was a honeymoon period for Pat and Sheila. When she was an old woman living in Switzerland in the 1970s, Sheila told Isobel Armstrong, who was helping her select a new poetry collection, that she and Pat had been 'like animals', their marriage based entirely on sexual attraction. But they had more than passion in these early days. They gave each other freedom; for the first time in his life Pat had no financial worries and, for the first time in hers, Sheila, now bound to an easygoing husband instead of a controlling father, had what she called, 'a sweater and an attic', which symbolized, for her, the freedom to write poetry. Snug in the rented house in Kent, where Fred Wilson sometimes visited and showed her how to mull claret, she was happy and, at last, productive. For although she loved her husband's company and their exciting holidays, her non-writing life was a sideshow. The real stuff of existence was poetry: writing it, reading it and talking about it to the literary friends whom she now began to cultivate with a sometimes disquieting intensity. She had been denied such company for too long to be able to take it for granted.

If anyone had pointed out that in cultivating other writers, she was showing signs of being her mother's daughter, Sheila would have been horrified. She did pursue them with all of Ethel's avidity, but from entirely different motives. Ethel wanted only to be recognized as a friend of the famous. She boasted about the writers in her own family, those best-selling novelists, Dinah Craik and M.E. Braddon, and the contemporary writers whom she knew, including the founders of the Irish Literary Revival. Ethel had met Lady Gregory 'at one of Sarah McNaughton's delightful Bohemian parties', in the summer of 1911 and it was this 'Egeria of the Irish Renaissance', Ethel claimed, who urged her to write a book. It is doubtful if the resulting memoir, *All That I Have Met*, with its cast of rich English aristocrats and dubious socialites, was quite what Lady Gregory had in mind. During the First World War, W.B. Yeats had visited Ethel at home, causing 'a small sensation among the lovely ladies at my Seymour Street parties with whom he was a cult'. In 1924, Ethel asked the poet for a signed photograph of himself. He obligingly sent one, inscribed none too intimately, 'To Mrs Beddington', together with a letter in which he recalled a glass-covered demonstration beehive which he had admired in Seymour Street. Ethel was always demanding signed photographs of famous acquaintances. She displayed them in her drawing-room and referred to them as 'my breath-taking and unique "Gallery of the Great"'. Her approach was shameless. She greatly offended the former prima ballerina, Lydia Lopokova, by asking for a photograph with dedication. The dancer refused this request but Ethel was unabashed. 'Perhaps I confused you by using the word "dedication"? forgetting that you are a foreigner,' she replied. 'I shall use your signature to paste on the portrait of you which I have here.'

Sheila didn't want signed photographs with dedications, she wanted help. In February 1937, Bethel Solomons introduced her to two writers who, smitten by her beauty and grave personality as much as by her talent, propelled her towards publication by introducing her to the writer Francis Hackett and his Danish wife Signe Toksvig. On the day that she first met Sheila, Signe recorded in her diary that 'Mrs Wingfield' was 'very bright, simple, outgoing young woman. Liked her at once. Half Jewish. Good sides of this.' Signe was very philosemitic. She adored Bethel – 'beautiful high strung, high-raced Bethel' – and, whenever she came across someone of exceptional intelligence, assumed him, or her, to be Jewish. She knew about Sheila's background from Bethel. In his autobiography, *One Doctor in His Time*, he revealed that Sheila was 'the daughter of Colonel Beddington, a fine Jewish character'. Claude, not as comfortable with his Jewishness as Bethel was with his, would not have cared for this description. Neither would Sheila.

The Hacketts had known Bethel since 1932, when Signe had a hysterectomy at his hospital, the Rotunda. Both Francis and Signe had spent most of their lives in the USA and had met and married in 1918, when they were colleagues on *The New Republic*, a progressive weekly magazine. Francis, born in Kilkenny, the son of a Parnellite father, was deeply committed to the new Irish Free State and, in 1926, he and Signe came to live in Ireland, an eleven-year sojourn which, according to Signe's diaries, had its ups and downs. Although they both wrote prolifically during those years – novels and biographies, translations, reviews and broadcasts, as well as entertaining at their home Killadreenan in County Wicklow and attending to a large garden – they felt stifled in de Valera's Ireland. This intensified after Signe's novel, *Eve's Doctor* (1937), whose doctor hero was based on Bethel Solomons, and Francis' autobiographical novel, *The Green Lion* (1936), were banned under the 1929 Censorship of Publications Act. Bouts of ill-health and money worries also contributed to their decision to leave Ireland for Denmark in 1937.

While living in Ireland, the Hacketts mixed, as Bethel did, with W.B. Yeats, Oliver St John Gogarty, Sean O'Faolain, Desmond McCarthy, James Stephens, Joseph Hone, Frank O'Connor, the Glenavys, Estella Solomons and Seumas O'Sullivan. Using these connections, Francis and

Signe worked even more assiduously than Bethel on Sheila's behalf. In the 1937 July–September issue of *The Dublin Magazine*, O'Sullivan, pressed by Francis, published seven of Sheila's poems, including 'Odysseus Dying' and 'Winter' – her publishing debut in the poetry world. The same issue of the magazine carried two poems by Patrick Kavanagh, whose first collection, *Ploughman and Other Poems*, had been published the year before, to mixed reviews.

Sheila was a world-class flatterer. Only a few days after meeting Signe, the latter wrote in her diary, 'Mrs Wingfield wrote a superlative letter about *E.D.*' [The about-to-be-banned novel, *Eve's Doctor*.] Since the theme of the novel was the influence of Catholic teaching on gynaecological practices in Irish hospitals, not a subject likely to appeal to the fastidious Sheila, one can only imagine that Sheila was trying to cultivate a useful connection. She succeeded. Following a second encounter, Signe's verdict on Sheila was, 'Pleasant. Less bright. Rather grave and thin she was but I feel sure we'll be friends if we have the chance.' The chance came; a month later, in March, Signe went to England and spent a day with the Wingfields in Kent: 'I was too tired but really liked them. She's *too* keen to publish and be reviewed but that may be naiveté. I believe in our friendship,' she wrote in her diary, that last sentence showing a willingness to ignore any suspicion that Sheila might be using her. On that visit, she wrote a postcard to Francis, in Ireland: 'Both Wingfields perfect – he's really nice – we'll see them this summer at Powerscourt. I loved both.' And then, in April, Sheila visited Signe at Killadreenan and was, according to Signe's diary, 'A perfect success in every way. Or I'm crazy or she'll be a real friend.' In June, Signe stayed with Pat and Sheila at Stonepitts for four days and, by that time, was certain: 'Now I have a friend.'

In spite of a busy social life, Signe was lonely in her Irish exile. 'Invisible walls shutting one out everywhere, stronger than the visible ones, loneliness and loneliness,' was how she described the country in a letter to Bethel, after she had, thankfully, left it. She loved her husband – 'He is the whole, entire meaning of life' – but was hurt by his inattention. She longed for intense, intimate friendship with women who were her intellectual equals, a sentimental yearning that was at odds with her critical nature. She dismissed the Dublin Arts Club: 'Dreary crawthumping, fastkeeping bourgeois there. A tomb of joy,' and Ireland itself: 'I maintain that this tense, raw suspicious Ireland is not good enough for me.' Before she met Sheila, she was equally scathing about Powerscourt. 'Trees and views grand – gardens and house drear and imposing in a wrong way.' Members of the 'literistic tribe' also failed to impress. Harold Nicolson was 'an odious ass'; Elizabeth Bowen 'stupidly affected'. Signe was a woman who needed to be needed, that was what friendship meant to her, so it's easy to understand her delight when Sheila came her way. Here was a beautiful, intelligent, charming woman who was impressed by Signe's authorship and wanted her advice in becoming a published writer herself. But, during the spring of 1937, Signe did something that consigned herself and Francis to the very edges of Sheila's life. She introduced their protégée to a woman who, even in frail old age, was a more influential patroness than Signe could ever hope to be, a woman so influential in promoting young writers that Virginia Woolf had said of her, 'Since Helen of Troy, I don't think any woman can have launched so many ships.' This woman was Lady Ottoline Morrell.

All through her life, Ottoline Morrell had been thought of as peculiar. 'It is no fun being an oddity for it makes one eternally lonely,' she wrote in her diary. 'Unfortunately, I combine being an oddity with being very proud, and that makes one aloof.' She made no effort to look anything other than extraordinary, swathing her thin chest in diamonds and pearls inherited from relations and trailing richly-coloured capes and shawls. Nijinsky described her as 'so tall, so beautiful like a giraffe', while to Gertrude Stein she was like a 'marvellous female version of Disraeli'. Although she felt herself to be alone in the world, she had a gift for intimacy, which led her not only into love-affairs but into quickly-made, close friendships. The Hacketts were a case in point. She had not known them for very long before she appointed Francis as one of her four literary executors and drew the Hacketts into her influential Bloomsbury circle. It was probably at their suggestion that Sheila sent Ottoline some of her poems, so that the latter had read them before she was introduced to the poet herself. It was typical of Ottoline's thoughtfulness that she arrived at her first meeting with Sheila armed with letters of introduction for her.

And so began an intense friendship between the ailing literary hostess and the as-yet unpublished poet, which lasted until Ottoline's death, just over a year later, on 21 April 1938. During the year that they knew each other, they corresponded almost daily and Sheila, usually not a hoarder, kept twenty of Ottoline's letters, fragile sheets of tissue-thin handmade paper, covered in a pale, spidery hand that is often illegible. Ottoline also introduced Sheila to Desmond McCarthy, who admired Sheila's poems.

She was now starting to arrange them in book form. 'I am so grateful,' Sheila wrote to Ottoline, 'and will continue to be so, whether or not any publisher takes it.' Her chances of publication improved greatly when Ottoline arranged another introduction, this time to John Hayward, a formidable literary scholar and maker and breaker of reputations. He was the poetry adviser to the Cresset Press, a board member of John Lehmann's *London Magazine* and the friend, and sometime flatmate, of T.S. Eliot. He was also Eliot's literary executor whose brief was 'to suppress everything that is suppressible'. Hayward was a muscular dystrophic and confined to a wheelchair but this did not stop him going to dinner parties at Claridge's, 'showing off his gorgeous red silk waistcoat which had obviously been embroidered by the tailor of Gloucester', as admired by Sheila.

'This strange and fateful woman', is how Sheila described Ottoline. In spite of an age gap of thirty years or so, they had much in common. They were both 'reading girls' who had been persecuted for preferring books to mindless socializing. How well Sheila understood Ottoline's feelings when, as a young girl, she was teased by her brother's officer friends because she 'always had her head in a book', the sort of activity that Claude, too, had criticized. The young Ottoline had worn a red cape lined with pockets in which to hold books because she could not bear to be without them. Like Sheila, she was a fearsome self-educator and prone to emotional crises and bouts of ill-health. Also in common was that Ottoline was half-English and half-Irish. Her mother, before her marriage to Lt General Arthur Bentinck, had been Augusta Browne, the daughter of the Dean of Lismore. By 1937, Ottoline was sixty-three, increasingly deaf, her jaw disfigured following an operation for cancer, and nearing her death. Garsington, the Oxfordshire manor-house where she had entertained Bloomsbury's finest, had been sold in 1928; Ottoline and her husband, Philip, now lived at 10 Gower Street, a smallish London house where, as Sheila wrote in *Real People*, 'Near the end of her life, she moved like a tall ghost in black satin, clanking silver tea-pots and tea-kettle instead of chains.' Her Thursday afternoons were muted occasions.

There had been a falling out with Yeats shortly before Ottoline and Sheila met, following the inclusion in the 1936 *Oxford Book of Modern Verse*, edited by Yeats, of a poem by Walter Turner. Ten years previously, Turner had caricatured Ottoline in his book, *The Aesthetes*, and had not been forgiven. This wasn't the first time that a writer whom she had befriended had lampooned her in fiction: Aldous Huxley and D.H. Lawrence had been equally guilty. There was something about Ottoline's genuine but exaggerated benevolence that made the recipients of it venomous, although it was not difficult to become the victim of malice and mockery in the hot-house that was Bloomsbury. Ottoline showed courage and loyal optimism in not washing her hands of the lot of them. It was the ungrateful Bloomsburyites, in fact, who deserted her. 'Lord! What a grind these Ottoline parties are,' Virginia Woolf wrote to Stephen Spender in 1934, as Ottoline's Thursday afternoons began to lose their lustre. Of her former acolytes, only James Stephens still attended nearly every Gower Street tea party, but had become such a bore that he kept other people away. Immediately on first meeting Sheila at Stonepitts, Ottoline invited her to tea at Gower Street and Sheila wrote to her, 'I am much looking forward to seeing you on Thursday week, and am wondering if I might bring my husband who is longing to meet you.' Out of this request, which was granted, grew the myth, perpetuated by Sheila and retold time and time again after Pat's death, that her 'philistine husband' had forbidden her to have anything to do with 'literary scum'.

Sheila never denied that she had sought the invitation for Pat to accompany her to Gower Street, but everything else relating to this period in her life, when she was on the verge of having her first book published, was subject to a baffling reinvention after Pat's death. In Sheila's version of events, she is summoned to Gower Street, Pat in tow, because Ottoline, whom she claimed she had not yet met, has heard about the merits of her poetry. This is how Sheila continued the story in a letter to the poet and critic Robert Nye, written forty years after the Gower Street tea party. In 'ignorance and stupidity' she had taken Pat with her to Gower Street. 'The drive back to our rented house in Kent was unforgettable. He (at the wheel) was silent for thirty-five minutes. After which he extracted a promise from me "that you must never while I'm alive, associate with that literary scum." I argued and pleaded but in vain.' She then tells Nye that Ottoline had pressed her to take up 'in a friendly and correct way', with a young poet who had offered her cucumber sandwiches at Gower Street since, if she did so, 'my future would be made'. However, 'much in love' with her husband, she had agreed to his embargo. In her RTÉ interview with Anne Roper, she repeats the story of the literary embargo, and identifies the assiduous young sandwich offerer as Lawrence Whistler, who, in 1934, had won the first King's Gold Medal for Poetry, at the age of twenty-three.

I had my doubts about this story from the beginning. What Sheila and Pat's daughter, Grania, loved most about her father was that he could get on with anyone. The colonel of his regiment had stressed what a wonderful companion he was and even the highly critical Signe Toksvig thought that this unliterary man was 'really nice' and as perfect as his wife. If Pat could be such a hit with the Hacketts, that extremely bookish couple whose advanced views on sex and psychoanalysis, among other uncomfortable topics, might not have gone down too well with staider members of Pat's class, it's hard to imagine him uttering the words 'literary scum'. I got in touch with Miranda Seymour, Ottoline Morrell's biographer, who told me that Ottoline's grandson, Philip Goodman, had kept all of his grandmother's Visitors' Books. With great patience, Mr Goodman went through the relevant books for 1937–8 and revealed a very different picture. According to their records, Pat and Sheila visited 10 Gower Street in 1937, on 22 April and 20 December. On their first visit, the other guests were James Stephens (as always) and a Monica Redlich.

On the second occasion, four months before Ottoline's death and after she had given up her regular 'Thursdays', the only other guest was Robert Gathorne-Hardy, one of her literary executors and the editor of her unpublished memoirs. No crowd of famous writers, no Lawrence Whistler; just a sick old lady who was probably delighted to have Pat Wingfield breathe some life into her musty drawing-room. So that stern edict can only have been an invention, since Pat himself made a return visit to Gower Street. Sheila didn't invent the story of her 'philistine husband' until that husband was dead, but then persisted with it for the rest of her life. In her mind, the nonsensical episode had become fact and the reason why, as she saw it, she had been a tragically isolated literary figure. To further the myth, as she did towards the end of her life in heart-rending letters to Robert Nye – 'All my life, working like a Le Carré mole underground and with no person to criticize or advise or help in any way whatever, I've had to take in strictures and/or advice by sheer osmosis. There was no soul to help' – Sheila had to cover her tracks. So, in her memoirs, Bethel Solomons, the Hacketts and Seumas O'Sullivan, are written out of the story and while Ottoline is presented admiringly in *Real People*, it is as a fellow invalid rather than a literary patroness. She couldn't admit to Ottoline introducing her to John Hayward, and through him to the Cresset Press. She later told Robert Nye that they had met through sharing the same surgeon.

Sheila and Ottoline saw each other constantly. Sheila was one of the very few people who was allowed to read the manuscript of Ottoline's memoirs. 'You are unique … your sense of loneliness – isn't that a sign of your being great? – You are a voice. There are so very, very few,' was her fulsome reaction. How lovely it must have been for Ottoline, the butt of so much malice, to have this young admirer who never stopped telling her how wonderful she was. 'You have more charm, wit, goodness and brains than all my women acquaintances put together,' Sheila assured her. In the short time between their first meeting and Ottoline's death, Sheila became almost a part of the Morrell family. The last weeks of Ottoline's life were spent at Sherwood Park Clinic, where she was being unsuccessfully treated for some vaguely diagnosed poisoning of the nervous system by the clinic's director, Dr Cameron. According to Miranda Seymour, Cameron was 'a society quack with an ugly record of alcoholism and a jail sentence for running over a child'. It's possible that Ottoline's death was caused by the liberal injections of Prontosil which he prescribed. Sheila did not care for the clinic, 'a nursing-home of flat gravel paths and slimy stone and dark evergreens and high-ceilinged bedrooms', and resisted Ottoline's encouragement to be treated there herself. For, by this time, Sheila's own health was causing concern. After Ottoline's memorial service, her daughter, Julian Goodman, wrote to Sheila, 'I was very worried by your appearance. I mean, you did look far from well,' adding 'I think you are the only woman I have liked at once – without reserve.' Sheila was indeed far from well, suffering from a mysterious illness that caused her chronic pain but seemed to have no physical cause. Just as she was to fulfil her greatest ambition, she was flung into a health-crisis which would cloud the rest of her life.

6. MRS WINGFIELD AND MR YEATS

'Hon. Mrs Wingfield is not a person to be encouraged.'
Letter from W.B. Yeats to Lady Dorothy Wellesley, November 1938

'My first book of poems had been praised by Yeats.'
Sheila Wingfield, *Real People*

When Sheila started to suffer excruciating pain in the summer of 1937, Dr Cameron was about the only doctor not called in to give a diagnosis, although Ottoline Morrell, seriously ill herself, 'had one day gone on her knees to my father to beg him to send me to "her place", which she believed in devoutly, to be cared for'. Back at 33 Grosvenor Street, Sheila was visited not only by Ottoline but by troupes of doctors. These included the Royal Physician, Lord Horder, who thought that the pain was psychological in origin; a Mr Wolff who didn't and advised her to become pregnant; the 'King of Gynaecologists', Mr Gilliatt, who disagreed with Mr Wolff; and a Dr Venesi, who came over from Paris and diagnosed a very bad inflammation. Yet another verdict was that a scar was pulling on a ligament. Years later, Sheila would refer to 1954 as her 'last year of health', but, in truth, 1937 was the first year she was beset by an illness which was never satisfactorily diagnosed. From that time on, every doctor she saw acknowledged that she endured great physical suffering but could never put a name to it, let alone cure it.

She was to learn that the pain was at its worst whenever she started another book or when a book was nearing publication, but also learnt to ignore the implications of this. From those first painful attacks in 1937, doctors recognized that some sort of mental conflict might have something to do with the case. Sheila wrote to Ottoline, 'They are all now gently psychoanalysing me but can find no hideous hidden secrets or worries – except that they think I pay more attention than I should to writing poetry and not enough to my children.' This was agonizing to contemplate. Another letter to Ottoline: 'For half my soul believes that family, children, the home and that [underlined] steady happiness are the paths of existence, while the other half knows that art and the intellect – those are the real, ultimate values, so that I never know which is the substance and which is the shadow.' A generation later, another poet expressed the same thought more pithily. 'When I was happy domestically, I felt a gag in my throat,' Sylvia Plath wrote to her friend, the poet Ruth Fainlight, in 1962. Female poets sometimes have problems adjusting to their circumstances, which is perhaps why they become poets.

Claude must have been more convinced than ever that literature meant trouble. For here was his daughter, who could have been leading the perfect life as wife, mother and member of high society, diagnosed as a neurotic because she would insist on writing poetry. And here was his house, invaded by baffled doctors and that peculiar Morrell woman, trailing cloaks and feathers and whole libraries of books, whose visits Sheila looked forward to more eagerly than she did to visits from her children. In spite of the pain, 'real proper, bad pain as soon as I move about much', it was clear that this strange illness was of some advantage to Sheila, because the whole confused chorus of consulted doctors advised rest. What a perfect excuse to go somewhere peaceful and get down to work. Sheila favoured the Empire Nursing Home in Vincent Square, where her room had a balcony 'and the nurses and food couldn't be nicer'. She wrote to Ottoline, but perhaps didn't mention to Claude that 'This regime of no housekeeping and [underlined] the children away – gives me a chance to get down to steady work, and some new things have just gone off to Francis [Hackett] for his criticism.'

She got down to steady reading too, three volumes of Ottoline's memoirs, Jane Austen, Plotinus, Conrad's *Heart of Darkness*. Her literary tastes were classical; it is not surprising that she believed that *Ulysses* and *Finnegans Wake* 'should be classed with the work of Gongora and Gaudi as a defiantly dead end'. Another refuge was the Felix Hotel at Felixstowe, on the Suffolk coast, a part of the country she had grown fond of during the winter shoots of her youth. She stayed there in the last months of 1938, and was snugly happy. 'This vast, plum-coloured Victorian pile is warm and comfortable and expensive and worth it,' she wrote to Ottoline, together with reports on her always extensive reading. A troubling pattern was emerging. The sweater and the attic had become the convalescent home and the hotel suite. She had begun to feel that she could devote herself to her twin passions of reading and writing only when she was ill and therefore 'free' of her family. The price of this freedom was that her husband and children began to seem like obstacles in the way of her ambition. Thinking of them like this worried her, anxiety made her ill, illness meant more doctors, more resting, more anxiety, and so it went on in an endless circle, never to be resolved. She had been conditioned by Claude to give a good performance as a wife and mother and, as a witness to the disaster that Ethel had been in these roles, wanted to excel. But she knew that the 'steady happiness' of domestic life was at odds with her hunger to be a poet; no wonder that the men in white coats had to be called in.

More than sixty years after Sheila battled with the problem, women are still trying to work out 'how to have it all', still suffering from the loss of nerve which affected women of Sheila's generation. But it was worse in her day, especially for a woman of her social class, who was expected to live mindlessly and, if she dared to become a poet, was described as a 'poetess wife'. Sheila had been enslaved by Claude for so long that she found freedom overwhelming. She was a courageous woman but lacked buoyancy; her letters to Ottoline demonstrate how easily she was cast down. Why did Sheila, so often in her life, suffer from that undiagnosable illness? Was it a case of hysterical exhibitionism, or a sort of ongoing panic attack because she wanted to be a published poet but was terrified of the consequences? Or did drugs have something to do with it? Drugs were quite freely dispensed during the early part of the last century; cannabis was made illegal only in 1928, and, until the Dangerous Drugs Act of 1920, you could buy morphine over the counter. The Bright Young Things of the Jazz Age bought their cocaine, the source of perfectly legal kicks, at Harrods, where it was sold as a stimulant or tonic. Did Sheila become hooked on painkillers and then, subconsciously, make herself ill so that she would be given more? Within a few years, she was certainly dependent on various white tablets. These she kept in exquisite pill-boxes inside a chic beauty-case, which she took everywhere.

In spite of, or perhaps because of, her delicate physical and emotional state, Sheila was determined to have a book of her poetry published. She asked Seumas O'Sullivan to arrange her poems for a first collection but he told her that she could do the job better herself. Sometime before the end of 1937 she did so and, through Ottoline's useful introduction to John Hayward, had the collection accepted by the Cresset Press for publication towards the end of the following year. Sheila, convalescing at her luxurious boltholes, spent the months before publication sending copies of the poems to eminent literary figures, hoping for testimonials that might be used for the book's flyleaf, as well as encouragement. One of these copies was sent to W.B. Yeats.

'You were silly like us,' W.H. Auden gently admonished the poet in *In Memory of W.B. Yeats*, forgiving him his human failings. But when Yeats was alive, Auden had been more critical. He called *The Oxford Book of Modern Verse*, edited by Yeats in 1936, the worst book ever issued under the Clarendon Press imprint. Even one of the poets included in the anthology, Oliver St John Gogarty, agreed that Yeats's choices were, well, silly. 'Only titled ladies and a few friends admitted,' Gogarty commented. As always, he is making fun of Yeats's snootiness: 'Yeats is becoming so aristocratic, he's evicting imaginary tenants.' Yeats tended to be smitten by titled ladies, which is why he included in the Oxford anthology seventeen pages of Buddhist poems by Lady Dorothy Wellesley, whose hospitality he enjoyed at her house in Sussex.

To be fair, Yeats found room in the anthology for an untitled infatuation of his, Margaret Ruddock, who did not live in a hospitable stately home. Yeats's septuagenarian lustfulness was put down to the supposedly youth-restoring Steinach operation he'd had, a procedure which Frank O'Connor said that in Yeats's case was 'like putting a Cadillac engine in a Ford car'. Yeats left out of the anthology poets whom he didn't like – Seumas O'Sullivan, Monk Gibbon – regardless of the merits of their work, and war poets, including Wilfred Owen, because, he said, 'passive suffering is not a theme for poetry', and that Owen was unworthy of the poet's corner of a country newspaper. Desmond McCarthy called the anthology 'a book of strange choices and strange omissions'. Most critics shared this view but in spite of their mauling, the anthology was a bestseller on both sides of the Atlantic. Yeats, however, was stung by the criticism; he wrote melodramatically to Dorothy Wellesley that it made him feel that he had no nation.

Gogarty wasn't alone in being amused by Yeats's aristocratic pretensions.

The poet Marianne Moore attended a lecture which Yeats gave in Brooklyn, New York in 1932 and found him, 'hearty, smiling, benevolent and elegant … He has the hand of a hereditary royalist who never picked up a stone or touched his own shoes.' So when Yeats received Sheila's poems, and a letter asking for his opinion of them, from the Honourable Mrs Wingfield, whose husband was the heir to Viscount Powerscourt, it was predictable that he would look kindly on them. He wrote to Sheila on 10 September 1938: 'If you are Irish, I am glad that this country possesses one more distinguished mind.' Inviting Sheila to visit him, he went on, 'You have style, distinction, and a precise and subtle vocabulary.' On the original of this letter, Sheila later wrote, perhaps to explain the ensuing fiasco to a future biographer, 'This was Yeats's answer to my candid question, "Have these verses any merit?" It was no more personal a letter than that, i.e. a request for a professional opinion.'

Candour had nothing to do with it. In persuading Yeats to comment on her work, Sheila was being disingenuous. By the time she sent him the poems, publication was already underway. *Poems* was due to appear in two months' time. In her reply to Yeats, from the Old School House, Godden Green, to which she and Pat had recently moved from nearby Stonepitts, she failed to mention this. She told Yeats that his words were 'of untold value as a guide'. Of the poems themselves she wrote: 'My first effort … now I can hardly bear to look at them – they seem far too effusive and pretty and gaudy: I have outgrown them for a way of feeling that is plainer, more austere, and much deeper. My present work is a single poem of about 4000 lines on a theme that seems really important – if only I can even get it down, it may turn out to be something worthwhile.' That 'first effort', which she so modestly disparaged and which she claimed to have outgrown, was probably already in proof form at the Cresset Press offices.

Poems, published when Sheila was thirty-two, carried admiring endorsements from James Stephens, Walter de la Mare and, finally, the Nobel Laureate himself. The encouraging words which Yeats had written, in what he believed was a personal letter, were made public. His reaction was immediate and furious. From France, he wrote icily: 'Dear Mrs Wingfield, I find that you have published an extract from a private letter of mine without leave.' He then told her that the poet Katherine Tynan had once committed a similar offence, not to advertise herself [he adds pointedly] but as part of her autobiography. I forgave her because as the daughter of a working farmer she was not sensitive on such [matters?]. But that you who have not the excuse of ignorance or poverty should do this vulgar thing fills me with all the more regret because I have liked your work and found some pleasure in our brief acquaintance.

Yeats kept a copy of this letter, the typescript much crossed-out and handwritten corrections inserted. Five days after writing it, he sent another letter, this time to Dorothy Wellesley:

Hon. Mrs Wingfield is not a person to be encouraged. She has used as an advertisement for her new book an extract from a private letter of mine. I have written her a corker. If she was not likely to be Lady Powerscourt some day I would not have bothered but I am all schoolmaster where Ireland is concerned.

Gogarty would have been amused by this. In the normal course of events, the fact that Sheila was a future Lady Powerscourt would have put her beyond Yeats's criticism. But Yeats wanted to give Lady Dorothy, to whom he signed his letters, 'Your friend, who feels so much more than friend', the idea that, contrary to public opinion, he wasn't dazzled by every titled lady he came across. Things might have been different had Sheila already been Lady Powerscourt and able to invite Yeats to stay in that fabulous house. For Yeats loved great houses, and the comforts and cosseting to be found in them, as much as he loved their chatelaines. Sheila, in her rented house, was at a disadvantage.

She tried to soothe the deceived poet in a letter written on 23 November, in which she presented herself as a literary ingénue:

I am most grieved to have given you offence by quoting you without your permission. When I received your delightful letter about my work, I very naturally showed it to my publisher, and asked if permission could be got from you to quote from it. I was told it was too late to ask for permission before publication, but I was assured that to quote from it was the ordinary thing to do, and that no elder writer objected to this and that it was the general practice. I fully believed this assurance, for I was a total newcomer to the profession of letters and could only trust in the advice of experts. With my deepest regrets for having made an unwitting but very grave mistake.

And this, one feels, should have been the end of the matter. But Yeats was in a captious mood and his response, written the day that he received Sheila's apology, rumbled:

No, it is not the practice among authors and publishers of repute. If I could keep you out of it, I would bring the matter before the Society of Authors. If what your publisher said was true, all careless, friendly correspondence between authors about their books, especially between the known and the unknown, would come to an end. The thing is damnable. I cannot get out of my head an American author who will think I refused to [something scratched out and illegible] his poverty what I granted to you because you are a woman of position. I may have to make some public protest, or get the matter discussed some [where?]. If I can discover how to leave you out of it. You are the victim of vulgar advice.

One gets the feeling that he is not going to try all that hard to keep Sheila's name out of the public protest he has in mind. And now Pat, that most unlikely meddler in poetic affairs, comes into it. Throughout the previous year, when Sheila had been ill and unhappy, Pat had behaved beautifully, settling her into her suite at Felixstowe, coping with the house and children. This new situation was an embarrassment; he had not counted on his wife being accused by Ireland's most famous poet of bamboozling him, but he did his placatory best. He wrote to Yeats – unfortunately this letter hasn't survived – and Yeats's reply is less menacing than his letter to Sheila. He tells Pat that he has asked the editor 'of a publication for which I occasionally write' to raise the matter 'of quoting private letters as advertisement for books' in his journal, but without mentioning Sheila's name or the title of her book. Were the editor to do this, Yeats himself would take part in the discussion. This is more conciliatory than his previous threat to make a public protest and he seems to think that even this milder scheme is a non-starter, since the editor probably won't take him up on the idea 'through fear of some publisher withdrawing his advertisement'. Yeats adds, reasonably and politely enough, 'If this habit of the less reputable is not checked it will not be possible to write a letter of encouragement to a young writer.'

Pat's intervention had a calming effect but Yeats's criticism could hardly have been more wounding: his repeated use of the word 'vulgar', the assertion that her publisher was less than respectable, branded Sheila as an upstart, an arriviste. Sheila was always alert to any intimation that she was not quite acceptable, especially when it came from someone like Yeats, who, like most of his class, was genteelly anti-Semitic. He had, for a time, flirted with the ideology of fascism to the extent that the Fianna Fáil Minister, Sean MacEntee, referred to the poet as 'that old fascist'. If not an actual fascist, Yeats was certainly a fellow-traveller. In a thoughtful book on the poet's politics, W.J. McCormack discloses that, in 1934, Yeats accepted a German literary prize and allowed a production in Nazi-controlled Frankfurt of his play, *The Countess Cathleen,* directed by a man who wore his SS uniform at all times. As late as 1938, in an interview with the *Irish Independent*, Yeats endorsed German legislation on property repossession, the removal of Jewish ownership. The subtext of his letter to Sheila was to let her know what she knew already, that, by Wingfield standards, she was a bit déclassée.

Poems was well received. Austin Clarke praised the book in a radio broadcast and read out the short poem 'Odysseus Dying' and part of the longer one, 'The Hours'. In the *Sunday Times* review which had so angered Yeats, Desmond McCarthy approved of Sheila's 'precision of style', while in the *Spectator*, John Hayward wrote, 'I think she deserves encouragement.' Insiders would have been aware that Hayward himself had encouraged the book's production. The *Poetry Review* had obviously got wind of the Yeats drama. Its review of Sheila's book was pure mischief: 'It comes out already praised by James Stephens, Walter de la Mare and Yeats (on the dust jacket, the sentences reproduced, presumably, with their writers' consent).' It then suggests that a fee may have changed hands for this commendation: 'One likes it not. How little Miss Wingfield's wine needed any such doubtful bush.' Yeats would have like it even less. The praise he had given in what he thought was a private letter was now quoted in reviews in *The Irish Times, Granta, The Irish Press* and the *Manchester Evening News*. And to compound his annoyance, the book's dedication was 'To The Givers of Encouragement', among whom Yeats was now irretrievably listed.

Before their falling-out, the reluctant giver of encouragement had mentioned his 'brief acquaintance' with Sheila, but seemed to know little about her background, since he asked if she were Irish. Sheila was a schoolgirl when the fêted poet had mingled with the 'lovely ladies' at Seymour Street. He didn't make the connection between Mrs Beddington and the poet he knew only as Mrs Wingfield. He would have known Pat though, at least by sight, since both men were members of the exclusive Kildare Street Club. Yeats had always admired high-born members of the Ascendancy, whom he saw as proud and heroic. He deplored the passing of Ireland's stately homes and the sidelining of their owners and future owners, men like Pat Wingfield who possessed 'a sort of hardiness and the absence of social fear', as Elizabeth Bowen wrote of the Anglo-Irish in her 1940 essay 'The Big House'. Pat's status made him the ideal mediator between the two poets but it was humiliating for Sheila, in whom social fear was never absent.

Before Yeats could begin a campaign of non-encouragement against Sheila, he died, on 28 January 1939, in the south of France. No longer restrained by Yeats's disapproval, Sheila reprinted his words of praise on every subsequent volume of her poetry, including her final *Collected Poems*, published in 1983, more than forty years after Yeats's death. Dorothy Wellesley also lost no time in making use of her poet-admirer's letters. In 1940, she published *Letters on Poetry from W.B. Yeats to Dorothy Wellesley*. This put Gogarty in a teasing mode, once again. 'It is full of interest and shows how clearly Yeats could love a lady,' he wrote of the book. It might have mollified Yeats that in 1943, Lady Dorothy, although long separated from her husband, became Duchess of Wellington on the death of her father-in-law, for Yeats loved duchesses even more dearly than ladies.

Although Sheila recycled Yeats's praise and wrote in *Real People* that her 'first book of poems had been praised by Yeats', she invented an unpleasant story about him, which she told first in *Sun Too Fast* and then repeated, in slightly amplified form, in her interview with Anne Roper. In the first version, Sheila, then a young woman, gets into a first-class compartment of the Holyhead–Euston train, in which a 'tall man with an undecided mouth', is already seated. Friends seeing her off recognize him as Yeats and warn Sheila that he has just undergone Steinach's rejuvenating operation and to expect a pounce. No advances are made – 'vanity was crushed' – but Yeats sneers, 'I wouldn't help a young poet if he were starving in the gutter,' as though he had somehow guessed that 'there was a copy of my first and so far unpublished verse burning my suitcase in the rack'. Later, in the restaurant car, Yeats 'embarked, in a loud voice, on a detailed story of two Galway fishermen of homosexual habits', to the embarrassment of other passengers. Having invited Sheila to join him for tea, he leaves her to pay the bill. In the Anne Roper interview, the story gets nastier. Now, Yeats leaves the train 'in the company of two Galway fishermen who lived together'. This slander was Yeats's posthumous reward for having written encouragingly about Sheila's early work. Pat paid a heavier price for his perceived wrongs. One day, Sheila would remove the Wingfields from Powerscourt and, after Pat's death, create a portrait of her husband as a drunken philistine, who loathed literary people because, according to Sheila, they were 'well above him and of whom he was jealous and whom he would never be able to understand'.

For the moment though, apart from the unpleasantness with Yeats, all was well with the Wingfields in their rented house in Kent. Once Sheila's book was published and the reviews favourable, her mysterious pains abated. She and Pat took the children on visits to Powerscourt, and to Bellair, where Irish Grandma still thrived and where she was delighted with her copy of *Poems* inscribed, 'To Darling Grandma on her 80th birthday, with all rejoicings and with the very truest love, from Sheila.' In London, Sheila sometimes lunched with Walter de la Mare at Hackett's restaurant in Dover Street and, as often, de la Mare invited her to lunch with his wife at Hill House in Buckinghamshire. In Kent, the Wingfields were visited by Mervyn, who ignored the fact that his son and daughter-in-law didn't actually own the house and excavated an Elizabethan fireplace hidden behind the plaster. In the summer of 1939, the publishers of the Gayfield Press, Blánaid Salkeld and her son, Cecil ffrench Salkeld, included Sheila in their series of broadsheets of 'Representative Irish Poets' and Sheila continued to work on the long poem she had mentioned to Yeats. Yet, from 1937 onwards, her mental and physical health became a worry to her friends. Francis Hackett lectured her gently, 'But how on God's earth can you suppose that you can sail, shop, mother, housekeep and flâner, and still summon the Muse? She isn't telephone central.' Sheila kept this letter and another one from Francis that ended romantically with 'Adieu poète'. In spite of Signe's infatuation with her, it was probably Francis who became her close friend, possibly even lover. He had a reputation as a womanizer and his letters are among the very few that Sheila kept.

Those early poems are among Sheila's best, already showing the 'simple strength' and 'precise form', which Herbert Read admired a decade later. 'Odysseus Dying', in particular, is remarkable for its highly original reworking of the archetypal ancient Greek text, 'the founding epic of nostalgia', in Milan Kundera's words. Sheila's version was to become her most anthologized poem and the one which those who were otherwise unfamiliar with her work, could quote. It perhaps contributed to the popularity of the name 'Penelope' among parents, including my own, of new-born girls, in the late 1930s and early 1940s. From this first collection, she started as she would continue, publishing poetry which, in Alex Davis's perfect description, had a 'Spartan lyricism'. One might call her poetry 'imagistic', had Sheila not insisted that she didn't know what the word meant and had never been influenced by a poetic movement. Somehow or other, she took to heart Ezra Pound's dictum that 'the natural object is always the adequate symbol'. She hated abstraction and wrote, in Anne Fogarty's words, in a 'vividly concrete mode'. She wasn't the only twentieth-century female poet who didn't conform to the popular image of her type as being driven purely by emotion – Laura Riding was another – but Sheila's voice was the purest. She specialized, as Fogarty remarked, in 'the jettisoning of the personal'.

This was an unusual stance among female poets, many of whom seem to see their calling as constructing a version of femininity by means of the confessional. Most of Sheila's poems are gender-free, such is their sturdiness of tone. Another poet, Elizabeth Bishop, a contemporary of Sheila's whose style was equally spare and reticent, has achieved a more lasting fame. In *Modern Women Poets*, Deryn Rees-Jones writes that 'Bishop's detached persona and cool and detailed poetics did much to counter the image of the woman poet which had grown up in the wake of Sylvia Plath's death in 1962.' Sheila was not as influential. Rees-Jones includes five of Sheila's poems in her book, two of them from her first collection, but was unable to publish any of Bishop's since she had made it clear that her work was not to be included in any women-only anthologies. It is doubtful that Sheila would have appreciated being categorized as a woman poet.

In 1938, even if the Muse wasn't 'telephone central', she had definitely been summoned and had arrived. The 'Hon. Patrick Wingfield's poetess wife', might have gone on being both wife and poetess without too much mishap had not war intervened, and, after the war, enormous and unforeseen changes.

7. ON A PINK BEACH

'I am going to send in my resignation as it seems a waste of the little brain I have, for I can do much work of national importance of a higher order.'
Letter from Claude Beddington to Sheila, 17 August 1940

'News has been received from enemy sources that Major Mervyn Patrick Wingfield, son of Lord Powerscourt, is a prisoner in Italian hands.'
The Irish Times, 15 May 1942

'War War it has come,' is the second line of *Beat Drum, Beat Heart*, Sheila's magnificent poem of war and peace. It was published in 1946, but when exactly it was written is unclear. Sheila sometimes claimed that she wrote it 'many years before World War II' and that she added only six lines during that war, 'to bring it more up to date'. Typically, she didn't say which six lines. In the poem's third section, 'Women in Love', there's an eleven line sequence which, Sheila explained in a note in the published work, refers to 'a latter-day Miss Havisham, whom I knew well in a sub-tropical island'. The island sounds very like Bermuda, which Sheila hadn't visited before 1940, but the sequence, although it is a fine and melancholy tribute to a neatly self-controlled spinsterish life – 'No defect of paint, no spiderweb, no branch out of trim' – carries no reference to the ongoing war. Confusingly, she had told Yeats, in the autumn of 1938 (when the Macspaunday poets were also writing about the coming war, in verse whose theme was one of exhausted resignation and waiting for the end), that she was working on her long poem, *Beat Drum, Beat*

Heart. (Its almost universally positive critical reception will be discussed later.) It's more plausible to believe that Sheila was indeed working on the poem in 1938, against the backdrop of the Spanish Civil War, Picasso's *Guernica* and Chamberlain's 'peace in our time'. It's hard to imagine a poet concentrating on anything except war then, even a poet like Sheila, preoccupied with the state of her health and the book she was currently reading. She must have noticed, in that 'unhappy autumn', as Elizabeth Bowen called it, that trenches were being dug in Hyde Park, a short stroll away from Claude's house at 33 Grosvenor Street.

Claude, that decorated veteran of two wars, did more than notice. He took action. Sheila was his only surviving child, pregnant with his third grandchild, and he wasn't prepared to lose her. Claude was an optimist, or pretended that he was, and would never have expressed any doubts that Nazi Germany would be defeated. Where his daughter was concerned, however, he was in no mood to take chances. He knew what was happening to European Jews, even fully-assimilated Jews like the Beddingtons, who didn't think of themselves as Jewish. He wanted to get Sheila away, and Bermuda, where Claude had helpful business connections, was chosen for her evacuation. So, in 1940, Sheila, 6-year-old Grania and 5-year-old Mervyn, nicknamed Murphy, sailed to New York on *The Samaria* which, a year later, converted into a troopship, would bring Pat to Egypt to join the Libyan Arab Force. From New York, Sheila and the children travelled by flying boat to an 'enchanted coral speck in the north Atlantic', the island of Bermuda which soon became Sheila's 'true love'.

Her rented cottage had a murmurous address: Valdemere, Paget, Bermuda. It was halfway down a sandy hill that descended to the sea. In her garden, she trained chalice vines to twine around the veranda and planted striped red and white amaryllis each side of the path. There were no cars on the island; Sheila drove a dark-blue buggy – 'a mousetrap on wheels' – drawn by Gypsy, 'my little American standard-bred pacing mare', who was looked after by Manuel, the Portuguese gardener. The account she wrote in *Real People* about her time on the island is uncharacteristically gushing: the churchyard of Smith's Parish Church 'is the prettiest in the world'; the local hospital, 'that sunniest, cleverest, most cheerful, best-equipped hospital in the world'. There is not 'one ill-used or unhappy person in the place', nobody who is 'poor or badly-dressed'. She wrote this blissful account some years later, in 1952, from a cold Ireland, bedevilled by shortages and poverty. At the time, she voiced a few complaints about the paradise isle, which Claude, living in a London of air-raid warnings, rationing and terror, concernedly tried to address. On 17 August 1940, he sympathized with her over 'the awful damp heat … and getting so little rest and that your legs are so swollen. I do feel so much that I am not with you to help'. So much so that he wrote again on the following day to say that he was sending her a Nurse Turner. This was Sheila at her most pampered and unsympathetic. Cocooned on her pretty island, doing little for the war effort except, with Grania's help, rolling up bandages for the troops, she seemed to have no idea that it was hardly the time to complain about swollen legs and fatigue.

Claude was seventy-two. Now living at 3 Grosvenor Square, he was, as usual, in the thick of things, determined to play a part in this war, as he had in two previous conflicts. Nothing, apart from Sheila's grumbles from a far-off pink beach, dismayed him. 'Wonderful news about Pat being promoted to Capt and adjt [in the 8th Hussars],' he wrote to Sheila proudly, while he greeted the announcement of higher income tax with 'Thank God! Now at last we can beat Hitler.' His only grouse was that, because of his age, he was considered fit only for Home Guard duties. Signing up for Dad's Army was not his style; while pleased with his blue denim uniform, he felt that he could do 'much work of national importance of a higher order'. Another reason why he thought he should be given another job was that he had a touch of bronchitis and guarding the draughty Admiralty Arch, alongside other elderly gentlemen, was bound to make it worse.

Claude began to badger the Admiralty to let him undertake naval work on *Cachelot*. Once his persistence had worn the Admiralty down, he set about hiring a sailing crew of five and a Lewis gunner. In that same letter in which he regretted not being with Sheila, he can't resist sharing his excitement: 'At last I got splendid lot,' adding that he was going to Brixham on the following Monday to sail, 'in command'. He assures Sheila that 'I have only to take her to somewhere – which will take three or four or five days, then I come back to London.' Just over a week later, Bermuda's Colonial Secretary received a telegram from Margaret Adams, Claude's secretary:

TERRIBLY GRIEVED TO SAY COLONEL BEDDINGTON SHEILA WINGFIELD'S FATHER KILLED BY ENEMY ACTION IN HIS YACHT THIS MORNING DIED INSTANTLY PLEASE BREAK NEWS TO SHEILA GIVE HER ALL MY LOVE AND SYMPATHY AM ARRANGING CREMATION AS HE WISHED AT MILFORD HAVEN.

Claude had been killed by machine-gun fire from two enemy planes when *Cachelot*, renamed the *Orca*, was about five miles out to sea off the Welsh coast, probably dropping depth charges. Nobody could understand why Claude alone had been shot until 1952, when Sheila referred to the incident in *Real People*. This prompted a letter from a reader whose brother had worked in the Brixham shipyard. He told her that Claude, realizing that his crew had no time to man the Lewis gun, ordered them below. Against everyone's advice, Claude had been wearing a white yachting cap, which presumably made him an easy target. The death of this hero brought fulsome tributes: a photograph in *The Illustrated London News* showed Claude dashing and distinguished in a trilby and fur-collared overcoat; an obituary in *Country Life* insisted that 'He died as he would have wished to die, in the service of his country, a very great and gallant gentleman and the kindest hearted and warmest friend any man could wish to have.' Claude's ashes were scattered at sea and his name inscribed on the Tower Hill Memorial, close to the City of London. *Cachelot/Orca* was later owned by Captain Jack Carstarphen, who renamed her *Maverick*. He claimed that Claude's ghost would always give him a warning tap on the shoulder when the ship was in danger.

In his will, Claude left nothing to Ethel, despite Sheila's earlier understanding to the contrary. He was generous to the rest of his family, with bequests to his blood relatives, his son-in-law and grandchildren, and to past and present members of his staff, including £10,000 to Margaret Adams and an annuity of £156 for life to 'my devoted and faithful servant Namo Kallasagaram'. The bulk of his estate went to Sheila. She was a rich woman now but a lonely one. A month after her father died, she gave birth to a son, Guy Claude Patrick, with none of her family near. She became ill with that nameless illness and, towards the end of 1940, underwent an operation of some kind. Learning about this, on 14 January 1941 Ivon Brabazon wrote to her: 'I wish you would tell me more about it and how long it would actually take you to get better again, as these are rather serious affairs it seems to me and I do not like being left in the dark.' But where Sheila's health was concerned, everybody was left in the dark, whether they liked it or not.

On 14 March that year, Irish Grandma sent Sheila a sprig of shamrock from Bellair, a bittersweet reminder of Ireland. Bermuda was becoming less idyllic; families of fighting men began to dread the ring of a telephone in case the Cable Office was on the other end. Two square miles of the

island, a tenth of its total area, were loaned to the USA for use as war bases
and women volunteers cut out hospital pyjamas in accordance with Red
Cross instructions. The pink beaches were splotched with black oil from
sunk tankers; there was the noise of anti-aircraft guns and the sight of
badly-burnt merchant seamen wheeled into operating rooms. American
sailors, not quite sober, wobbled along the streets on bicycles.

Grania's first memories of Sheila are of this time. The self-portrait
that Sheila painted in *Real People* of the devoted young mother who
sprawled on the grass of her Kentish garden while Grania and Mervyn
put foxgloves on her fingers, or who watched anxiously at Powerscourt
while her small children played in the long grass, dangerously close to a
scythe-wielding gardener, has gone, if she ever existed. In her place is a
critical, harsh mother who won't leave her children alone. Grania recalls
that these children were relieved when the cottage became too small for
the household and they were moved to a neighbouring one. Unfortunately, there's a governess there too, as strict as Sheila has now become,
who makes Grania walk along the beach with a placard pinned to her
back. It read, 'I did not eat my supper'. From this time on, Grania became
an expert in avoidance, keeping out of Sheila's way as much as she could.
She would have understood what Sheila would one day write about her
own mother, 'Whenever her attention was directed at me it boded ill.'
Grania was a child of her time and social class which meant that she'd
been brought up almost entirely by nannies. When the children got older
and the nannies departed, parents and children, now rather late in the day
uneasily acquainted, found each other mutually unfathomable.

Sheila's life, in spite of Bermuda's pink sands, was becoming more
clouded. As Guy's babyhood passed, she began to realize that the little boy
was profoundly deaf and that, unwittingly, she was to blame. While pregnant with him, she had sat next to a friend who had German measles,
unaware of rubella's effect on unborn children. And then, Pat went missing
in Libya. He had been sent to North Africa in 1941 because, having lived
there for a time before the war, he could speak Senussi, the language of the
Libyan Arabs. Nobody had been notified of his arrival in Libya, and it was
only through a chance meeting with a British officer in a bar that he
became officially attached to the Third Battalion of the Libyan Arab Force
as second in command to Colonel Victor Paley. It is hard to imagine Pat,
tall and fair, nipping behind enemy lines improbably disguised as an Arab,
but this was just the kind of job, both larky and dangerous, that appealed

to him. His commanding officer, writing to Sheila to tell her that Pat was missing, described him as 'a bold and fearless soldier and quick and alert', as well as 'a most charming and delightful companion'.

Pat had been captured, sixty miles south of Benghazi, on 29 January 1941, in an attempt to reach his divisional headquarters. He didn't know that on the same day the Germans had occupied Benghazi and taken control of the road leading to it. Benghazi was an unsettled theatre of the Desert War, changing hands five times before being liberated in the battle of El Alamein. Pat was captured by the Italians, who had come to the aid of the Italian army in Libya, an Italian colony since 1912. The Italian lorry driver who transported Major Wingfield to Prison Camp number 29 in northern Italy, gave him a present of a tin spoon. Pat used this spoon, his only eating utensil, throughout his three and a half years as British prisoner of war 34959. Sheila was told that Pat had been taken prisoner a month after the event but the terse *Irish Times* news item didn't appear until 15 May: 'News has been received from enemy sources that Major Mervyn Patrick Wingfield, son of Lord Powerscourt, is a prisoner in Italian hands.' Sheila wrote in *Real People* about the trips she made to the USA on Pat's behalf but didn't explain what she hoped to achieve.

The wartime letters between Pat and his sister, Doreen, the Hon. Mrs Fitzherbert Wright of Holbrook Hall in Derby, known affectionately to her brother as 'Dar', tell part of the story of his captivity, but not all of it. Like so many men who had been through hell in the prison camps, Pat never talked about it later or attended reunions. He was a prisoner of the Italians until the Italian armistice in 1943. During his time in Italy, he wrote to Dar that he was 'very well but very bored'. The camp was dirty but the guards were bribable. Smuggled-in wireless sets received messages sent by MI9 (Military Intelligence) at the War Office and mail and packages arrived, although slowly and haphazardly. Pat was grateful for the 'lined shoes' and blankets which Dar sent him and optimistically asked her not to send any more corduroy trousers as 'I doubt I shall be able to bring them home'. He was convinced, during the first part of 1943, that the war would end soon. His letters to Dar finish, 'Hope you had a good Xmas, will see you before next one,' and 'By the look of things we ought to be meeting soon and what a party we will have.' He studies the books on farming which Dar sends him, in readiness for the day when he will inherit Powerscourt. In a rare, downbeat moment, he reflects that 'Guy is nearly three years old and I have never seen him.' Dar's letters to Pat make no attempt to shield him from bad news. 'Did you know that Billy Fitzwilliam, Lord Headfort and Hans have all died, also Paddy Chichester was killed just before Xmas, and Arthur Fitzgerald's eldest son John too.' This list of casualties may have been her way of indicating to her brother that he was better off away from the fighting, however frustrating his captivity.

The Italian armistice, which was immediately followed by the German occupation of northern Italy, took the POWs in the seventy-two Italian prison camps by surprise. From their clandestine radios came unfortunate advice from the War Office 'to stand fast until liberated'. Those who obeyed were put under German armed guard within forty-eight hours of the armistice, and were soon on their way to POW camps in Germany. Pat was among those who disobeyed orders and made off. The easier option would have been for him to travel northwards and cross the Italian Alps into Switzerland, a feat accomplished successfully by 4000 escaping POWs. But Pat wanted to rejoin the fighting, so travelled southwards, with the intention of meeting up with the advancing Allied lines. His luck ran out, although 6500 escapees were successful. After sixteen weeks on the run, he was spotted by a German tank, jumped over a bridge to escape capture, broke his ankle and was easily caught. During his weeks of freedom, he had been helped by Italian civilians, given a pair of trousers, food and a place to sleep and hide. His Italian hosts behaved with great courage; the German occupiers had made it clear that anyone harbouring escaped POWs would be executed.

From a prison camp for officers in Hamburg, where he was to spend the rest of the war, Pat continued to write to Dar with his customary cool grace. 'It was maddening getting caught again after so long out and having got so far,' he wrote, with typical understatement. His optimism remained intact. He was grateful that his feet had recovered and that postal deliveries were more efficient than in Italy: a letter from Sheila had taken only a month to reach him. He related news of fellow escapees as though they were tourists ambling towards their destination: 'Bill Barber was last heard of at the end of December quite well and flourishing … Gregg I have no news of but believe he was with a party which was making for Switzerland.' His sign-off is undiminished in its cheerfulness: 'Hope to see you all again soon.'

From Pat's letters, resolutely ignoring the horrors of his daily existence and unrealistically planning his homecoming, Dar could not have guessed what conditions in the camps were like and, until recently, neither could anyone else. With the publication in 2000 of *The Last Escape: The Untold Story of Allied Prisoners of War in Germany 1944–45*, by John Nichol and Tony Rennell, we can fill some gaps in Pat's story. The authors examined recently declassified files, discovered old diaries and interviewed veterans. The story that emerged was one of War Office incompetence as much as German brutality. As the Red Army advanced towards the Reich in the autumn of 1944, the Germans cleared the POW camps of nearly 166,000 British and Commonwealth servicemen and 92,000 Americans, and marched them westwards into the worst German winter for fifty years. The Red Cross warned the British War Office that the men would starve unless mercy convoys were sent across the lines, but was told that lorries and petrol weren't available. After months of hesitation, 100,000 food parcels were parachuted in, but by then between 2500 and 3500 men had died. After the war Pat hardly ever mentioned these forced marches.

Ivon Brabazon was having a better war than Pat Wingfield. He had been close to Churchill since 1918 when, having just become an MP, he was appointed Churchill's private parliamentary secretary at the War Office. Churchill made him Minister of Transport in 1940. It had been Ivon's idea, against expert advice, to use the Tube stations as air-raid shelters, a plan which saved the lives of many Londoners. The following year, he was promoted to Minister of Aircraft Production but was sacked a year later, following his outspoken criticism of the USSR – he had suggested that there wasn't much to choose between Russia and Germany. Banished to the House of Lords, he took the title Lord Brabazon of Tara after Tara Hall in County Meath, where he had grown up. He continued to be disarmingly tactless in his ongoing correspondence with Sheila: 'Sheila dear. Thank you for your telegram. I valued it so much from one who I have loved so long and with whom I have spent such happy days.' The telegram, presumably, was to congratulate him on his elevation to the peerage. Letters between the two continued after Pat had been taken prisoner. Sheila never admitted to an affair with Ivon but she planted some erotic signposts in her second memoir. The envelopes containing Ivon's latest move in their game of postal chess 'set my heart thumping'. She quotes a passage about Ivon from Henry Longhurst's book, *Only on Sundays*, in which Ivon admits to being 'the only peer ever to have been mated by post'. She wrote that all of Ivon's letters to her were signed, 'Ever Thine Nelson, Or else Nimzovitch,' but she was exaggerating. A letter that began 'Wonderfull [sic] dear Sheila', and went on to announce Ivon's intention of hunting and sailing with her when they met again, closed only with 'Goodbye, my love'.

The wartime dying went on. After Claude, Irish Grandma, mercifully before the deaths of her two 'golden grandsons', John and Edward Nutting, Enid's sons. The loss of her two young cousins had significant consequences for Sheila. Irish Grandpa had left Bellair to Enid but neither she nor her surviving son, Anthony, wanted the house, site of Sheila's happiest memories. Enid made it over to Sheila at a very reasonable price. Sheila wanted to return to the Bog of Allen as much as her mother had wanted to leave it. Bellair stood for peace and tranquillity, both more precious now than ever, after the tumult of war. Besides, Sheila was forty, and had never had a home to live her own life in and to fill with books. It would be a life without Claude, her once omnipresent protector, but his death promised freedom of a kind; Virginia Woolf confided in her diary that if her father were still alive, she wouldn't have been able to write. Sheila planned to write at Bellair, and to set Pat up in farming. Thus he could put to practical use everything he had learnt in the farming manuals while a prisoner of war.

This didn't happen immediately. When Pat was repatriated to England, he weighed eight stone, had lost all his teeth and was fearful that he might be impotent. He was cared for by Dar at Holbrook Hall; Dar, not unreasonably, took it badly that Sheila didn't make the journey from Bermuda to welcome her husband home. Instead, after what Sheila describes as 'vicissitudes and obstacles', Pat went to Bermuda and stayed for six months, recuperating in mind and body. Anybody looking at a photograph of Pat and Sheila taken for a Bermudian newspaper soon after Pat's arrival, could be forgiven for thinking that Pat had spent the war loafing on a pink beach, while his wife had endured unspeakable horrors. Posed by a calm harbour, Pat, raffish in shorts, a white jacket and carrying a straw hat, looks fit and sturdy and no older than he had done before the war. His teeth have been excellently repaired and he is smiling happily. It is Sheila who has aged; her lipsticked mouth is a taut, dark gash in her white face and her eyes seem haunted. She seems to be making some misguided effort to be sexily alluring, for she is wearing high-heeled, peep-toe shoes and a delicate ankle chain which draws attention to her legs, her worst feature. She and Pat seem disconnected from each other, which is perhaps how they felt, as did so many husbands and wives, separated and changed in different ways by the long war years.

Arriving back in England, after a pleasurable stop-over in New York, the atmosphere at Holbrook Hall was scratchy with disapproval. Dar disapproved of Sheila because of what she saw as the latter's lack of wifely devotion; Pat despised his brother-in-law Fitz, who had spent the war in Derbyshire, uneventfully farming. It was with relief that the Wingfields at last made their way to Ireland, the country that they both loved best – at least they had that in common. Here, at Bellair, Pat would farm and Sheila would write. While she had been in Bermuda, Irish literature had had a good war. In 1940, Sean O'Faolain and his fellow-Corkman, Frank O'Connor, had founded *The Bell*, a literary journal which offered a more exclusive view of Irishness than the dogged nationalism of de Valera. In 1941, the Irish literary scene had been further enlivened by John Betjeman's posting to Dublin as press attaché to the UK Representative to Éire, Sir John Maffey. Betjeman saw his job as fostering good cultural relations between the two countries and, in 1942, masterminded an Irish edition of the literary and political magazine, *Horizon*, edited by Cyril Connolly. This saw the first journal publication of part of Patrick Kavanagh's poem *The Great Hunger*. Also in this issue were articles by Kenneth Clarke on Jack Yeats, Sean O'Faolain on 'Yeats [W.B.] and the Younger Generation' and Frank O'Connor on 'The Future of Irish Literature'. In an editorial, Connolly sought to dispel anti-Irish feeling in England by pointing out that, in spite of its neutrality, Ireland was suffering as many, if not more, discomforts than England: 'Bread is rationed, tea and coffee are very scarce, trams run slowly on inferior fuel.'

Sybil Powerscourt, somewhat exaggeratedly noted by Diana Manners for her suffering in the First World War, had an equally hard time in the Second, her difficulties worsened by old age, poor health and anxiety about her imprisoned son. The gloom lifted for a while when, in June 1943, Powerscourt was used as the setting for the Battle of Agincourt scenes in Laurence Olivier's directorial debut, the film of *Henry V*. In the re-enactment of the battle, members of the local Defence Force acted as infantrymen. Among the extras was Patrick Kavanagh but Sybil would not have heard of or recognized him. In this new atmosphere of tentative cultural diversity, Sheila, a poet with a divided heritage, could have flourished. But she had scarcely settled her family into easily-managed Bellair, within striking distance of her sweater and attic, before the familiar golden chains started to clank.

8. IN GOLDEN FETTERS

'I could not settle myself with my book or my work in any of those splendid rooms, nor can I fancy anyone enjoying existence in these golden fetters.'
Elizabeth Smith of Baltiboys, visiting Powerscourt in 1849

If only Sheila could have stayed at Bellair, which she always referred to as her birthright. She felt uncomplicatedly Irish there, free of that duality which Elizabeth Longford called 'a doubled richness but divided commitment'. Although Sheila loved the place, she set about changing it. Out went the accumulated clutter of Irish Grandma and generations of Mulocks: 'Spears (there are always spears); a multitude of medicines, some I am convinced pre-Indian Mutiny and perhaps an unknown cause of it.' Irish Grandpa's collection of tiger-skulls, arranged in rows on top of the bookcases, went too and his billiard-room became a dining-room. A cinquecento carved marble chimney piece was installed in the double drawing-room and more windows were let into the thick walls. During these renovations, a prehistoric Irish elk's head was found buried in the foundations of the house. In Bermuda, Sheila had become used to American-inspired comforts and imported some of these to the Bog of Allen: central heating, fitted carpets and several additional bathrooms. The walls were scooped out to provide shelving for Sheila's book collection, 'eight thousand in the double drawing-room alone', if she is to be believed. An act of defiance by the reading girl, although the books were made more decorative by being covered in different wallpapers by Sheila and Grania.

'Books were my bulwark against the sadness of this land,' Sheila wrote but, for once, seemed in no need of a bulwark.

Despite rationing and shortages, Ireland in 1946 was not as bleak as England. At Bellair everyone and everything was comfortingly familiar; orchards, meadows, riverbanks; hay piled high in the haggards; Joe Cornally, one of the gardeners, attacking the grass wearing one of Irish Grandpa's suits, much cut-down and as ancient as himself. Tom Salmon, the farm manager, had been her grandparents' chauffeur and had taught Sheila to drive. Bridget, the housemaid, compared the mess made by the installation of the new bathrooms to the time when 'the old mistress [Irish Grandma] had all the chimneys torn asunder', which is to say that she had the flue linings replaced. When Sheila wondered, 'How could I fail to enjoy living in a country where the past kept pushing its fingers, often its whole hand, through the fabric of the present?' she wasn't talking only about archaeology but about memory. Memory, said Proust, is the only place where permanence resides and, at Bellair, all Sheila's memories were unclouded: the unconditional love offered by her grandmother and Aunt Enid; the excellent sausages sold at Ballycumber post office; Claude, organizing a regatta on the Brosna river and awarding a prize to the catcher of the smallest fish. She and Pat became quite companionable again, shooting wild duck, or driving to Dublin at sunrise to buy carpets in Grafton Street. Virginia Woolf's prescription for creative contentment was 'a room of one's own and £500 a year' and Sheila had rather more than that. And suddenly, hardly settled into Bellair, she found herself with a hundred rooms of her own. Sybil and Mervyn died within three months of each other and Pat and Sheila became the owners of Powerscourt.

The deaths of her parents-in-law were so unexpected that there were rumours that they had been poisoned. Typhoid fever caught from the cook was a likelier explanation. Sybil died first, on 6 December 1946; Mervyn was too ill to attend her funeral although, just over a week later, *The Irish Times* reported that he was out of danger and that his condition was improving. The improvement didn't last; he died on 21 March 1947, having survived a bitterly cold winter in a house that Sheila considered to be 'one colossal icebox'. His funeral, conducted by the Archbishop of Dublin, in the little burial ground in the Powerscourt demesne, was attended by a representative from the Taoiseach's office and by the UK Representative to Éire, but not by Sheila, marking the first of her baffling non-appearances at important family gatherings. Mervyn's obituaries harped on his public roles: chief commissioner in Éire of the Boy Scouts, chairman of the Associated Hospitals Committee, Lieutenant for County Wicklow, Justice of the Peace. They gave no hint of the Mervyn whom Sheila so lovingly and entertainingly described in *Real People*, the man who fed biscuits to his ornamental birds and 'loved to feel their cold bills in his hand', and who once made the curious admission that 'I am never so happy … as when sitting on top of a London bus, thinking of all the worries I've had.'

Powerscourt in that biting March was even chillier than usual. Many of its sheltering trees had been felled during the war to ease the national shortage of fuel but you could have tossed whole forests into those marble fireplaces without warming up the high-ceilinged rooms. It was impossible to install central heating without harming the house's structure, so Sheila decided that she and her family would retreat to the snugness of Bellair from November until Easter. That sharply critical Victorian visitor to Powerscourt, Elizabeth Smith of Baltiboys, thought that it was too grand to live in, whatever the reason: 'The place as a place is fine, the house as a work of art, handsome, and the interior of it a shew and a shew only, for no one with simple happy tastes could endure to live in rooms so gorgeous.' Sheila didn't have simple happy tastes. She set out to make Powerscourt even grander and more gorgeous than ever, while other Ascendancy families were feeling the economic pinch, moving from their dilapidated Big Houses into gate lodges, along with other belt-tightening exercises.

Sheila began a rebuilding programme for which Bellair had been merely a rehearsal. In Ireland, it was a frustrating time to call in the builders, there was such a drastic shortage of cement and timber that a quota system was in place. Exceeding it, Sheila pleaded with the appropriate government ministry to let repairs continue, citing pitted drainpipes, a leaky roof and primitive plumbing and electricity. 'The Minister looked at me calmly. "There are sufficient ruins in Ireland without having Powerscourt another one," he said. "I'll set the matter right." ' It was three years before what Sheila called the reconditioning of Powerscourt was completed. At the end of it, there was an entire floor of bedrooms, each with a bathroom and dressing-room. A lift and a ladies' lavatory were also installed downstairs, unique innovations. A butler and liveried footman were hired. A 21-year-old American visitor, Cynthia Cawley, whose mother had known Sheila in Bermuda, spent a weekend at Powerscourt with her parents in 1947, and was dazzled when the butler announced, 'My

Lord, my Lady. Dinner is served.' In spite of a hot water bottle, Cynthia's mother was so cold when she got between the glacial sheets that she piled on so many blankets as to make her swelter alarmingly during the night.

In 1938, *Tatler* had described Powerscourt as 'one of the show places in all Éire', but it was not at all to Sheila's taste when she moved there. The stairway bristled with the sixteenth-century German chandeliers known as *Hirschgeweih Weibl* – 'stag-horn ladies' – formed from antlers supporting figures of women. Twin canon and suits of armour flanked the hall door. Cassels had imposed an eighteenth-century veneer on the old, rough, defensive castle of the fighting de la Poers. Sheila wanted something more modern and luxurious. So the ground-floor sitting-rooms which, decades ago, had been idiosyncratically distempered in strong raspberry pink and bright inky blue, were repainted in the bland pastels popular at the time. Massive statues were removed: 'Quite a few simpering, female nudes were sent packing from the Saloon – with heavy machinery and much difficulty,' and rehoused in dark corners of the garden. It wasn't enough. The belongings of previous Wingfields, many of whom had been obsessive collectors, confronted her 'with a challenge to the death'. Less than a year after moving in, Sheila held a massive clearance sale.

Advertised in *The Irish Times* as a 'highly important fine art and furniture auction', it was conducted by the Dublin auctioneers, Allen & Townsend, who explained that the reason for the auction was to sell off surplus articles 'because of the partial refurnishing of the house'. Sheila's dislike of 'a gigantic elephant's skull with one tusk missing, a bullet hole in the occiput and a red velvet antimacassar on top of its head' is understandable. It was an ugly reminder of the elephant-foot wastepaper baskets at 26 Seymour Street, whose 'shine on the toe-nails' and 'bumps and roughness inside the dead skin' had decidedly put her off dead elephants as decorative objects. But why sell off the Sheraton writing table enclosing library steps (it made £24), a 77-piece French china dessert service (£35) and nine Empire rosewood chairs (£189)? The sale was meant to last for five days but was so successful, attracting English as well as Irish buyers, that it was extended for another five.

Everything had to go: mattresses, bolsters and pillows; an untrained 4-year-old filly and a Brougham pony trap. In this frenzy of riddance, George Laffan, a sculptor and Dublin antique dealer, spotted a bargain on top of a bookcase, so caked with dried mud that that perhaps only a sculptor would have noticed it. Laffan recognized its value and bought it for less than £100. Underneath the mud was an exceptionally fine bronze sculpture of a cat, *c.* 1250 BC. The story of how it came to Powerscourt was recorded by the 7th Viscount in his 1903 book, *A Description and History of Powerscourt*. His younger brother, Lewis Strange Wingfield, while covering the Egypt war of 1882 as a *Times* correspondent, had taken the cat from the ruins of a railway station. The 7th Lord Powerscourt was aware of the cat's value but fifty years later, the bronze was covered in mud and forgotten. The Powerscourts were such avid collectors it was perhaps inevitable that the odd treasure might be overlooked. Even the 7th Viscount, that ardent acquirer of artworks, had made the occasional slip-up, once selling a Vermeer for a few hundred pounds. (The painting now hangs in the National Gallery of Washington D.C.) The subsequent *Irish Times* report of Laffan's purchase implied neglect and carelessness on the part of the Powerscourts, which rankled with Sheila. In *Sun Too Fast*, she dismissed Lewis Wingfield as 'a volatile and effeminate person who was a tenth-rate painter'. In fact, he was a member of the Royal Hibernian Academy and had studied painting and surgery at Antwerp. He had appeared on stage at the Haymarket Theatre in London, became a correspondent for *The Daily Telegraph* and *The Times* and sent his dispatches out by balloon during the siege of Paris in 1870. He wrote novels and a travel book and died in London in 1891. Among his paintings was a set of eight panels, representing scenes from the poems of Thomas Moore, which were installed in the upper stage of the Saloon at Powerscourt. Sheila had the panels dismantled. The past meant nothing to her; Claude had seen to that by dismantling his own ancestry. He had reinvented himself from scratch, as Sheila began to do. She would have auctioned off her own family history if she could.

Apart from her mortification over the Egyptian cat, Sheila was delighted with the reconditioning. When the several pairs of gates had been regilded, the old furniture sold and the butler and liveried footman in place, she invited Pat's elderly aunts to admire the changes. Grania could see that the old ladies were heartbroken to see their family history erased as well as embarrassed by Sheila's extravagance at a time of austerity and hardship. Sheila's old friend, Harry d'Avigdor Goldsmid, gave her the admiration she craved. After his first visit to the renovated house in 1952, he wrote to Sheila, 'It was a tremendous pleasure to me to see that great house so cared for, so preserved and embellished ... You were very lucky to have such wonderful material to which to apply your innate creative ability.' While Harry saw it as a tribute to Sheila's taste, her husband may have seen the reconstruction of his ancestral home as a demonstration of his wife's ruthlessness and power. Not that there was much he could do about it, his parents' almost simultaneous deaths had landed him with massive death duties, which meant that without Sheila's money, Powerscourt would have been sold. It was worth putting up with pink-carpeted bedrooms to keep it in the family. Why did Sheila take such a high-handed approach in dismantling centuries of eccentric decoration? Perhaps it was to turn Powerscourt into somewhere she could feel comfortable and have put her own stamp upon. Or maybe she wanted to show Pat that she was in charge and could do whatever she liked. By rebuilding Pat's property, she certainly made it vindictively clear that she had no intention of being thwarted.

She hated having to leave Bellair for half the year but, as the 9th Viscountess Powerscourt, was fully aware of her responsibilities. Sybil had been chief commissioner of the Irish Girl Guides and Sheila succeeded her in the post, in July 1947, wearing a uniform which, in its flamboyant inventiveness, showed her to be her father's daughter. This uniform was a beautifully tailored navy blue suit, tightly belted to show off her narrow waist, and sparkling with gold braid. Her matching hat had a rolled brim and a cockade. Her uniform was like a theatrical costume in which she could play the part of an Anglo-Irish aristocrat, ignoring the side of her that wasn't remotely Anglo-Irish. This was quite unlike the approach of another Ascendancy wife, also a writer and a considerable heiress, who had made no secret of her Jewishness and might have been a useful role-model for the ill at ease Lady Powerscourt. This was Ellen Odette Bischoffsheim, (1857–1933) second wife of the 4th Earl of Desart. Her fortune allowed him to restore his Palladian house, Desart Court, in Kilkenny. Lady Desart encouraged the setting up of a branch of the Gaelic League in Kilkenny, pointing out that her own people had also revived a forgotten language. She was later awarded the Freedom of the City of Kilkenny and, along with fifty members of the Ascendancy, including Mervyn Powerscourt, appointed to the Senate by Cosgrave.

Ireland's record in sheltering Jewish refugees during the war had been abysmal and this attitude persisted in peacetime. On 9 October 1945, Sir Basil Newton of the British Foreign Office reported that Joseph Walsh, of the Irish Department of Foreign Affairs, had told him that 'there were

5000 Jews in Dublin and that the ostentatious behaviour of some of them was not making them popular. He evidently did not wish to see any considerable immigration of Jews into Éire'. Walsh's remarks were part of a private discussion; no government minister referred to Jews as undesirable aliens in public. But, as Dermot Keogh points out in his study of Jews in twentieth-century Ireland, 'anti-Semitism remained a peripheral subcurrent in Irish society'. As Sheila entertained her husband's friends and associates, she may have caught a whiff of that casual prejudice, perhaps overhearing somebody joke that the seaside resort of Bray was now called 'Little Palestine' because so many Jews had bought houses there. Bray, only twelve miles from Dublin, was also a popular holiday spot for that city's Jewish population. Holidaymakers were once greeted with this graffito on a Bray railway bridge: 'Give us back Bray and we'll give you back Jerusalem'. Did Sheila, like Osip Mandelstam, another poet who had to toe the line, feel like 'a double-dealer with a divided heart'? Powerscourt had been saved from ruin with money made by Claude and his Jewish forebears. This was kept quiet, just as Claude himself had once been pushed into the shadows in the newspaper reports of his daughter's engagement, which mentioned only that 'the bride-to-be comes of a well-known Irish family on her mother's side'.

Beat Drum, Beat Heart was published by the Cresset Press in 1946. Herbert Read was so excited by it that he stayed up all night to finish it and then pronounced it 'the most sustained meditation on war that has been written in our time'. Other reviewers were also enthusiastic: 'The emotions of love, its strength and contradictions, are intensely suggested' (*Times Literary Supplement*). 'A work of unusually high poetic merit, and has earned the praise even of that sternest, and least compromising of critics, Austin Clarke' (*The Irish Times*). Vita Sackville-West praised it in *The Observer*, leading Sheila to write to her and begin an important new literary friendship. Some years later, when they had become friends, Kathleen Raine wrote to Sheila that the poem was 'an astounding piece of work, as if you were at that time possessed; or as if you had then written everything that was in you, poured out all your blood to the last drop'. Only Geoffrey Parsons, reviewing the poem in *Tribune*, disliked it. '[It] rambles on for two thousand flat ragged lines.'

Although Read saw *Beat Drum, Beat Heart* as a meditation on war, the poem has unsettling things to say about peace, as Alex Davis has pointed out. Its domain is doubleness, 'all twofold things', as the poet puts it: terror/

boredom, tranquillity/discontent. It's full of split loyalties, confused feelings and ambiguities:

> Angel and beast in me are one: because
> The midway heart is held between
> What's private, base, and what's diffused and rare.

The heartbreak of war is captured perfectly in the image of departing soldiers leaving their wives who are 'Bent back at the waist/To kiss them alone.'

But that's balanced by lulling descriptions of women at peace, which have a disturbing hint of Robert Lowell's 'monotonous sublime'. Although its references are far-ranging, the poem is rooted in Ireland. Alex Davis compares its account of the 7th Lord Powerscourt's creation of his Italianate garden in the section 'Men at Peace' with Yeats's 'Ancestral Houses' in his poem, 'Meditations in Time of Civil War', and pinpoints the reference to Ireland's War of Independence (1919–21):

> And the mistress in bed seeing on the wall
> The flash of the fired barracks across the way.

Recognizable images of Ireland are threaded through the poem's four sections:

> ...gloss
> of rain on pavements; and each market friend
> Who stood and argued, argued without end.
> ...walls so loose and easy-built
> That much of them have fallen.

It's an honest poem and, reading it, you feel the nonsense being shaken out of you. We all recognize our ownership of a 'midway heart'.

Beat Drum, Beat Heart opened doors for Sheila in literary Dublin. On 18 February 1948, she delivered an address, 'Certainties and Uncertainties in English Poetry' to the English Group at Trinity College, in which she concluded that English poetry didn't exist. However, she was never part of the city's bohemian circle. It's impossible to imagine the immaculately dressed Lady Powerscourt joining in 'the late-night sessions which went on in the back rooms of small hotels talking, talking all the time, the glasses filled regularly', as described by another Anglo-Irish writer, Theodora Fitzgibbon, but she knew its regulars, especially Joseph Hone. Hone was Yeats's first biographer, so endearingly absent-minded that he once ate the string tied around his asparagus, as well as the asparagus, without noticing. He lived near Enniskerry in Wicklow and came to an arrangement with the postman to deliver letters to Sheila free of charge, since Powerscourt was so near. Hone was a guest of Sheila's in May 1949 when, under Taoiseach John Costello, the Irish Free State became a Republic. The Garda Barracks at Enniskerry asked to borrow a celebratory tricolour from Powerscourt. Since Pat had kept up his father's impressive flag collection, he sent one tricolour down to the barracks and ran up another on the Powerscourt flagstaff. This delighted Sheila who defended everything Irish, including de Valera, 'the most humane of statesmen'. Her next collection of poetry, published that same year, suggests a poet who has a happy, easy attitude to the country she lives in, an attitude not all that common to the Anglo-Irish gentry at the end of the 1940s.

9. BAD BEHAVIOUR

'The only solemn pact I ever made with myself was as a child, when I
swore that I would never misunderstand my own children. Alas, it was
an oath I have been unable to keep.'
Sheila Wingfield, *Real People*

Placid contentment wasn't in Sheila's nature, and once she had finished
transforming the house, she became discontented with the duties that
went with it. Following in Sybil's footsteps kept her busy. She offered
hospitality and camping facilities to scouts and guides in the Powerscourt
demesne. She hosted lavish parties during the Dublin Horse Show week
in August and helped make the Powerscourt gardens more alluring to the
tourists who, since Mervyn's time, had been allowed to visit them. She felt
that she must be involved in the running of the estate and its 'multiple
problems, most of which I had to deal with', which meant worrying about
the price fetched in the Dublin market for fruit ripened in Powerscourt's
'acres of greenhouses'. All this despite the fact that she employed estate
and farm managers and a team of gardeners, as well as a large household
staff. The new Viscountess Powerscourt gave a good impression of an
industrious Big House chatelaine but it was only an impression. However
busy and preoccupied she was, if she wasn't writing or living among
writers, she felt somehow indefinite. And how could she write when she
had so much else to do, including that twice-yearly trek between Bellair
and Powerscourt, which involved the staff being sent on, with the silver-
ware, in a lorry, before the family arrived? She would have liked to have

invited other writers to stay in Powerscourt's expensively redecorated bedrooms but not many of them came. One who did, however, was John Hayward, always ready to live life on the grand scale.

The Powerscourts' marriage was going badly. Sheila didn't disclose just how disastrously until years later, in 1981, long after their separation and Pat's death. She wrote to her son, Guy: 'After years in a Hamburg prisoner of war camp, he came out raving mad against me (always polite when in public, but at other times, God help me). Such starvation turns everybody's brain. So we must not hold this against him.' She went on: 'A very long time after marriage I learnt that your father was an alcoholic before I married him (a thing no one tells a young bride and I was so in love with his good looks and so on) … he never came to bed at night sober once, as far as I remember.' Nobody, apart from the couple themselves, knows what goes on within a marriage but no one who knew Pat ever remarked on his heavy drinking. It was Sheila, they noticed, who always had a glass of vodka to hand as well as that beauty case, rattling with pills, and it was Sheila who was often bad-tempered and unpredictable. Pat was the more entertaining parent; he took the children to shoot rabbits in an open-topped car, or played the drums and bagpipes for them.

There were few women more isolated, more at the mercy of parental whim, than the daughters of the Irish Big House. Molly Keane's wickedly entertaining novel *Good Behaviour* (1981), features a cold, overbearing mother, based on Keane's real mother, whose iron-clad rules make her daughter's life a misery. This seems exaggerated until you hear non-fictional accounts such as Grania's. For a brief, happy time, she was sent to Downham, an English boarding school in Hertfordshire, but Sheila soon decided that the school fees were too expensive and brought her daughter home to be educated, or rather un-educated, by a governess. Grania spent most of her time working out how to escape from Sheila's critical eye. She gave her pony more exercise than it needed, although, before she set off, there would be a close inspection of her clothes. After that, she was free until eleven o'clock when, according to another rule, she had to come home to drink a glass of milk. One morning, terrified of being late, she made her pony jump over barbed wire so as to take the quickest route home.

Hunting was an even better means of escape. Grania had to lie to Sheila about whom she had tea with afterwards since whoever her hosts were, Sheila was sure to disapprove of them. Practice turned Grania into a plausible liar. When there was no hunting, it was easy enough to give a hypercritical mother the slip in a house the size of Powerscourt. Grania spent her days reading in one of the several new lavatories, choosing a different one every day to avoid detection. She got round other rules too: forbidden to wear make-up, she smeared calamine lotion on her face and sneaked bottles of Evening in Paris from Woolworth's. But Sheila went on choosing Grania's clothes until her daughter got married and Grania had no say in the matter. It was at those times when she realized that life didn't have to be as it was at Powerscourt, that she felt most unhappy. Once, when she was fourteen, she stayed for a few days with another family: 'Nobody criticized anybody else; everyone seemed to get on with one another.' Soon afterwards, she tried to run away, making it part of the way down the main avenue. It was exciting to see cars searching for her later, lights flashing, but she had no money, no plans, no means of getting anywhere else. She went back to the house.

Surprisingly, she wasn't punished. The Wingfield family doctor had advised against it and perhaps the drama of the episode made Sheila realize that she hadn't been the kindest of mothers. She herself had understood how harsh her own mother was when, as a schoolgirl, she had visited 'Cousin Hester [who] proved so kind to her three daughters that whenever I saw her I felt an overpowering rush of affection and would burst into tears.' It was a chastening experience to discover that she was making her daughter as unhappy as Ethel had made her. Of course, she wasn't quite as horrible as Ethel; she had never forced Grania to eat tapioca or wear surgical boots that she didn't need, and she had given her bound copies of her favourite comic, *The Eagle*, and taught her how to bat. Ordinary maternal affection, however, was beyond her. Although Sheila wanted to treat her own children better than Ethel had treated her, perhaps, deep down, in the blackest corner of her heart, she begrudged them a happier childhood than hers had been. Sheila longed to understand her children and perhaps she did, up to a point, but she couldn't stop herself from mistreating them.

Like Ethel, she seemed to lack a maternal instinct, if by that we mean an ability to put yourself in your child's place. Like Ethel, she frequently humiliated her daughter. 'Have you brushed your teeth?' she once asked Grania before the assembled guests at a house party. Sheila had no idea what intimacy meant; she kept Grania waiting outside her door while she dressed, sending her outside again if she came in while Sheila was still in her petticoat. Sheila could not tolerate being seen before her presentation of herself – immaculate, stylish – was complete. Then she would appear, her carefully made-up face immobile and expressionless. Grania never thought that her mother was good-looking; there was something life-denying about her perfect grooming that cast a pall over everything. What Grania wanted, more than anything else, was to go to art school. Sheila forbade it and so Grania stayed at home, frustratedly doing the flowers and rebelliously spending her £100 annual stocking allowance on art books. A long time afterward, Sheila assured Anne Roper 'we could have invited anyone we liked and did', but that's not how Grania remembers life at Powerscourt. There were few visitors; on most evenings, she dined downstairs with Pat while Sheila skulked in her bedroom. When she did come down, she sat silently by herself, her face a mask. Grania can't remember ever seeing her mother smile.

Mervyn had an easier time of it. There were harsh but familiar rules for sons of the Big House, who were sent away to school in England at a young age. They had to cope with homesickness but escaped the lonely, flower-arranging fate of their sisters. Mervyn, a handsome and charming boy, was clearly Sheila's favourite. During his school holidays, she spoilt him rotten. But, as he grew older, she tried to force him into the heroic shape of her dead brother, Guy Beddington, even renting Guy's digs for him when he went up to Cambridge. Her expectations were impossible for Mervyn to fulfil and he left Cambridge after a few terms. That other Guy, Sheila's youngest son, severely deaf, could not be sent to a conventional English boarding-school. He was sent away though; between the ages of six and ten, he was a boarder at the Central Institute for the Deaf in St Louis, 2000 miles from home. During those years, he came back to Powerscourt only in the summers, Sheila claiming it was too expensive to fly him back at Christmas and Easter.

The Institute's methods were designed to make its pupils part of the hearing world. Sign language was forbidden, the emphasis being on lip-reading. Guy's early 'oralist' training, frowned on today, when many deaf people, refusing to be pushed into a speaking life, use sign language and demand to be accepted as they are, was the right one for him. Guy is a talkative man, who speaks and understands German as well as English, and is very musical. He was happy enough at the Institute, happier there than during the summer holidays at Powerscourt, when Sheila wouldn't let him climb trees or play with the children of the estate workers. When he came back to Ireland permanently, after four years in America, his life disimproved. Taught at home by a tutor, he had nobody to play or learn with. No efforts were made to find him playmates and everything he did seemed to irritate his parents. Guy was a slow eater and this infuriated Pat. 'Swallow that mouthful,' he would yell, making the little boy even more nervous and upset, so that the food turned dry in his mouth. If Guy apologized for some small misdemeanour, Sheila would snap, 'What's the use of saying sorry when you'll do it again?' He liked it better when his parents weren't there.

Years before, when Sheila had become ill with what might have been nervous exhaustion, she had written anguishedly to Ottoline that she couldn't decide whether the true path of existence lay in domestic joy or the bliss of achievement. She no longer had doubts: domesticity, her churlish husband and her disappointing children, whose lives had to be controlled at all costs, could not compete with poetry. The well-received publication of *Beat Drum, Beat Heart*, years after she had written it, obscured the fact that it was a long time since she had produced anything else. There were all her household duties, of course, and her tendency of giving in to other distractions. John Hayward, observing her games of postal chess with Ivon Brabazon, told her, disapprovingly, 'Don't be so jolly stupid. Get on with your writing instead.' Her days were full, so she took to writing between 3 and 7 am; her only free time, she claimed. Grania disputes this. She remembers her mother as a hot-house flower, a creature of breakfast trays and bed jackets, who stayed in bed until late in the morning and who could do whatever she liked, whenever she wanted. But Sheila isn't the first woman writer who felt, justifiably, that her writing was disapproved of, if not actively discouraged, by her husband and best carried out in the secret hours before dawn. The biographer, Iris Origo, whose long marriage was, for the most part, happier than Sheila's, used to write at odd moments when her husband was out of the house or asleep, so as not to annoy or irritate him. There was no doubt in her mind that were he to see her at work, he would be both annoyed and irritated.

It wasn't just Pat who was discouraging (or, at least, not actively encouraging); Sheila was now writing in a generally unwelcoming climate. Ireland's wartime literary blossoming had been blighted by an increasingly conservative social and political atmosphere. In England, the new Apocalypse Movement, headed by Dylan Thomas and George Barker, saw a return to a romanticism in poetry which made Sheila's austere style out of step with the times. In 1948, Liam Gogan of Heinemann charmingly rejected her new collection. Gogan told her: 'It is difficult to see this poetry being appreciated today, outside of certain well-defined literary zones in America. I am afraid you have made quite a number of good poets rather pallid and deflated for me.' Sheila wrote to Vita Sackville-West about her difficulties in getting published and that practical woman suggested that she pay for publication herself. 'If you were willing to do this,' she advised, 'I feel sure that you could place them [her poems].' Gradually, however, things improved for Sheila. Two new poems, 'Winter' and 'Epitaph' were included in an anthology of modern verse, *The Voice of Poetry 1930–1948*, and the *Evening Standard* published two more of her recent poems, 'History' and 'Romantic Landscape'. Then, in 1949, the Cresset Press brought out the new collection which Liam Gogan had turned down. Called *A Cloud Across the Sun*, there's a sense of nestling contentment throughout the book, in spite of its ominous title, with references to 'mussel-coloured houses by the dunes', Clonmacnois and Ross Abbey, as well as glimpses of the poet's life although, unsurprisingly, these fall short of revelation. 'No Entry' comes closest with

> ...my work, whose beat
> Hurts with its knock and actual daily pulse
> Of stinging joy, short ease and constant doubt.

Once again, Yeats's praise for her first collection, published eleven years earlier, is quoted on the jacket.

Reviewers praised the poems' 'purity and succinctness' and 'austere sincerity'. Dorothy Wellesley, now Duchess of Wellington, had a new poetry collection, *Selected Poems*, published at the same time, allowing a review of both aristocratically-authored books to appear in *The Irish Times* under the headline 'Ladies' Day'. The Duchess was as shameless as the Viscountess in appropriating Yeats for promotional purposes. In her preface, she wrote,

> The following introduction by W.B. Yeats was written for a selection which he made from the Author's poems in 1936. Unfortunately most of the edition was destroyed by fire during the great London air raids. In the circumstances it may be of interest to reprint this here, as an instance of his own taste in styles and subjects, and also of the generosity of a great Poet towards the work of one of whom he then knew nothing beyond her poems.

In fact, Yeats had met Lady Dorothy – introduced by Ottoline – at about the same time that he first read her poems. But, to add some drama to his introduction, he wrote that having read Dorothy's *Poems of Ten Years*, he learnt to his surprise 'that she [the author] was neither harassed journalist nor teacher'. Delighted as well as surprised, one assumes.

Sheila's greatest enthusiast, as far as her poetry was concerned, was undazzled by her rank. The poet, novelist and memoirist, Monk Gibbon, had admired her work since 1940, when Lady Fingall had sent him *Poems*, for which he thanked her profusely: 'I think she is a real poet … Something fine and grave and inevitable … Her lines zing. And also she is not afraid of having a heart.' Ten years later, in the 1952 March–April edition of the journal *Poetry Review*, he published 'The Poetry of Sheila Wingfield', a long, critical appraisal of her work. Sheila could not have asked for a more understanding and astute critic. Gibbon felt that her poems 'lie outside time in a sort of timeless present'. Sheila's voice, he asserted,

> … is her own and she uses it to say things that I cannot remember any other poet having tried to say … The soul of this particular poet shows plenty of fight. Whatever she says seems to come from a deep, smouldering intensity of thought and mood.

On 'Odysseus Dying' Gibbon wrote that 'though the concept of this poem is reflective, its impact upon us is the impact of living facts'. He found *Beat Drum, Beat Heart* 'weighted with the sense of life's irony and imperfections: it is tragic; but it is perhaps less tragic than I have made it out to be'.

Gibbon may not have known Sheila when he wrote this essay but he did some years later, because Beatrice Glenavy, writing to Sheila in 1962, mentions 'Monk Gibbon, who lives around the corner – I am sure you loathe him! He says himself that everyone loathes him.' In the margin of the letter, against this comment, Sheila wrote YES, a harsh judgment on such a distinguished champion of her work. Glenavy was two-faced as well as unkind. When she published her memoir, *Today We Will Only Gossip*, in 1964, the universally loathed Monk Gibbon is transformed in the acknowledgments into 'my friend Dr Monk Gibbon', and is thanked for 'his valuable assistance and good advice'. Gibbon, by all accounts a peppery character, was used to being snubbed, most nastily by his cousin W.B. Yeats who excluded him from *The Oxford Book of Modern Verse*. Twenty years after Yeats died, Gibbon wrote *The Masterpiece and the Man: Yeats as I Knew Him* (1959). There he presented Yeats as ruthless, malicious and breathtakingly detached. His portrait of the much-idolized poet, resembled, according to Conor Cruise O'Brien, 'an unsavoury and all powerful building contractor in the Bronx, his finger in every pie'. Why Sheila didn't warm to this man who loved and understood her poetry and who mocked the national hero who had humiliated her, is hard to understand. An awkward character herself, perhaps she felt uncomfortable with people who were equally difficult.

She was better disposed toward John Betjeman although she had never met him. She was planning to write her first memoir, *Real People*, encouraged by John Hayward who, by now, was ending his letters to her with the peculiar sign-off 'Your obedient mid-husband'. She asked Betjeman, whom she knew to be an admirer, to supply a preface, although she gave him no idea what the book was about. Betjeman wrote bemusedly to Hayward, 'I am, apparently, to write a preface on what you tell me about the book. This is a bit difficult for you and me.' Optimistically, he asked for a copy of the book or typescript. Neither existed, for, although Dennis Cohen of the Cresset Press had given Sheila an advance of £50 and had drawn up a contract which offered her royalties rising to 15 per cent and gave him rights to the American edition (which doesn't seem to have ever materialized), the book wasn't ready for publication until 1952. Meanwhile, something had to be done about Grania.

10. AN EVASIVE AUTOBIOGRAPHY

'A hint of silent cruelty as if one were to shoot ornamental birds from a
distant window with an air gun.'
Harold Nicolson reviewing *Real People* in *The Observer*, 1952

Sheila's attitude towards money swung between bouts of heady extravagance, such as restoring Powerscourt, and periods of heartless stinginess, like the times she kept Grania out of the boarding-school she loved and kept Guy away during most of his school holidays, rather than pay his airfare home. This kind of financial shilly-shallying is perhaps not surprising, given her upbringing. Claude had brought her up in a selfishly generous way, showering her with everything she didn't want: expensive clothes, the very best guns and fishing rods, while depriving her of everything she did: books, and more books. No wonder she was confused about the power of money.

This confusion is apparent in a passage in one of her memoirs, about Fred Wilson, that inspiring lecturer on antiquities at the Victoria & Albert Museum, who died in 1949, in his eighties and in great poverty. Soon after the war, Sheila had visited him in the shabby house in Ealing, west London, where he lived on a tiny state pension and took care of several even more destitute relatives. Sheila's portrait of this household is moving but she follows it with a description of the antique Waterford tumbler that he gives her during this visit, at a time when he had scarcely enough to eat. She then mentions that, in his will, he left her a little Indian crystal head which she had admired a quarter of a century ago. Nothing about this makes sense: why is a poor old man giving a valuable present to a rich woman, when he could have sold it, together with the Indian crystal? And why doesn't she do anything about his miserable circumstances? That she sees nothing wrong in telling the story about how she left the house in Ealing clutching a valuable piece of Waterford glass is even stranger.

In 1950, with Grania's debutante season on the horizon, Sheila decided to make up for her daughter's underfunded and scrappy schooling. She could have sent Grania to a finishing school, a popular option, but, instead, decided to take her on a six-week European tour. They would go by car, with Pat as chauffeur, and take 15-year-old Deirdre Wingfield, Grania's second cousin, and Sheila's goddaughter, for company. Deirdre had grown up in Westmeath, not far from Powerscourt, but hadn't seen much of her godmother. She didn't in the least want to go to Europe with relations she hardly knew, especially since it meant leaving her English boarding-school during term-time and missing the first half of her O-level preparation. She was worried, rightly as it turned out, that she wouldn't be able to catch up. But her mother made her go; Deirdre's father, Pat's cousin Anthony Wingfield, was not well off and, as a hard-working farmer, could offer his family very little social life. Six weeks abroad with Sheila, who insisted on nothing less than sumptuousness wherever she went, must have appeared to Deirdre's family like a glittering opportunity for her. Sheila wanted the trip to have a dual purpose: to give the two girls a touch of European sophistication and polish and to allow Pat to search out the many courageous Italians who had cared for him during his time on the run in the war. What a hazardous venture; she must have been in a desperately restless state to be able to contemplate spending hours in a car with two schoolgirls who hardly knew each other and a husband with whom she was no longer on the most loving terms. Not for the first time, Sheila failed to predict the consequences of her actions.

They set off from Powerscourt in Pat's roomy Dodge. Arriving in London, they stayed at the Dorchester, the first in a series of luxury hotels which overawed Deirdre, who nevertheless noticed that her godmother took a lot of pills from a selection kept in pretty jewel boxes. Then Paris, Avignon, Carcassonne, the south of France and into Italy. Pat did all the driving, chewing his tongue in concentration. Grania sat next to him so that she could tell him when it was safe to overtake; not old enough to drive herself, she wasn't a reliable guide, which led to some friction. Otherwise,

there wasn't much conversation in the car. Although most European travellers were restricted in the amount of money they could take abroad at
that time, Sheila already had some money in Italy because of the compulsory sale of Claude's villa at Ospedaletti. She bought herself a ring in
Milan and in Venice the party stayed at the Danielli, the most expensive
hotel in the city. Somewhere north of Rome, when Pat stopped at a garage
for petrol, the pump-attendant recognized him; he had lent him a pair of
trousers during the war.

It was a Holy Year and Rome was packed with Irish visitors; the
Dodge with its EIR number plates was warmly greeted. But the two girls
were not allowed to share in the general high spirits. Everywhere they
went, Deirdre recalls, they 'stood in front of pictures for hours'. Only later
did Deirdre appreciate Sheila's knowledge of art. They were never
allowed to have fun; Sheila, as was her habit at home, went to bed before
dinner and Pat went out immediately after it, whether to meet his
wartime protectors or for merrier purposes, nobody knows. How things
had changed since the last time Pat and Sheila had been together in Italy.
Then they had been honeymooners, entranced by each other; now they
could not tolerate an evening together. Deirdre hated the way that Sheila
bullied Grania, criticizing her for not holding her handbag correctly, for
forgetting her gloves, or for wearing the wrong ones. Then, as later,
Deirdre couldn't feel relaxed in her godmother's company although, as
the years went by, she came to like and admire her. Grania enjoyed
standing in front of pictures more than Deirdre did, but because of
Sheila's carping, had just as miserable a time. Pat's gift for lowering the
level of tension was stretched to the limit during this tense holiday which
nobody enjoyed.

In October, Sheila, with Grania in tow, first visited Sissinghurst, the
house and famous garden of Harold Nicolson and Vita Sackville-West.
Sackville-West had once been, in Virginia Woolf's words, 'very splendid
and voluptuous and absurd' as well as, more meanly, 'florid, moustached,
parakeet-coloured'. It was a more muted Vita who welcomed Sheila to
Sissinghurst. She was then fifty-eight, suffering from arthritis and a
dilated heart, although she was still formidably busy, writing a weekly
gardening column for *The Observer*, broadcasting for radio and working
on a new novel, *The Easter Party*. Woolf had once said that Vita had 'a pen
of brass', and her novels and poems are certainly rather clunky, although
popular in their day. Her robust writing on gardening is another matter,

worth reading for its originality and soundness, even if your gardening is confined to a window box. On that first visit to Sissinghurst, Sheila thought that Vita's grey curls were 'shortish and haphazard enough to give her the look of a well-disposed Roman emperor'. She didn't seem to notice that Vita wasn't well, although James Pope-Hennessy, writing about Vita the same year, thought that she looked 'amazingly, frighteningly ill'. During the years of their friendship, it was always the older woman, in poor health and with financial worries, who comforted and consoled the younger one.

Vita was a tender-hearted friend to Sheila but perhaps wouldn't have been had Sheila been Miss Beddington rather than Viscountess Powerscourt. Vita and Harold were often described as unashamedly elitist. Their critics go further. To John Carey, Harold 'was a rabid snob and squirming snakepit of prejudice' and he gives examples of his 'poisonous and permanent anti-Semitism'. Harold favoured a national homeland for the Jews in Palestine since it meant that they could all be kept in one place and, long after the Holocaust, said of a Jewish acquaintance that he aroused his sympathy for Adolph Eichmann. Vita excelled him in snobbery; she was against educating the lower classes since it encouraged them to have notions above their station. Such prejudices were not uncommon among members of their class and not nearly as unusual as their sex lives. Vita was openly and, in her youth, sometimes scandalously lesbian while Harold was less flamboyantly homosexual, at a time when to be so was illegal. None of this features in Sheila's descriptions of Harold and Vita, published after both were dead. She knew that Vita was a lesbian, everybody knew that; Grania thought, on that first visit to Sissinghurst, that Sheila might have taken her along to act as chaperone. At some later stage, Vita asked Sheila to go on holiday with her to Greece. Sheila declined, worried, as usual, what people would think of her, especially as Vita's love affairs were always of interest in literary circles. But Sheila wrote in *Sun Too Fast*: 'It is only with Vita and her family that I have ever felt such deep tact and consideration ... or known such gentle manners.' There was also a connection between the Wingfields and the Sackvilles; an ancestor of Vita's, the last Duke of Dorset, had been killed in a fox-hunting accident in County Wicklow, in 1815, while visiting the then Lord Powerscourt.

What contrasting portraits of marriage were offered at Sissinghurst and Powerscourt. Vita and Harold loved each other in every way except sexually, their homosexuality being another of their many shared interests.

'I simply feel that you are me and I am you,' Vita once wrote to Harold and neither of them faltered from this opinion. Their love showed itself in mutual tolerance: Harold usually spent the week in London, where he thrived on parties and gossip, while Vita stayed at Sissinghurst, contentedly awaiting his arrival at the weekend. Pat and Sheila had never felt like that about each other, even in the early days of their marriage, when they had loved and fished and stayed on a small boat together. Now all they had in common was worry over the upkeep of Powerscourt. Sheila hardly ever joined Pat in his hunting, shooting world and he had never cared for literature. The Powerscourts, like so many Ascendancy families, had a bit of a history when it came to ensnaring heiresses and by now Sheila was beginning to feel like the latest victim.

She and Pat were both committed to Powerscourt but it wasn't theirs in the way that Sissinghurst belonged to Vita and Harold. They had bought Sissinghurst when it was a ruin of a castle in seven acres of mud and rubble, without water, electricity or one habitable room. Vita and Harold were hands-on owners, not only creating and maintaining the glorious garden but painting cupboards. Had she been a boy, Vita would have inherited Knole, a house even grander than Powerscourt. Knole could never be her property but it became her muse, the setting for her novel, *The Edwardians* (1930) and of her family history, *Knole and the Sackvilles* (1922). Perhaps she was lucky in having no responsibility for Knole; it inspired rather than shackled her. She might be dispossessed, but she was free. Sheila noted 'the confidence and freedom that lapped round one like warm air' at Sissinghurst. Such an atmosphere was inconceivable at Powerscourt, a house weighted down by its own history and the straitjacket of duty. There was something futile and changeless about it.

Some of that confidence and freedom of Vita's came from having compatible people around her; most of her friendships were with other writers, including the ubiquitous Dorothy Wellesley. To Sheila, Vita appeared to be heaped with honours and praise and at the centre of the literary world. In that same year, 1950, when Sheila first visited her at Sissinghurst, Vita received an Honorary D.Litt from Durham University and entertained the sort of people who rarely came Sheila's way, including Leonard Woolf and Ivy Compton-Burnett. Some of Sheila's admirers thought that her isolation was beneficial. The literary critic and editor, George Fraser, wrote, in a preface to her 1977 poetry collection, *Her Storms*, that 'I think it [living outside the literary world] helps to give her poetry its very special tone. No voice could be more individual, no personality more tantalizingly evasive.' Perhaps. But Wicklow was beginning to seem tiresomely parochial, all Girl Guides and opening fêtes and having to spend her time with people who were mainly interested in horses and cattle farming. These included her husband and children, who never expressed an opinion on a book. Who could blame them, since, if they had, Sheila would probably have reacted with scorn?

She made an effort to widen her circle but, in middle age, there was something intimidating about her and about Powerscourt itself. Its formality and grandeur deterred some writers from visiting. John Betjeman declined an invitation in 1951: '… owing to poverty we are having to sell this house in May, and if we get a good enough price for it, move into a smaller house in the neighbourhood'. He wrote this letter in March, two months before the move, so it doesn't seem much of an excuse for not making the journey to Ireland. The tone seems rather reproving, as though the well-heeled aristocrat had no right to be making claims on the less well-off man of letters. During the 1930s, Betjeman had spent most of his holidays with his friends the Longfords at Packenham Hall in Westmeath. There he found an intellectual atmosphere and a chance of meeting up with people in his own circle, such as Evelyn Waugh and Maurice Bowra, opportunities which would not arise at Powerscourt.

In 1977, Sheila sent a copy of *Real People* to the historian A.L. (Leslie) Rowse, who, along with Robert Nye, became the target of self-pitying and rambling letters from the ageing Lady Powerscourt. She told him, 'I've never even met John Betjeman who did the short foreword.' A similar invitation was issued to the novelist, Francis King, who has said that he didn't accept because, 'I know that had I done so, I should not have been able to relax for a single moment.' He admired Sheila because 'she challenged me to be at my intellectual best', but this kind of challenge is hard on a house guest. Except for John Hayward, Sheila doesn't mention her friendships with writers in her memoirs. It would have been difficult to mention them since she always insisted that she kept her promise to Pat to avoid mixing with 'literary scum' – 'He was so severe and stern about it I thought I'd better say yes – but you can imagine my grief.'

Throughout her life, she vigorously pursued men of letters. In her seventies, she wrote with embarrassing frequency to both Nye and Rowse, urging them to visit her in London or Switzerland, where she then lived for part of the year, at her expense. Like Betjeman and King, decades earlier, they didn't take her up on it. Her invitations managed to sound both needy and imperious, an alarming combination. Whatever George Fraser's romantic view of Sheila's 'outsiderness', there's no doubt that her isolation preyed on her. Two days before Christmas, 1951, Sheila signed a letter to Vita, 'Your broken-down Sheila'. Vita, always sympathetic, wrote back: 'With all my heart I send you a perfectly useless love.' Christmas is often stressful and Sheila also had to start arranging Grania's debutante season. She had a book as well as a daughter to bring out, with the usual toll on her health that was always her response to imminent publication. Heavy reliance on drugs did not make things easier.

Real People was published in the spring of 1952. Ten years earlier, another Anglo-Irish writer, Elizabeth Bowen, had written an almost equally shadowy memoir, *Seven Winters*, which R.F. Foster considers to be 'a masterpiece of non-information'. It is also, perhaps, misleading in the way that Bowen interprets events. But at least Bowen is at the centre of her autobiography, whereas Sheila, in hers, is merely an onlooker. *Real People*, as John Betjeman wrote in its preface, having presumably at some stage got hold of the proofs, is a 'selfless autobiography'. And, if Sheila is hardly there, Ethel is a hinted-at disappearance. Few readers could have known to what Sheila was referring when she wrote, 'It was at this time that a cloud of unhappiness which had overshadowed our lives lifted.' That cloud was the author's unmentioned and unmentionable mother, who was still alive and living far from unhappily, since she refused to countenance sadness, in a flat in Grosvenor Square.

Although she didn't acknowledge Ethel's existence, Sheila filched material about her Mulock ancestors from Ethel's previously published memoir, repeating almost word for word Ethel's story about the effect of her father's faultless Italian on hotel waiters. *Real People* was Sheila's furious, if belated, response to her mother's memoir, and removing Ethel completely from her story a satisfying revenge. The very title of Ethel's book, *All That I Have Met*, would have annoyed her as much as all the suspect anecdotes about Sheila's childhood. It's taken from Tennyson's poem, 'Ulysses': 'I am a part of all that I have met'. Ethel could identify with this, she'd latched on to so many people in her time. Another line of the poem about Ulysses' mariners, 'That ever with a frolic welcome took/The thunder and the sunshine ...' would certainly have appealed to her optimistic and adventurous nature. But the *Odyssey* was one of Sheila's favourite stories, later the subject of one of her earliest and most highly-praised poems, 'Odysseus Dying', and Ethel had appropriated it first.

Pansy Pakenham reviewed *Real People* in *Time and Tide*, whose literary editor was John Betjeman. Instead of 'selflessness', she discovered Sheila's 'charming ego'. *Kavanagh's Weekly* was similarly charmed: 'Miss Wingfield seems to have had a happy life. As a result she gives forth great charm but no intensity. She has not got an analytic mind. In this she shows her femininity.' Such pronouncements were possible in 1952. Only Harold Nicolson, himself a brilliantly inventive autobiographer, reviewing the book in *The Observer*, sensed the spikiness beneath the silky surface: 'A hint of silent cruelty as if one were to shoot ornamental birds from a distant window with an air gun. It is this almost indiscernible malice that makes *Real People* more fascinating than the usual silver-spoon reminiscences.'

Sheila's poetry was by now finding a larger audience in England than in Ireland. In June the *Times Literary Supplement* (*TLS*) published 'A Tuscan Farmer' and, a month later, the *New Statesman* accepted 'The Hunter'. These minor triumphs were overshadowed by Grania's coming-out ball in August, on the eve of the Dublin Horse Show. As the Hon. Mrs Mervyn Wingfield, Sheila had always been referred to as her aristocratic husband's 'poetess wife' in newspaper social columns. Once she became Viscountess Powerscourt, her literary achievements were seldom mentioned. In all the descriptions of Grania's coming out, in all the photographs of a gaunt but handsome Sheila hosting the ball for nearly 500 people in the Gresham Hotel, there is no disclosure that Lady Powerscourt is the writer Sheila Wingfield, whose well-received memoir had been published that same year. In these circles, women who had careers caused a certain social awkwardness. Reports of Sheila's dinner party describe only her 'pale gold and rose brocade gown with halter neckline and full skirt', while *The Queen* magazine's account of the ball puts the Ascendancy womenfolk in their rightful place: 'lovely wife' (the Countess of Donoughmore) or 'handsome wife' (Lady Goulding). This was the 1950s, the decade when women of every class were pushed into the role of homemaker and desirable helpmate, schooled in 'the arts of the civilized slave', as Robert Louis Stevenson described Victorian women. It would be another decade before women began a tentative rebellion and recognized their house arrest as 'part of the problem that had no name'. The guest list for Grania's ball is very similar to those of the house parties which Sheila had attended as a reluctant debutante: a sprinkling of titles, military types, double-barrelled ingénues. As Lady Powerscourt, it was easier to get on in their society than it had been as the oddly exotic Miss Beddington. It's unlikely that anyone in those circles had read a word of anything she had written, which was both a relief and an annoyance.

It was a busy August. Harry and Rosie d'Avigdor Goldsmid visited Powerscourt, full of praise for Sheila's achievements there. Afterwards, Sheila wrote to Harry, 'Thank you for heartening us just when we were beginning to feel that our decision to restore this place, and our attempt to keep it going as a living organization, was not only unwise but probably insane as well.' This is perhaps the first inkling we have that Sheila was beginning to think of Powerscourt as a ruinous place which only inspired dreams of leaving. In September, she gave a broadcast on the BBC Home Service. It was called 'A Parent' and was a loving and amusing tribute to Claude, covering much of the same ground described in *Real People* and painting a picture of a clever, delightful man who loved sport and practical jokes and was 'the best parent in the world'. At the end of the year, Claude received another tribute: in the Sunken Garden, beside Tower Bridge in London, an extension was added to the 1914–18 war memorial to make room for more names, Claude's among them. In spite of this significant act of closure, Sheila would never be through with Claude.

But by then she had found another father figure. She claimed to have first met Sir Chester Beatty, the wealthy New-York-born philanthropist, collector of antiquities and founder of the Chester Beatty Library in Dublin, while trying to get in touch with his granddaughter in order to invite her to Grania's coming-out ball. This was in 1952, the year before the library's completion, and if Sheila and 'CB', as he was universally known – and how poignant a set of initials for Sheila – did indeed meet in that year, during which his second wife, Edith Dunn, died, their friendship developed very quickly. By December, CB, aged seventy-seven, was writing admiring letters to Sheila from his winter home in Nice: 'You have remarkable judgment in picking out the paintings of quality,' which suggests that Sheila had frequently visited his collection. CB was everything that Sheila found appealing in a man: brilliant at business and with an adventurous past; fabulously rich owner of rare oriental treasures; someone who made no secret of his respect for Sheila's judgment and supplied her with presents and adulation. When Sheila wrote about CB in her second memoir, she turned him into a fearless world explorer when, in fact, as his biographical details in the British Library dryly reveal, he 'built an expert team of geologists and mining engineers whom he sent abroad with specific instructions on the areas to explore: he never travelled to these places himself'.

Sheila was finally beginning to branch out beyond the fêtes and horsey festivities. During the early 1950s, she became a member of several societies. She joined the British Association for the Advancement of Science, the Prehistoric Society and the London University Institute of Archaeology, involvements which took her away from the tensions of home, and from her writing. She excused this displacement activity as giving her the opportunity of running across some basic truth 'by dashing in various directions'. John Hayward would surely have seen it as a lack of discipline. Section H of the British Association dealt with three areas which fascinated Sheila: anthropology, archaeology and folklore. Following her membership of the association, she developed a friendship with the formidable Margaret A. Murray who, at the age of ninety, became president of the Folklore Society in 1953. Inspired by her, Sheila began to prepare an article for the society's quarterly magazine, *Folklore*. It never appeared; perhaps she didn't finish it. In April 1953, she attended a three-day meeting on archaeology in London and can't have spent much time in Ireland before returning to England to launch her daughter's London season. Grania was presented at Court, a dismal experience since, due to the recent death of Queen Mary, the event was very subdued. Grania hardly knew anyone in London and had a miserable time at the parties and dances she had to attend, only cheering up when invited to the country for the weekend.

That September, Vita and Harold stayed at Powerscourt for a few days. Its gardens were to feature in Peter Coats's *Great Gardens of the Western World*, for which Harold was writing the introduction. Due to recent storms, the gardens were not at their best; Sheila wrote, 'All I noticed in our lavish borders were a few bent bedraggled Michaelmas daisies of the commonest sort,' but the terraces and the view remained impressive and Vita and Harold were two writers who would never feel intimidated by the grandeur of the Big House. Vita, in particular, was disappointed in anything less than total magnificence. During that autumn, Sheila was in England again, this time in Liverpool for a British Association meeting. Over curried chicken, she and Margaret Murray discussed, among other topics, baby substitution during the reign of the Stuarts, Coptic musical notation and the Old Testament as a source-book on witchcraft. From there, Sheila went to Salisbury for a four-day outing of the Prehistoric Society. In the empty church of Sarum St Thomas, she was 'moved by the same emotion that so often pierces me in old churches and cathedrals. This is not an awareness of God's benevolence but, on the contrary, a choking realization of man's generosity of soul in forgiving God the tragedies of life'. There's another instance of her upside-down view of religion in one of the poems from *A Cloud Across the Sun*, 'Epiphany in a Country Church':

> What does it matter if our wise men stress
> The Barn as false, the Feast as wrong?
> I hold the Magi were the wiser, yes,
> To be believed in for so long.

Dame Leslie Whately, director of the World Association of Girl Guides and Girl Scouts, made an official visit to Dublin in November. She attended a meeting of the annual council where Sheila presented an outline of guiding in Ireland during the year. As always, at these events, Sheila was a dazzling distraction in her loops of gold braid. At Christmas, or so Sheila wrote, 'Bellair was full of children and friends,' a description disputed by Grania for whom Bellair, being more isolated than Powerscourt, was even more lonely. Sheila, who had clearly enjoyed being away from home for much of the year, decided to be more venturesome in future. In September, she had written to Francis King, who had a flat in Athens, that she was 'avid for Agamemnon's tomb'. Having learnt the lesson from the European trip that group travel was a trying experience, she intended to make the journey to Greece all by herself.

11. WAYS OF ESCAPE

'It turned out to be my last year of health, and imprisonment by illness
serves to identify the past.'
Sheila Powerscourt, *Sun Too Fast*

Sheila probably kept a diary for most of her life, using it as an appointment book and aide-memoire, but only a few of her diaries have survived. Appropriately called 'Viscount', these are identical and pocket-
sized, bound in red leather. They were found, ten years after her death, in
a secret compartment of the desk she left to her executor. Every year, she
had laboriously copied information from the inside cover of one diary into
that for the following year – her blood group, names and addresses of doctors and lawyers, her stocking size and passport number. Less than fully
informative and not at all confessional, the surviving diaries are often
encoded, as when the pale blue pages are covered with a series of asterisks
followed by the word 'chlorom' or 'chloro'. At a guess, these indicate doses
of chlorpromazine, an anti-psychotic drug and tranquilliser, or chlorme-
thiazole and chlormezanone, barbiturates which are used as sedatives and
muscle relaxants. At the front of her 1964 diary, among the usual instructions regarding doctors and lawyers, Sheila wrote, 'Never give chlorpromazine or convulsions may follow. Morphia O.K.' Sheila usually resorted
to capital letters when she thought something was significant. 'O.K.' is
also underlined three times.

Like another female poet, Edna St Vincent Millay, Sheila was a serious
junkie, although not quite in Millay's class. The American poet, for a time,

took nearly two-hundred milligrams of morphine daily and, even during periods of comparative sobriety, drank a litre and a half of wine each day. Judith Thurman, reviewing a biography of Millay in *The New Yorker*, wrote that 'her motor ran on adulation'. So did Sheila's and since, for adulation addicts, there is never enough of the stuff to satisfy, their cravings may take other forms. In 1954, the only year that she lived in Ireland for which a diary exists, Sheila's drug addiction hadn't yet become a problem. This was the year that she would wistfully remember as 'my last year of health', but, at the time, it must have seemed like her first year of comparative freedom: her children were almost off her hands, her two houses restored and Pat established in Hereford cattle-breeding circles.

But what a caricature of staid Big House life the diary records: 'Lunch party for 12. Château Yquem. Eggs mornay. Chicken and mushroom sauce. Choc. profiteroles.' '3 pm Open Fête at Rectory.' How exciting, by contrast, are the occasions she escapes from Powerscourt. She spends an evening at a taverna in Athens with Francis King and his friend Colonel Velandios, lunches with Dennis Cohen at L'Etoile restaurant in London and then goes on to visit John Hayward in the flat he shared with T.S. Eliot at Carlyle Mansions in Chelsea, a long way in every sense from that rectory fête. She had also finished a new poetry collection. Twenty years later, she recalled: 'After months of choosing, revising, and for the fiftieth time re-correcting past and recent work, I had at last finished a book of selected and new verse. This was important to me and had taxed my deepest resources.' As always, she gives the impression that, although she had wanted to be a poet from the age of six, writing poetry was the most arduous sacrifice on her part.

This new collection was called *A Kite's Dinner* and contained only eight new poems. Its title comes from a passage in Quarles's *Emblèmes*: 'The heart is a small thing, but desireth great matters. It is not sufficient for a kite's dinner, yet the whole world is not sufficient for it.' Sheila credited Father A. Gwynn SJ for tracking the passage's provenance to an anonymous twelfth-century source, but in a *TLS* article of 6 May 1955, Joseph Hone claimed that he had done this detective work, at Sheila's request. Sheila delivered the typescript to Dennis Cohen on 1 March and then went on to Carlyle Mansions. By this time, she and John Hayward were close friends and he had stayed at Powerscourt. John encouraged and promoted her work, not always with the greatest propriety, as we shall see, until the inevitable falling-out. By the time she came to write affectionately about him after his death in *Sun Too Fast*, she knew only too well that 'It was hard to guess in advance who was in, who was out, among his friends, including oneself.' Anthony Powell, like Sheila, found John Hayward fascinating, not least because Hayward had no difficulty in attracting pretty women despite his 'somewhat terrifying manner and appearance'. Powell's biographer, Michael Barber, thinks that Hayward may have inspired the character of the crippled photographer, Saul Henchman, in Powell's last novel, *The Fisher King*.

As soon as she'd delivered the new poems to her publisher, Sheila flew to Athens. Like Virginia Woolf, as a young girl she had taught herself Greek, and the heroes and villains who lived in ancient Greece crop up in her poems as anecdotally as Irish market days and gossipy fishwives. Sheila could have visited Greece in 1936, during the cruise on *Cachelot* but, for some reason, she and Pat left Claude's yacht at Suez, three weeks before it put into Piraeus. Perhaps she didn't want to see the beloved landscape for the very first time with her ebullient father, who, in *We Sailed from Brixham*, mentions the Greek stop-over only in terms of parties and food and drink, adding, 'Classical Athens has been so overwritten for the last hundred years that it deserves to be allowed to rest in peace.' So, at the age of forty-eight, Sheila went to Greece on her own; a homecoming in its way, for Greece was the landscape where she lived in her dreams.

The blissful account of her holiday given in *Sun Too Fast* is full of omissions. Francis King, whom, we learn from her diary, she saw several times in Athens, is not mentioned in her memoir, nor is the poet Richard Murphy whom she met at a lunch in King's flat. King remembers their meetings well, as he does another occasion when, lunching with some friends at Costis, a fashionable Athens restaurant, he saw Sheila come in with a group of rich, married women whom he knew, and whom he suspected of being lesbians. 'I assumed that she [Sheila] shared their sexual interest but I could have been wrong. She might merely have been going around with them because they were rich, smart and good company.' Irony of ironies: Vita had suggested going to Greece with Sheila, who had declined because of her friend's reputation and now here she was, inspiring speculation among Athens' people-watchers. During another lunch that King gave for Sheila, he noticed that 'She totally ignored a scruffy but highly intelligent young Englishman, but was all over another friend of mine called David Jeffreys, who was elegant and at ease, knew all the right people and was tutor to the then Crown Prince.' When King referred to Richard Murphy's father, W. Lindsay Murphy, as 'distinguished', Sheila said, 'Can anyone called Murphy be distinguished? Ninety per cent of New York cops are called that.' In fact, W. Lindsay Murphy was an upper-middle-class Anglo-Irishman who had had a successful administrative career, including a stint as Governor of the Bahamas. His wife, the former Betty Ormsby of Galway, had a family tree which would have impressed even Sheila, since it included a French marquis, the poet Geoffrey Chaucer and William the Conqueror. Their son, Richard, twenty-seven when Sheila met him in Greece, was the director of the English School in Canea. The post was a British Council appointment and his application had been supported by Harold Nicolson. She was undeniably a snob but a very badly informed one.

The wealthy women with whom Sheila lunched at Costis lived in Kolonaki, the ritziest, most exclusive part of Athens or, as Sheila put it 'where the old families lived in their old houses'. They included Dora Lykiardopoulou, her friend Irini, whose father had donated the Benaki Museum, housed in a beautiful mansion outside Athens, to the state, and the charming and forceful Dora Stratou, who ran a touring Greek folk troupe and was an authority on ancient Greek music. This group of cultured women took Sheila to parties and on excursions and found the time for long conversations on the horror of the war years in their country and the problem of Cyprus. In spite of the Kolonaki connections and visits to the British Embassy at the invitation of the British Ambassador, Sheila described herself on this holiday as a poor but happy traveller, getting about the country by bus and staying in the smallest rooms of modest hotels. Well, not quite. The hotel in Athens where she decided to 'live frugally and eat the view', was the King George, which boasted of being able to satisfy the demands of 'even the most discerning traveller'. But simple joys were definitely part of it. At Mycenae, she climbed over rocks slippery from recent rain and clambered 'through waist-high and impeding wet green barley'.

In contrast to her account in *Sun Too Fast*, her diary tells a different story, recording that this fit and energetic tourist took heavy doses of 'chlorom', for six days of her holiday. Even if drugged, however, she had a wonderful time; more than a month after her return to Powerscourt, she wrote to Francis King, 'Part of me is irrevocably and irrecoverably still in Greece. And I simply can't put the whole of my mind to the matters I ought to be attending to.' Only part of her mind was on her children's

Bellair House, Ballycumber, Co. Offaly
(*courtesy of the Irish Architectural Archive*).

'Remember, your mother is the most beautiful woman in London.'
Drawing of Ethel Beddington by John Singer Sargent, 1914
(*courtesy of the Courtauld Institute of Art, London*).

'I was a plain child and horribly dressed.'
This photograph of Sheila in 1913 contradicts her view.

Ethel with her children Guy, Sheila and Niall,
photographed for the Beddington Christmas
card in 1913.

Guy Beddington shortly before
his death in 1925.

Irish Grandma.

Sheila and Pat photographed on their engagement, 1932.

Wedding in Jerusalem, December 1932. Claude and Niall are witnesses.

Powerscourt House, Enniskerry, Co. Wicklow
(*courtesy of the Thomas Gunn Collection,
Irish Architectural Archive*).

Pat and Sheila at home in Kent *c.* 1933
(*courtesy of the National Portrait Gallery,
London*).

Mervyn's christening at Powerscourt, September 1935.
With First Greystones Troop of Rover Scouts (Lord Powerscourt's Own).

Sheila and Pat with Grania and Mervyn at Powerscourt, before World War II.

Bermuda, during World War II:
Sheila with Mervyn and Grania.

A marital reunion: Pat and Sheila
in Bermuda, after World War II.

Sheila, impeccably turned-out
horsewoman.

The new Viscount and Viscountess Powerscourt in 1947.

Two photographs of Sheila
in middle age, second with
unsuccessful 'postiche'.

futures. In April, Mervyn had joined the 1st Battalion of the Irish Guards, as a 2nd lieutenant, stationed in Surrey. This delighted Sheila; she gave her son double the usual officers' allowance, compensating him for the indignity suffered by Pat a quarter of a century earlier, when he had had to leave the regiment because his father couldn't afford to keep him in it. That same spring, Sheila gave a house party at Powerscourt to coincide with the Dublin Spring Show. Among the guests was Hercules (Heck) Langrishe, whose grandfather had been a friend of Pat's father, Mervyn Powerscourt. By the time his grandson met Mervyn's granddaughter, Grania Wingfield, the two families had lost touch. Twenty-seven-year-old Heck was a suitable boy in every way. Heir to a baronetcy created in 1777, he was an Old Etonian who had served in the 9th Lancers and was now studying farming at the Royal Agricultural College, Cirencester. Heck was invited back to Powerscourt for the house party which took place during Horse Show week. By the end of the season he was engaged to Grania, and was described by Sheila in a letter to Francis King as 'quite the nicest young man we've ever known'.

In June, Sheila gave an address to the Parents' Association of the Zion Schools at Bloomfield Avenue in Dublin. The schools had been established in 1931 with financial support from the then Cumann na nGaedheal government, to provide an education for Jewish children. (The last Zion school closed in 1980.) No record of Sheila's speech has survived and it may be assumed that she gave it in her role of chief commissioner of the Irish Girl Guides, rather than because she was half-Jewish, since she never disclosed this. Dublin's Jewish community was often staunchly nationalist. To give just one example, the artist Estella Solomons had been a member of Cumann na mBan and had played an active part in the 1916 Easter Rising. Like Estella, Sheila had married 'out' but unlike her, in doing so had become a member of the Protestant Ascendancy, 'English but in no way English, Irish but in no way Irish', as Spencer Curtis Brown put it, and certainly in no way Jewish.

Meanwhile, Sheila's friendship with CB deepened. She was helping him to grade his collection of Chinese makimonos, hand scrolls which are read from right to left. Though she modestly insisted that she had had no training, 'trying to disillusion him was a hopeless job … CB relied on my independence of mind, although this was merely the courage that comes from ignorance'. The great collector was placing the untrained amateur in exalted company. He wrote to her from Nice regarding a collection of 'sixty of the latest makimonos' held in his Dublin house and in need of revaluation: 'I think the committee of experts – you, Wilkinson, Merton and myself – can probably size up the thing as well, if not better, than they do in museums.' J.V.S. Wilkinson was the librarian of CB's oriental collection and Wilfred Merton his honorary librarian for the western manuscripts and books.

Throughout June, Powerscourt became an outpost of Hollywood as the costume drama, *Captain Lightfoot*, starring Rock Hudson, was filmed in the house and grounds. In *Sun Too Fast*, Sheila cast a bright, withering gaze on the proceedings: 'The picture turned out, I believe, an undistinguished production.' Days after the film crew had packed up the papier-mâché candelabras, 'the kind of vases you hope not to win at fairs', the snaking cables and the wardrobe trailers, the Horse Show house party, including Heck Langrishe, arrived. Immediately after the Horse Show, Sheila attended the World Conference of Girl Guides in the Netherlands. The conference provided a slashingly funny chapter in Sheila's memoir but its immediate effect was fatigue. The diary records a lot of 'chlorom' taken. Dora Lykiardopoulou, her friend from Athens, visited Powerscourt in the first week of September and Sheila took her to the Chester Beatty Library and to Bellair. Dora also received a lecture on the Irish caste system; Sheila told her that whereas the Irish country people appreciated the true gentry, they despise the parvenu as being ' "only a half-sir", and in this social limbo the unfortunate man and all his descendants will remain, however much land or money they acquire'. Sheila herself, from good parvenu stock, rather gave the lie to this theory.

The news that *A Kite's Dinner*, still in proof form, had been made the quarterly Poetry Book Society (PBS) choice came, via the telephone at Enniskerry post office, Powerscourt's line having been savaged by storms. Sheila noted that 'thirty years of practising my chosen craft had resulted in this nice little tap on the shoulder. (It also meant guaranteed sales).' The PBS selectors for 1954 were John Hayward, Edwin Muir and Janet Adam Smith. In a scrapbook of her press-cuttings, next to the *Irish Times* announcement of the PBS selectors, Sheila wrote, 'As I was a candidate personally known to him, John Hayward correctly withdrew from this judges' panel and T.S. Eliot took his place.' And there was more invention to come. In *Sun Too Fast*, Sheila asks her publisher's secretary, over the faint, ghostly telephone line, 'Who were the judges?' Even more faintly, the voice replied, 'T.S. Eliot, Janet Adam Smith and Edwin Muir.' The aforementioned *Irish Times* announcement had appeared the previous March, so Sheila knew perfectly well who the judges were and was perhaps embarrassed that among them was her poetry editor who, unabashedly, selected a book in which he had been closely involved. Eyebrows might have been raised had it been known that the same judge returned from visits to Powerscourt laden with Wingfield trinkets. It's probable, however, that all three selectors were acquainted with some of the poets who submitted their work.

The *PBS Bulletin* gave Sheila space to write about her working methods. Familiar themes emerge in her short article: her life as a secretly reading girl; her love for her father; the sacrifice of her time – 'Now, as the years go by, increasing private and public duties allow even fewer free hours in which to concentrate on my craft' – and her painstakingly slow progress; eight years to write *Beat Drum, Beat Heart*. But a new topic is introduced, one which will gain importance as the years go by, that of illness as an escape from life: '... on several occasions I was grateful to weeks in a sickbed because of the fine opportunity for writing they offered'. The potted biography which followed the article mentioned that she and her husband, 'who succeeded his father as Viscount Powerscourt in 1947', ran two farms and bred Hereford cattle. Even when she's writing about her creative struggle, she can't resist pulling rank. The *Bulletin's* readership, participants in literary quizzes held at the National Book League, readers of their own poetry – 'limit 3 minutes' – at the Poetry Society's Audience Nights, must have been bemused by one of their number who presented herself, albeit unintentionally, as a lady dabbler.

October saw the autumn exodus from chilly Powerscourt while Pat went to Hereford to meet up with other breeders. Sheila's diary records, 'Staff go down to Bellair and lorry, silver etc.' *A Kite's Dinner* was published in December, 'The Choice of the Poetry Book Society', printed on its cover. As usual with Sheila's poetry collections, there was no author photograph and no biography on the back-flap but, unusually, the early praise from W.B. Yeats was not given an airing. Instead, on the inside front cover, Herbert Read wrote a short appreciation of *Beat Drum, Beat Heart* and the new, shorter poems. Of these, two of the eight, 'A Tuscan Farmer' and 'Venice Preserved', celebrate Italy and may have been written during the bad-tempered holiday of 1950. The latter poem begins, 'Under the tingling bongle-booming/Of St Mark's', but doesn't sustain this gorgeous rhythm; Sheila was always better at simpler imagery.

On 3 December 1954, the diary entry is 'Merrion Nursing Home (operation).' Was this the 'botched Dublin op. ... done thirty-five years ago for a trouble which is excessively rare and quite incurable', as described to Robert Nye in 1983, and which left her 'in constant misery of incurable pain'? She stayed in the nursing home for only a week, which suggests that she didn't undergo major surgery. However, her health declined sharply during this period, although the disease was never diagnosed, just as that earlier medical crisis in 1938 had baffled every doctor called in to cure it. After that stay in the nursing home, Sheila became a chronic invalid, to the point of hiring an ambulance whenever she wanted to shop at Switzers department store in Dublin, seventy miles away from Bellair. So a year that began with her leaping girlishly over rocks in the Greek countryside, ended with her indulging in some very eccentric cosseting. Using an ambulance as a taxi smacks of hypochondria – a real invalid wouldn't be able to go shopping in any kind of vehicle. More than being a genuine hypochondriac, she was a self-destructive woman who, somehow, and for complex reasons, made herself ill. Her mystifying pain, like the drugs she took, was another means of escape from a life she should never have chosen.

12. THE UNRELENTING DAY

'... To be at rest
Is but a dog that sighs and settles: better
The unrelenting day.'
From 'Poisoned in Search of the Medicine of Immortality',
by Sheila Wingfield

She was falling apart, or so she said. She wrote to Francis King, in February 1955, that the reason she hadn't thanked him for his Christmas card was that she had been 'on and off operating tables', since the previous December. She hadn't been anywhere near an operating table, but felt ill enough that spring to stop chairing meetings of the Executive Committee of the Irish Girl Guides. She seemed to insist on being defined by her ill-health. Over twenty years later, in his preface to her 1977 poetry collection, *Her Storms*, George Fraser had her 'swaying on a sick woman's litter', somehow not noticing that, during that year, the sick woman had made her usual trips to London and Bermuda from her home in Switzerland. By then, Sheila had convinced a lot of people that she was suffering from something serious, if not fatal, although she was too ladylike to give it a name. And so it went on; a doctor who looked after her in her extreme old age told Grania that although Sheila was obviously ill, he couldn't find anything wrong with her.

The publication of *A Kite's Dinner* at the end of 1954 provided further excuse for victimhood. When the reviews began to appear in the New Year, some were hostile, or woundingly brief, or implied that the poet was a has-been, or, worse, a nobody. In *The London Magazine* (April 1955), Elizabeth Jennings wrote: 'My general impression of Miss Wingfield's work is that she too rarely comes to grips with her subject-matter. It is not that her feelings are lukewarm or that her versification is uneasy. I think it is her language which is at fault. Her words often lack precision and inevitability and for this reason fail to linger in the mind.' This must have stung: Sheila had a reputation for being a precisian. However, Elizabeth Bowen, in a one-paragraph review in *Tatler*, quoted from 'Chosroe the Second', an earlier poem: 'It was a princely morning of bright winds', and observed that, 'lines such as these stay afloat in the memory'. By contrast, *The Observer's* Patrick Dickinson expressed surprise that *A Kite's Dinner* had been made a Poetry Book Society Choice at all, since it contained only eight new poems. He slighted the reappearance of *Beat Drum, Beat Heart*:

> Had this meditation on war been published in 1919, I think the critics of the twenties and thirties would have dismissed it as 'typically Georgian' for it has most of the faults assigned, often wrongly, to poets of that period; though in the meanwhile it has been possible, by attention to modern masters, to add one or two more.

After such a mauling, praise from Geoffrey Taylor in *Time and Tide*, where he had succeeded the recently sacked John Betjeman as poetry editor, wasn't particularly soothing, since he began his glowing review with: 'The poetry of Sheila Wingfield has made curiously little impact.' *The Sunday Times* listed the new collection under 'Chosen Verse' but described the poet as 'a relatively unknown writer'. *The Times*, in an insultingly late review, not published until the autumn, included the collection with five other books, among them Laurie Lee's *My Many-Coated Man*. The review appeared under the discouraging headline 'Six Modern Poets in Search of a Public'. It began, 'Who, one wonders, apart from modern poets, reads modern poetry?' and concluded that the answer was almost nobody. 'It says a great deal for the pertinacity of poets that they can still persuade publishers to print verse at all.'

Here was a new literary theme: the unreadability of contemporary poetry, and it was taken up by Kenneth Young in *The Daily Telegraph* in an article called 'Sense Returns to Poetry'. Young wrote: 'During the past thirty years the intelligent reader has ceased to read new poetry. If asked why, he would probably reply that poetry has become difficult, obscure and unrewarding.' Exceptions were John Betjeman, Laurie Lee, Frances

Cornford and Sheila Wingfield, all of whom Young praised for lifting the 'dead hand' from English poetry. By now, Sheila must have realized that newspapers, and even literary magazines, can be unreliable. Donald Davie's review of *A Kite's Dinner* in *The Dublin Magazine* was wildly inaccurate. In the margin of his review, which she pasted into her press cuttings book, where he had written, 'I am glad to report that she shows no signs of having read Dylan Thomas or Sidney Keyes,' Sheila scrawled 'I consider Sidney Keyes by far the greatest poet of my lifetime.' Davie went on to say, 'Of the metres she most favours the least dependable is the octosyllable.' Against this, Sheila wrote, 'WRONG. I never use octosyllabic line – but am partial (for some reason) to a line of 4 beats.' The reviewer concluded that Sheila had a 'mild and honest talent' and was 'unpretentious', which was 'meant to be quite high praise'. But would not be taken as such.

Unpretentious, failing to make an impact, or this unkind verdict from the *TLS*: 'At her weakest, she is, to be blunt, feminine-rural,' although the review did say that 'the best of these poems have a distinction which is likely to last'. All these notices hardly mattered, however, compared with the unsigned review which appeared in *The Listener* on 10 February 1955, and the reaction to it, which, over the next four issues of the magazine, turned its letters page into a battlefield. After a general criticism that 'Miss Wingfield's problem is obviously the clear definition of emotion in objective terms, and we cannot feel that she has so far solved it satisfactorily,' he (or perhaps she) disparaged the two-line poem, 'Funerals', which had first been published in *A Cloud Across the Sun*. Here is the poem in its entirety: 'Be done with show. Let the dead go to their lair/Unseen, a step barely heard on the stair.' The following week's issue brought a letter from Hilary Corke of Edinburgh University 'This little poem seems to me to use two pieces of traditional imagery in an original but not an extravagantly original way.' He then derided *The Listener's* reviewer as 'amateurish'. Under the heading, 'Our reviewer writes ...', the critic responded to this insult by discussing the meanings of 'lair' and 'stair' and by going on to say, 'Mr Corke's argument from tradition does not persuade me that it is natural to use a word connoting a deliberate human construction with one connoting an animal's dwelling.'

This was clearly going to run and run. The next letter, in a heavy-handed form of poetic satire, was from Hal Summers of Tunbridge Wells:

How darest thou, Sheila, unprovoked,
Commit a metaphor?
That sin the reviewer found thee in:
It is what he is for.
Henceforth let the image hide its head,
Let fancy's engine stall.
Lie down, lie down, the reviewers frown;
Let literalness be all.

The next week, Hilary Corke wrote again:

> Without wishing to turn 'Funerals' into a battleground, may I venture a short Rejoinder to the Refutation of my Animadversious? Words do not have either/or meanings in imaginative poetry, they have and–and–and meanings: that is how poetry works.

Another correspondent came to the poem's defence. From Cambridge, H.J.C. Grierson wrote:

> For me, as for Mr Hilary Corke, the emotional effect of Miss Sheila Wing-field's poem is conveyed by the words: 'Let the dead go to their lair'. It is the emotion conveyed by Socrates, in the *Phaedo* of Plato, and by our Lord in the Gospels. Socrates' body is not Socrates. Let the dead bury their dead. Do not fuss about funerals.

Sheila herself brought the debate to an end. In the issue of 17 March, wounded but defiant, she wrote:

> It would be unseemly for me to argue about the possible merits of my work as poetry; but I feel I can, with propriety, join the discussion started by your review of 'A Kite's Dinner', as the statements made seem to revolve round the important and central point of obscurity. In this I can at least declare my aims.
>
> These are threefold: first, to communicate the poetic experience; secondly, to avoid obscurity, as this hampers such communication; thirdly, to set down facts and feelings as austerely as possible, hoping the manner of doing it will create overtones, evoke sensory images, and arouse emotions in the reader.
>
> From the volume of collected verse (the result of thirty years' work), your reviewer quotes 'Funerals'. [She then quotes the two-line poem.] On the strength of these simple lines, he charges me with incomprehensibility, as well as theological and zoological inaccuracy. However, as Mr Hilary Corke, Mr Hal Summers and Sir Herbert Grierson find no difficulty in understanding me, and apparently approve this use of metaphor, I shall hope to find other readers who share their views.

And that was that, but the ferocious attack left Sheila bruised. Vita calmed her down, saying 'Well you've been compared with Socrates and Christ. What more d'you want?' Had Sheila been able to answer honestly, she might have said, 'Total and complete adulation.' The *Listener* episode taught her that there was no such thing as literary loyalty. The magazine's literary editor, J.R. Ackerley, was a friend of Francis King, who liked Sheila's poetry well enough to occasionally commission it, yet had offered *A Kite's Dinner* to a reviewer who tore it to shreds. There were rumours that this harsh critic was the same Patrick Dickinson, who was to give the book another bad review in *The Observer* the following month, this time under his own byline. It could be that Sheila's short biography, published in the *PBS Bulletin* – her title, her privileged lifestyle, her pedigree cattle – had made critical hackles rise. The objections to 'Funerals' are ridiculous. To read those two expressive lines is to sense, without difficulty, the hopeless finality of death.

The poetry establishment suspected the presence of George Fraser behind the *Listener* letters defending 'Funerals'. Fraser was about to bring out a poetry anthology, to be discussed in Chapter 13, which included work by Sheila and her new-found champion, Hilary Corke. Her other gallant, Herbert Grierson, was, like Fraser, a Scottish academic who had held professorships in Scottish universities before settling in Cambridge. This was the typical wheels within wheels situation which Sheila despised, men of letters at play, showing off and acting like schoolboys at her expense. Their defence of her short poem couldn't still her anger at not being taken seriously and of being accused of mistiness. Conversely, being the object of so much waggish attention gave her a new visibility. That spring, *The Listener* published 'Elegy for Certain Friends', after John Lehmann rejected it for *The London Magazine*, while *Time and Tide* published 'An Answer from Delphi'. 'Lines for the Margin of an Old Gospel' and 'Alter Ego' were chosen for *The Chatto Book of Modern Poetry 1914–1954*, edited by Cecil Day-Lewis, another Anglo-Irish poet, and John Lehmann, for which Sheila was paid £2 16s. 8d. Well might Vita have asked, 'What more d'you want?'

Whether she wanted it or not, she had to cope during this period with the major distraction that was Grania's wedding. This was to take place at St Patrick's Cathedral on 21 April and would be quite unlike Sheila's own subdued marriage service in Jerusalem, or her parents' untrumpeted signing at Marylebone Register Office. Grania, in keeping with Powerscourt tradition, was to be married by the Archbishop of Dublin, the ceremony followed by a reception at the house, where two Garda detectives would stand guard over the wedding presents on display in the first floor Saloon. The arrangements began with the father-of-the-bride getting a tongue-in-cheek reprimand from the Turf Club, which called on Mervyn to explain why he had arranged the date of his daughter's wedding for the same date as an important Curragh race meeting.

Then the bride herself caused a problem by choosing a Catholic friend as one of her bridesmaids. At Sheila's insistence – any departure from protocol enraged her – the friend was 'unchosen', but it was years before she found out why. And she never realized that she was the victim of the mother of the bride's insecurity. By the mid-nineteen fifties, there remained little anti-Catholic prejudice among members of the Ascendancy who, as their position in Ireland became more marginal, could allow themselves a more relaxed tolerance. But Sheila, a latecomer at the Ascendancy picnic, clung to an out-of-date model of correctness, which was offensively incorrect. Although she loved her future son-in-law, the thought of organizing this grand-scale wedding was terrifying, an occasion where events could conspire to show her up. She had never really belonged to this world of easy privilege, where everyone was so annoyingly unbothered about what anyone else thought of them. Sheila hated their sterile reverence for the past and never stopped feeling that she was held in contempt by people viewed by her as intellectual inferiors. She felt towards her Anglo-Irish neighbours the way she had felt towards the callow dancing partners of her youth. The antipathy was mutual. Discussing Sheila today, elderly men and women who attended the same race meetings and cocktail parties mention Sheila's name coldly. No, they hadn't known her at all well. They had heard that she wrote poetry but, no, they had never read any of it.

Sheila found help managing this grandest of Ascendancy weddings in the shape of Joy Telford, who, at the age of thirty, was one of the more mature students at Betty Lombard's Secretarial College, Dublin. When she met Sheila and Grania for the first time, in the Bailey pub off Grafton Street, Joy was so nervous that she walked into the men's lavatory by mistake. But they got on; Joy recognized that the Powerscourts were a family in need of her organizational gifts. She moved in with them for the following five months, first at Bellair and then at Powerscourt, learning to adapt herself to a house whose staff included a butler, footman, boot boy and chauffeur, and where everyone took two baths a day. She didn't qualify for her own lady's maid, so, although Powerscourt had a lavish laundry block, she went home to Dublin at weekends to do her washing. She prepared the guest list, finding her way through the complicated titles and, before choosing a florist for the Cathedral flowers, put on her shabbiest clothes so as to get a better price.

In letters to Geoffrey Taylor, Sheila claimed that, during the weeks before the wedding, she had been back on the operating table. This wasn't true but she had stayed in her room for most of the time and, in the appreciative reference that she later wrote for Joy Telford, said, 'It was imperative that someone very capable should be there to make all the arrangements ... as I myself was too ill to give more than minimum help.' From her bedroom, other members of the household were summoned to receive orders, or expressions of disapproval. Hardly ever making an appearance downstairs, Sheila always seemed to know what was going on. Somehow, she found out that Pat had asked Joy out to dinner, and immediately suggested to the young wedding organizer that she take a few days off and go home. Impressed, Joy thought, 'You clever woman.'

In spite of the bustle of the wedding preparations, Powerscourt remained its usual sombre self. There were no visitors, nobody went out in the evenings, and the gates were locked at half past ten. Joy noted the lack of warmth between Pat and Sheila but wasn't aware of any obvious friction; by now, they were used to mutual disappointment. Sheila's medication – Joy had no idea what it was – made her bad-tempered but Joy ignored her outbursts, just as she ignored complaints about her health. It wasn't just the locked gates that made the house seem like a luxurious prison; its deadly decorum was stifling. On one afternoon, Sheila confided wistfully to Joy, that she would love to have scrambled eggs on toast in bed. But when Joy offered to go to the kitchen and cook them, Sheila forbade it, saying that the staff would walk out. Meals, even when you were eating them by yourself, reading a book, as Joy sometimes did, had to be taken in the dining-room, a silent footman standing, unnervingly, behind your chair. Reacting against the countless gloomy restrictions, Joy took Grania on outings to Dublin. For once, Sheila's radar system didn't pick up information on these expeditions.

Sheila was a generous employer. She urged Joy to buy a handbag at her (Sheila's) expense and insisted that she wasn't to spend less than £30, at a time when the average wage was £10 a week. She introduced Joy to language and literature, earning her everlasting gratitude, and supplied her with a reference that boosted the young woman's prospects once she'd left Powerscourt: 'Her intelligence makes her quick to learn her employer's way of liking things done; and her charming manners, friendliness and tact make her liked all round.' In spite of Sheila's malingering and savage temper, Joy considered it a privilege to work for her. Sheila spent lavishly on her daughter's wedding, but, as was her habit, couldn't resist the odd bit of penny-pinching. So having ordered Grania's hand-quilted, white slipper satin crinoline wedding dress from Dublin's most famous couturier, Sybil Connolly, she scrimped on the bridesmaids' dresses, which were champagne-coloured net and came from Arnotts department store in Dublin. Sheila's goddaughter, Deirdre, was one of the cheaply-outfitted bridesmaids, as was Dar Wright's daughter Susan, whose own daughter, Sarah Ferguson, would one day marry the Duke of York. On the night before the wedding, Sheila sent Grania to her room before supper, while her bridesmaids were allowed to stay up. Sheila never stopped trying to dominate her daughter, even telling her how to plan her family, her advice being to have two children in quick succession and then a gap before the third, as she herself had done. When Grania produced three children, one after the other, Sheila asked her what had gone wrong; it didn't occur to her that Grania had her own ideas on family life.

On the wedding day, the bride's mother did not look her best. Her close-fitting little hat looked as though it had a painful grip on her skull and, for some reason, she kept on her mink jacket, which looked lumpy in the photographs. Her face, once beautiful in its calm immobility, now looked ravaged, as if she were forever beyond tranquillity. What Grania remembered most about her wedding day was the advanced age of most of the guests, almost all of them unknown to her. Later that year, Sheila checked herself into the Liverpool Royal Infirmary and stayed there for six months. John Hayward, Harold Nicolson and *New Statesman* literary editor, Janet Adam Smith, all wrote to her there, not knowing what was wrong, only that something clearly was. She hadn't told them, or her family, that the reason for going to the Liverpool hospital was to try to cure her drug addiction. It was not something one talked about then, or maybe even now.

13. WRITING ON THE WALL

'The day dangles an empty bridle.'
From *Beat Drum, Beat Heart*, by Sheila Wingfield

Sheila never talked about her long stay in the Liverpool Royal Infirmary and neither did anyone else. Regardless of the treatment, if it involved long periods when she could stay in bed and read, absolved of all responsibility, she would have accepted it contentedly. Whatever happened at the infirmary didn't cure her addiction; her diaries go on listing the necessary 'chlorom' well into her old age. When she returned to Powerscourt, she settled more firmly into the role of career-invalid, petulant and contrary and no help at all to Pat as he battled to keep the estate viable. It had been the Wingfields' home since 1603 and a financial drain almost from the start. Several previous Lord Powerscourts, on acquiring the title, had been faced with catastrophe caused by a predecessor's financial flightiness, but Pat was unluckier than most. His parents' almost simultaneous deaths, in 1947, had left him with double death duties.

In England, even the post-Second World War Labour government had allowed aristocratic families to stay in their houses with the assistance of government grants, a sympathetic gesture inspired by the shock of seeing so many English stately homes demolished after the war, or almost ruined by the effects of requisitioning. The Irish government made no such offer. Only three decades after Independence, it had a reasonable ambivalence towards the Big House, that beautiful but threatening symbol of the landlord class. It was difficult for even the most tolerant of

Irishmen to look at those lovely windows and smooth stonework without thinking about the starving tenants whom previous owners of such splendid architecture might have evicted from their hovels and tiny fields, or forced to emigrate. Within living memory, architectural masterpieces had been burnt down in the name of Irish patriotism; by the 1950s, those which remained, such as Powerscourt, were a source of both pride and embarrassment. If Pat had read Elizabeth Bowen's 1939 review of Joseph Hone's book, *The Moores of Moore Hall* (which he certainly wouldn't have done since it appeared in the *New Statesman*), he would have recognized her anguished list of problems: 'The debts, the debts, the roof, the tenants, the drains, the trees.'

Did Pat sense that his wife's fortune was invested in Powerscourt more and more reluctantly? Or did he begin to hate having to rely on Sheila's money, unpleasantly beholden to someone he no longer loved? During twenty-five years of married life, Pat had become familiar with Sheila's capriciousness and cold, dominant will. Not to mention her sudden fits of parsimoniousness – those nasty cheap bridesmaids' dresses were a classic example. He had to try and save Powerscourt by his own efforts. On 10 June 1956, the *Sunday Independent* reported that a cafe with a souvenir and country-produce shop had opened at Powerscourt. Admission charges to the estate had been drastically reduced (four shillings for adults, two shillings for children) to attract more visitors, and the new venture was encouraged by Bord Fáilte, which would like to see other Big Houses do the same. The newspaper quoted a Bord Fáilte spokesman who said that the organization would lend its moral support and place 'its full publicity facilities at the disposal of an estate owner who is thinking along these lines'. It envisaged delegates to international conferences, increasingly held in Ireland, being taken by coach to see 'magnificent mansions, in many cases architectural masterpieces, in their settings of woodland, mountain and rolling parkland'. Lord Powerscourt's enterprise 'would mean that the local craftsman would have a market on his doorstep', in the shape of customers at Pat's souvenir shop. Moral support was as far as the state was going to go; it was not going to give financial help to the landed gentry.

And now Ethel comes back into the story. She approached Harold Nicolson and pressed him to visit her 'gallery', that collection of signed pictures and photographs of the 'great and the good'. Harold wrote to Sheila, 'I replied politely but got out of the visit. I expect it is a pretty wonky gallery and she evidently wanted me to say that we should love it for the National Portrait Gallery,' of whose board Nicolson was a member. Sheila herself had seen Ethel, not long before, for the first time in more than thirty years. Lunching with the 20-year-old Mervyn, in a London hotel, Sheila 'noticed her [Ethel] raddled, flower-toqued and mute, in a large party of women all of whom looked like widows in their seventies once connected with the stage'. Ethel, whose sight was perfect, stared at her daughter and the grandson she had never known 'without any sign of recognition or emotion. I stared back equally unmoved. Her power of evil had waned to nothing.'

By then, Ethel had left her 'dream house' for a flat at 48 Grosvenor Square, the same square which had been Claude's last address, where she entertained impressively. Although estranged from her sister, Enid Nutting, she was close to Enid's surviving son, Anthony, and his children. One of them, now Sir John Nutting, remembers being taken to a pantomime by his lively great-aunt Ethel. He had liked sitting in Ethel's box but had been embarrassed by the way she shouted greetings to friends in the stalls. When he grew up, he found Ethel amusing and appreciated her caustic wit and the celebrity-packed parties in her flat where 'little Manhattans of newspapers' were stacked on the floor. When Ethel went to other people's parties, she brought along a shooting stick to sit on. Sir John did not think that 'raddled' was an adequate description of this game old lady. Ethel was a disgraceful character but it's hard not to admire her determination to cut her losses and make the best of things. When life gave her lemons, she made lemonade; estranged from her own grandson, she simply commandeered a great-nephew. The downside of this jaunty courage was her pathological refusal to admit to unhappiness, which she took to terrible extremes in not attending her sons' funerals.

Many poets make their own damaged psyches the subject of their poems. Sheila was not one of them. In that otherwise unfortunate article in the *PBS Bulletin*, she had stated her theory of poetry: 'What is personally felt must be fused with what is being, and has been, felt by others. But always in terms of the factual.' Her best poems, during this uncertain and unhappy period of her life, continued to be elusive, although never obscure; her style, in George Fraser's words, one of 'delicacy and obliqueness'. In 1956, she wrote a new long poem, *God's Nature, A Guessing Game*, not published in book form until 1964, when the title was shortened to *Guessing Game*. Its various sections appeared in issues of the

New Statesman from 1956 to 1959. The poem is a sombre, grown-up version of the old children's game of counting cherry stones to discover a
future career or, in the case of girls then, a future husband – tinker, tailor,
soldier, sailor, rich man, poor man, beggarman, thief. Sheila's variation
has some remarkable imagery and, for the first time in her poetry, there's
a shuddery mention of the Holocaust. The tailor's mind is clouded by

> … charred years
> Of being outcast; tears and a vast
> Final heap that wastes
> And heaves at Dachau, nearly
> Dead.

The *New Statesman* chose not to publish this section of the poem, but
what it did print still holds terrors. The sailor coming into port sees rats
gnawing at the spoiled cargoes on the wharves. The rich man, obviously
a Lord Powerscourt, who 'jokes and humphs', rules a damaged domain
whose gardens are trampled by visiting crowds, 'shuffling and mute'. The
effects of the thief's crimes are more like rape than robbery:

> The core of the house prised
> And grabbed. Weak
> And sore, you feel hands have fumbled
> Your heart's cage.

The Listener, reviewing the aforementioned *Chatto Book of Modern Poetry*,
congratulated its editors for including Sheila's poems since she had been
'wrongly neglected by recent anthologists'. Not any longer. In 1957,
'Winter', the first poem in her first collection, was included in *English
Love Poems*, edited by John Betjeman and Geoffrey Taylor and has been
anthologized many times since. 'Odysseus Dying' was equally favoured:
chosen for *The Oxford Book of Irish Verse*, edited by Donagh MacDonagh
and Lennox Robinson, which was published in 1958 and reprinted for the
third and final time in 1974. Its successor, *The New Oxford Book of Irish
Verse*, edited by Thomas Kinsella and published in 1986, omitted Sheila.
Frequent anthologizing of her work did not stop Sheila complaining,
falsely, to Robert Nye in 1980: 'Do you know that never has a whole poem
of mine been printed in any anthology.' In that same letter, she incredibly
claimed that Francis King, who had showed her every kindness, and
others in the literary establishment, deliberately kept her work out of

print. 'Lord how they loathe me and I'm jolly well against the wall.' To King himself, she hinted at an affair with Yeats, which King rightly considered dubious.

Her most important appearance in an anthology at this time was in *Poetry Now*, edited by George Fraser and published by Faber & Faber in 1956. Promoted as an anthology of younger poets, it nevertheless included three poems by the 50-year-old Sheila Wingfield: 'Poisoned in Search of the Medicine of Immortality' and 'Epiphany in a Country Churchyard', both from *A Cloud Across the Sun*, and 'Lines for the Margin of an Old Gospel' from *A Kite's Dinner*. By then, Sheila had befriended George Fraser and his wife Paddy, who welcomed poets to their Chelsea flat and urged them to read their work aloud to a critical audience of their peers. It is hard to imagine Sheila at these bohemian gatherings, where guests arrived with a bottle of wine or beer. More probably, her meetings with the Frasers involved her giving them lunch at Claridge's. *Poetry Now*, together with two other anthologies, *Poets of the 1950s* (1955), edited by D.J. Enright and *New Lines* (1956), edited by Robert Conquest, helped to make the emerging 'Movement' into a coherent poetic body. The Movement poets included Elizabeth Jennings, Philip Larkin, Donald Davie and Thom Gunn. Their style was anti-romantic, rational and sardonic, in contrast to the romantic and apocalyptic tone of 1940s British poetry.

Sheila was not a member of any movement or Movement – she always claimed not to know what was poetically in fashion – but her austere objectivity sits rather well with the Movement's work. George Fraser's preface to *Poetry Now* is candid and enlightening, his opinions of certain poets still persuasive almost fifty years after he voiced them. Of George Barker: 'He was a literary sensationalist, a poet of shock-tactics.' Of Dylan Thomas, who had died in 1953: '[He] was always ready to court richness, even at the risk of confusion.' Both Barker and Thomas were associated with the New Apocalypse poets of the 1940s, against whom the Movement poets reacted. Of Sidney Keyes, Fraser noted his 'harsh realism', that his gods were Wordsworth, Coleridge and Rilke and that 'He once described himself jokingly as "Misery's child".' Fraser called Keyes's style, 'literary neo-romanticism'. Much later, Philip Larkin said of Keyes that 'He could talk to history as some people talk to porters.' You can see why he was Sheila's favourite poet. Of Larkin himself, who, the year before, had established his reputation with his second collection, *The Less Deceived*, Fraser wrote that he 'suggests a chastened Yeats – a Yeats "done over again" in water-colour'.

Fraser made no extravagant claims for *Poetry Now* in his preface: 'On the whole, the pattern of my selection will make most sense to the reader if he thinks of me as attempting to answer the question: "What since 1939, in English poetry, has been new?" ' He concluded, 'I think this anthology contains a great many good poems of a surprising variety of sorts, and perhaps no great poem.' Among the seventy-four poets chosen were Larkin, Laurie Lee and Richard Murphy; Fraser was no inflator of reputations. This brush with the Movement didn't inspire Sheila to devote herself more thoroughly to the sweater and the attic. Instead, in November, she booked herself into the very smart and very expensive Hotel Metropole in Monte Carlo, convenient for meetings with CB, wintering in nearby Nice.

At the beginning of 1957 John Hayward's life changed and his championship of Sheila waned. On 10 January T.S. Eliot, who had shared Hayward's Chelsea flat for the last eleven years, came into John's room and gave him a letter to read. It announced that he was leaving the flat at once and was about to elope with his secretary, Valerie Fletcher. Eliot was sixty-eight, Valerie thirty. Hayward reacted calmly and the relieved Eliot kissed him. Hayward said later, 'Since I am the most un-homosexual man in London, I found this a most offensive gesture.' After that unwelcome kiss, a rift developed between Hayward and the flatmate he had always devotedly referred to as 'Mr Eliot'. In the 1963 reprint of *Four Quartets*, the note of acknowledgment to John, which appeared in the original publication, was gone. Eliot, like John Hayward, and, indeed, Sheila, ended relationships abruptly. Shaken by the rupture with Eliot, who, not long previously had chosen him as his literary executor, Hayward lost his enthusiasm for encouraging poets.

But Sheila had found a new champion. The actress Margaret Rawlings (1906–96), wife of Sir Robert Barlow and a vice-president of the Poetry Society, had become an admirer of Sheila's poetry. Margaret Rawlings had quite a following in Ireland, since she had appeared in several productions of Elsie Schauffler's play, *Parnell*, in the role of Katherine O'Shea, as well as in plays by Shaw. On 2 April 1957, *The Irish Times* reported that Miss Rawlings would next month give a reading on the BBC Third Programme of *Beat Drum, Beat Heart* by Sheila Wingfield, 'who is, of course, Viscountess Powerscourt'. Announcing this reading, *The Daily Telegraph* also mentioned the poet's title, as though it was the most important thing about her. In August, Margaret Rawlings, writing to Sheila from the Dorchester hotel in London, tells her of 'the overwhelming grief' she felt at reading a new poem of Sheila's, 'Darkness', which *Time and Tide* had accepted for publication in December and which would, some years later, begin her new collection. Its theme is death: 'Let me predict my funeral weather/Biting at black coats', and its mood lurches marvellously between fury and regret. Margaret Rawlings gradually took on a managerial role in Sheila's life. In September, John Lehmann wrote to her, rather than to the poet herself, saying that he would like Sheila to rework a poem called 'The Fantastic Keepsake' for *The London Magazine*. The outcome is unknown, but the poem does not seem to have survived in any form. And, infuriatingly, no record exists of a talk that Margaret Rawlings gave to the Poetry Society on 15 November, entitled 'Sheila Wingfield, her poetry and her personality'.

The personality in question was now suffering what seemed to be advanced hypochondria. Sheila resigned as chief commissioner of the Irish Girl Guides on the grounds of ill health, discontinued her subscription to the British Association and, in spring, let Margaret Murray understand that she would not be well enough to see her in the autumn, when that robust old lady planned to come to Dublin. Not many people who are ill in April are convinced that their health will still be bad the following September. Ill though she was, Sheila found time to write a letter to the Folklore Society's quarterly review, *Folklore*, about 'a tabu of the hunting-field', namely that of the correct terminology for describing the colour of a 'white' horse: 'However snowy somebody's mount might be, it still had to be referred to as a grey horse.' This was an unappetizing mixture of dishonesty – since in *Real People* she had written convincingly of the misery that hunting held for her – and snobbery. While scoffing at 'the very fashionable and moneyed members of the hunt', she makes it clear that she herself was one of them. One wonders how this inconsequential letter went down with *Folklore's* readers, who were possibly not well disposed towards fox-hunters, even those who respected ancient custom. Sheila was becoming something of a vexatious correspondent, although she hadn't yet taken letter writing to the extremes of her old age, when she wrote long, self-justifying scrawls to people she had never met. In 1958, the novelist and *Irish Times* columnist, Brian O'Nolan, gave her some sound, John Hayward-ish advice, suggesting that she 'should write more poetry' and 'not contaminate' herself 'with letters to the editor'. Perhaps Sheila took his advice, since new poems of hers were shortly afterwards accepted by

The Listener and *Time and Tide*. *The Listener* published *For My Dead Friends*, a long, desolate poem of four eighteen-line verses.

> The pen scratches and flies drone
> And towns suffer heat,
> And I know life can be weariness
> And the sour pleasure of the incomplete.

J.R. Ackerley, editor of *The Listener* also accepted 'Patriarchs', a poem which comes close to acknowledging her Jewish heritage: 'We live as if not knowing the Good News/Expediently, still cheating and still tricked.'

These poems were to form part of a new collection, which, in 1957, Dennis Cohen agreed to publish with the Cresset Press. He wrote to Sheila, not altogether tactfully, 'And to boost your morale, we will publish them at our cost, even if mine suffers correspondingly.' Margaret Rawlings had already consented to recite the new poems when, on 7 January 1958, Dennis changed his mind. He told Margaret, 'It would be a mistake to publish a book now which contains a number of poems which are not up to her best. It would do her no good.' He added that this was also John Hayward's opinion. Dennis immediately wrote to Sheila to tell her the bad news and so, brutally, did John Hayward: 'The plain and disappointing fact is that you've not yet accumulated enough material to make another book.' It seems odd, when so many of the poems submitted – 'Darkness', 'Patriarchs', 'On Being of One's Time', *Guessing Game* – are among the best that Sheila wrote, and had already found an audience in well-regarded periodicals, that the gentlemen at the Cresset Press were so slighting. Were they alarmed at the darker tone of the new poems or was John Hayward jealous of Margaret Rawlings's role in Sheila's life? When the new collection of thirty-two poems was eventually published in 1964, it was brought out by Weidenfeld & Nicolson; the Nicolson was Nigel, the younger son of Vita and Harold, who later gave the story of his parents' extraordinary union in *Portrait of a Marriage* (1973).

Cresset's rejection of her poems coincided with more illness, either real or imagined. Sheila wrote whimperingly to J.R. Ackerley that she was still an invalid. As a magazine editor with pages to fill, he wrote back, hoping that she would recover and send him another poem. She wrote a mystifying letter to Vita, who was on her annual winter cruise with Harold, this time in the Far East, saying that she had had a relapse (of what?) and was in a back bedroom of a Dublin hotel (why?). Vita poured soothing words over John Hayward's rejection: 'Critics are not infallible,' and, in case Sheila should think that the Nicolsons were having a wonderful time while their old friend was ill and unhappy, added, 'Japan is simply beastly. Horrible country, horrible towns, horrible little people. You wouldn't like it a bit.'

Sheila craved sympathy. She reminded Harry d'Avigdor Goldsmid that 'Illness is a great finder-out of real friends.' Harry was indeed a real friend; he agreed to become Sheila's literary executor, a job that Sheila assured him was, for 'a minimal minnow like me', not at all irksome. Harry would have only to keep an eye out for misprints or alterations, 'should there ever be a question of the reprinting of these books (a wildly improbable idea). And possibly the matter of letters from interesting folk of all kinds'. This, she assured him, would be 'very un-onerous indeed; only a question of adding only a few objects – two books and a bundle of perhaps-worth-keeping letters – to your return air luggage'. He could add this bundle to his suitcase during his next visit to Powerscourt or Bellair, a journey which Sheila urged him to undertake, but not quite yet since she was 'due soon for another dreary jaunt to a London specialist later this month [September 1959]'. Her letter ends, 'Love from Pat – and from Sheila, who is much comforted.' One wonders why, since she was soon to travel to England, she couldn't put her meagre literary estate in her own suitcase. But that would have been out of character; she needed other people to put themselves out for her. Which is what Harry found himself doing as the un-onerous task became increasingly burdensome, and this very busy man found himself entangled with publishing contracts and literary spats on Sheila's behalf.

The Powerscourt predicament was worsening, in spite of Pat's entrepreneurial enterprises. In 1960, he sold the mountain and waterfall for £10,000 to Ralph Slazenger, an Englishman who had lived in Ireland for the last eight years. Slazenger had made a fortune in 1958, when he sold the sporting goods company, founded by his grandfather, to Dunlops for either £1.5 million, according to Slazenger, or £3 million, according to the Irish newspapers. An engineer, he planned to establish a hydro-electricity plant using Powerscourt's waterfall. He also set up an electronics firm in Dublin. His wife, Gwen, unusually for a woman at that time, raised Aberdeen Angus and Hereford cattle on 800 acres at Durrow, in Offaly, very near to Bellair, where Pat farmed for part of the year. Inevitably, the two pedigree cattle breeders met and soon Pat was joining the Slazengers on family picnics. Sheila didn't accompany her husband on these outings; she disliked the Slazengers both then and later, when their lives became dramatically intertwined. She didn't much like Pat by this time either, although she wasn't quite ready to leave him. She had decided instead to do something that would hit him much harder than her eventual departure.

14. IRELAND'S IN THE WAY

'We always knew we were there for a limited period. Still I couldn't
bear to leave the place.'
Sheila Wingfield, interview with Anne Roper, 1987

Sheila refused to subsidize Powerscourt any longer. Without her
money, the cafe, craft shop, reduced entry fees and the sale of some of
the land weren't enough to save the estate. Pat was forced to put it up for
sale in 1961. There was a certain irony in that the Wingfields had managed to hold on to their home throughout the Troubles of the 1920s and
the Civil War, throughout the period of the Free State and the Republic,
only to lose it at the whim of a discontented heiress. Dublin fizzed with
rumours as to possible buyers: Princess Margaret and her new husband,
the photographer Anthony Armstrong-Jones; a Hungarian couple; a
German industrialist; Billy Butlin, the holiday camp king. Questions were
asked in the Dáil expressing concern that Powerscourt might be sold to a
foreigner, a source of bitter amusement to Pat, since the Dáil had never
shown any concern, or offered any help, during the years when he struggled to keep his estate in the family.

At last, and to general relief, *The Irish Times* was able to report, under
the headline 'New Company to Control Powerscourt', that Powerscourt
'will be preserved as a single entity and will remain in Irish hands'. The
buyers were, in fact, the Slazengers, who already owned Powerscourt's
mountain and waterfall. For £300,000, Ralph and Gwen acquired the
most spectacularly situated estate in Ireland, including the house and all

its contents, the demesne and deer park, more than 1000 acres of farm and woodland and about fifteen estate houses and lodges. Under the terms of the sale, the estate was transferred to the control of a new company, the Powerscourt Trust, of which Pat was to be a director. After the sale, the Slazengers went on living at Durrow Abbey for much of the time, and, although Pat moved to Bellair with Sheila, he went on using Powerscourt as though he still owned it. This arrangement suited both him and the Slazengers, but Sheila found it maddening. That summer, Pat hosted the pre-Horse-Show party at Powerscourt, as he had done since his father's death. He may have felt that losing the estate was like losing paradise, but there was much to be said for being able to swan in and out of the place without having to be responsible for its upkeep. There was something indomitable about Pat, an optimism that had helped him survive a prisoner of war camp and now a new Ireland in which his class was becoming increasingly irrelevant. Always ready to make new friends, he became closer to Ralph and Gwen Slazenger, whose family circumstances inspired him to go in for a spot of matchmaking.

In 1961, Mervyn (Murphy) Wingfield was twenty-six years old, with no regular job and a passion for racing cars. He had been in Canada at the time of the Powerscourt sale but was recalled in time for the pre-Horse-Show party. The estate was entailed and he was needed to sign some papers. The Slazengers' 17-year-old daughter, Wendy, was completing secretarial and modelling courses in Dublin, as well as breeding ponies at her parents' farm at Durrow and doing volunteer work at the Central Remedial Clinic. This exemplary and busy girl hadn't wanted to go to the party at Powerscourt and Mervyn probably hadn't wanted to either but, as in all the best romantic novels, fate intervened. Pat called out, 'Wendy,' followed by 'Murphy, come over here,' and that was it: the two quickly became inseparable. They shared a reluctance to conform to parental expectations and bruised childhoods as a result of their parents' insistence that they play certain roles. The Slazengers, after leaving England in 1953, had adopted the traditional Anglo-Irish sporting life and made their children do the same. So Wendy had found herself hunting in Westmeath, hating it and frightened to death. Sheila had tried, unsuccessfully, to mould Mervyn into the god-like shape of her dead brother, Guy, while Pat required him to socialize at the Kildare Street Club and take part in events sponsored by the Royal Dublin Society. So here were two confused young people with no idea of who they really were. Each saw the other as a kindred spirit who would help them find out.

It's easy to see Sheila as having vindictively forced the sale of Powerscourt simply to punish Pat; tempting to imagine her raging against what he stood for – the framed ancestors, the honours, the titles – all that dignified showiness when her own concealed past was so treacherous. But that wasn't the whole story since, in spite of Pat's efforts to make the estate viable, it was losing money and likely to go on doing so. Perhaps financial worry, as much as ill-will towards Pat, was behind her decision to sell. It was a huge responsibility and one that Mervyn didn't seem interested in inheriting. And then there were those moments of financial panic to which Sheila was prone, she might have looked at the accounts and imagined herself in the gutter before the year was out. But it was still an odd time to choose to sell up; the heaviest financial outlays were behind her and visitor numbers to the gardens were on the increase. Elsewhere in Ireland, the Big House was having something of a revival. In 1958, Desmond Guinness and his wife Mariga, founders of the Irish Georgian Society, bought Leixlip Castle in County Kildare, where they held literary house parties. One of Guinness's cousins, Aileen Plunkett, palatially restored Luttrellstown Castle in Clonsilla, County Dublin. Her sister, Lady Oranmore and Browne, breathed new, young life into Luggala in Roundwood, County Wicklow, a cottage mansion which Mervyn Powerscourt had sold to her father, Ernest Guinness, in 1937. Both sisters entertained extensively during the 1950s and 1960s; the two round dining tables at Luttrellstown could seat forty people and, at Luggala, actors and writers mixed with politicians and diplomats. Other Big Houses, such as Curraghmore, Birr, Dunsany, Glin, Kildangan and Mount Juliet, were also restored in this period. Perhaps Sheila noticed and resented that a new breed of sparkly, young, Big House chatelaines were putting her and Powerscourt, where she hardly ever entertained and where the gates were shut long before midnight, in the shade.

Only when Powerscourt was no longer hers did Sheila understand how much it mattered to her, and the degree to which she had inherited the Ascendancy attitude referred to by Elizabeth Bowen as 'I have therefore I am.' Having struggled for years to maintain Bowen's Court on her writer's income, Bowen herself had been forced to sell it in 1959 to a farmer who demolished it. After the loss of Powerscourt, Sheila retreated further into illness, causing CB to write to her in the spring of 1961, 'I do hope you are making some progress and are not suffering so much,' and, some weeks later, 'I do hope you are feeling very much better, and hope that very soon you will be graduating from having to come to the Library in an ambulance.' On 7 July, only days before the sale of Powerscourt was made public, Enid Nutting, that beloved aunt who had 'embodied durable affection' and sold Sheila Bellair, died. Now Sheila could actually live at Bellair all the year round, close to Heck and Grania, who were bringing up their three small children at Ringlestown House in County Meath. Guy was perfectly independent and Mervyn, whose youth had been restless, was more settled under Wendy Slazenger's influence. Instead of finding greater contentment as a result of all this, Sheila became more dissatisfied then ever with her husband. With nothing to call his own, he still charmed everyone, except his wife. Sheila began to plan further humiliation.

Sheila's first encounter with Wendy was, from Wendy's point of view, and as later narrated by her, unforgettable. Before her engagement to Mervyn was announced, they were both invited to stay at Bellair. As was her habit, Sheila didn't appear at the dinner table but, just as Pat finished carving the roast, the butler appeared to say that Lady Powerscourt wished to see Miss Slazenger in her bedroom. Pat told him to tell Lady Powerscourt that Miss Slazenger was eating her dinner, although keeping Sheila waiting made Wendy too nervous to finish it. When she finally went upstairs to Sheila's room, she felt engulfed in pinkness. Sheila was in bed wearing a pink bed jacket with pink feathers; beside her a pink television stood on a pink table. A bizarre scene, made stranger by Sheila's conversation. She told her future daughter-in-law that she must understand that Mervyn should have been born in Regency times, then he would have been 'all right'. But 'he wasn't and there will be problems'. Wendy didn't know what she meant. Her only experience of marriage was that of her parents; a couple so devoted that they never spent a night apart. Sheila also advised Wendy to dye her hair brown, as this was the colour Mervyn liked best. She didn't seem to notice that Wendy already had brown hair. Surprisingly, in spite of all this and Sheila's bossiness, the two women got on well, which Wendy put down to the fact that Sheila recognized that she wasn't a threat. It didn't take her long to notice that the people around Sheila were either frightened of her or expected her to pay for everything; this made her look on her difficult mother-in-law with something like sympathy.

Mervyn and Wendy were married at St Patrick's Cathedral on 2 October, after Wendy had been hastily christened at St Anne's church in

Dawson Street. The bride had no say in the guest list but was allowed to choose the music accompanying the newly-married pair as they left the Cathedral. Sheila, in a silk coat and tiny embroidered hat, turned up in an ambulance and Wendy couldn't tell whether she was drunk or drugged. There is a photograph of her at the reception at Powerscourt, looking on as Mervyn and Wendy cut a four-tier cake, which was taller than they were and topped with a silver vase filled with flowers. Sheila looks so alone that it's hard to believe there were hundreds of people in the same room. After that return to a Powerscourt which was no longer hers, she felt diminished at Bellair, particularly when the Irish newspapers began to publish admiring articles about Gwen Slazenger, in which she appeared as 'The Lady of Powerscourt', and praised her success in breeding pedigree cattle. Now barely on speaking terms with Pat, Sheila spent Christmas with Grania and Heck at Ringlestown. Warring parents were something that the Langrishes were able to handle smoothly, since Heck's parents had long been separated and visited at different times. Sheila talked vaguely of moving to Spain for the sake of her health, which was badly affected by Irish damp, but said that she had decided against it because there were too many flies in Spain. The family assumed that whatever Sheila did, Pat would be able to stay on at Bellair, where he contentedly farmed and fished.

There didn't seem to be an immediate problem; after all the talk of Spain, Sheila appeared to settle down again. In March, she had a minor career boost when John L. Sweeney, curator of the Poetry Room at Harvard College Library, asked her to record a reading of her poetry for the Poetry Room's collection, since three of her books were on the library's shelves. The Peter Hunt studio in Dublin would make all the arrangements, the recordings would never be used commercially – 'they are simply for the pleasure of those who visit the Poetry Room' – and she would be paid $50. The poems she chose to read included the ubiquitous 'Odysseus Dying', 'Ireland' and 'Poisoned in Search of the Medicine of Immortality'. There is a copy of the recording in the British Library in London and it is a pleasure to listen to. Sheila's voice is warm, conversational, slightly unsteady, and she reads the poems as though they were stories, which, in some ways they are, and in an intimate way which makes Odysseus sound like a member of her family. She does not sound like a woman who is about to turn her life upside down, but that was what she was.

Grania, now expecting her fourth child, was on holiday with Heck in

Italy that summer, when Pat telephoned to say that the housekeeper at Bellair had brought him a message. Sheila was selling the house and he must leave immediately. Grania returned to Ireland and with a large hired van, began removing Pat's belongings from Bellair, watched by the housekeeper who reported the removal of each object to Sheila, who in turn demanded that it be brought back because it belonged to her. Grania took no notice and refused to accept Sheila's peace offering: a set of reproduction antique chairs and the pink-painted television which had so intrigued Wendy Slazenger the year before. It seemed like madness for Sheila to want to hold on to Pat's belongings; she left Bellair as she had left Powerscourt, leaving everything behind, including new bed linen, still in its packaging, on the shelves of the linen cupboard. Pat seemed to have done nothing to deserve this second expulsion, except to be himself. But that was enough to infuriate his wife.

In spite of her disagreeable marriage, the high rate of Irish income tax and a cold, damp climate, it seemed neurotically reckless of Sheila to contemplate leaving Ireland. There were so many reasons to stay: her beloved house, filled with books and warmth, grandchildren nearby, her love of the country expressed in poem after poem. That she would leave all this seems like one more quirk of her contradictory personality. Except that there was something else going on, a 'personal worry', which she confided to the centenarian Margaret Murray, now a resident of the Queen Victoria Memorial Hospital in Welwyn, Hertfordshire. In *Sun Too Fast*, Sheila didn't disclose what this anxiety was, but reproduced Dr Murray's uplifting reply to a letter, which assured Sheila of loyal, undying friendship 'as long as life lasts', and advised, 'So heart-up, my dear, and occupy your mind with something different from what you did when you were well and happy.' Her advice was followed. Sheila did something very different: she moved to Switzerland.

She justified this move, years later, in a letter to Robert Nye: 'I'm not a tax-dodger, and was chased from Ireland and UK by the black crows who stood round my bed in '63 and said "Live in a dry, warm spot in winter."' In Irish mythology, the appearance of crows is a bad sign. The hooded variety is one of the many disguises of Badb, the war goddess, and to glimpse it signals slaughter or misfortune. In Sheila's poem, 'Darkness', at the poet's imagined funeral, crows fly over the graveyard with a 'quick clatter of black wings'. Their bedside appearance was bound to alarm. She didn't take their advice though; the place where she chose to begin a new life was not dry and warm in winter but cold and wet. Palma au Lac, Locarno, beside Lake Maggiore near the Swiss/Italian border, is an old town of narrow streets, vine-clad hillsides and a lakeside where 1500 species of plants grow. The Italian military architecture historian, Marina Vigano, thinks that its castle might have been designed by Leonardo da Vinci, who worked as a military architect in the town between 1478 and 1506.

But its icy winters melt into muggy springs; the only suitable time to be there, from Sheila's point of view, was in the hot, dry summer. Sheila usually went to Bermuda in the summer, even though summer there can be unpleasantly windy. If her health was the reason for this sudden exile, Palma au Lac, as inhospitable in winter as the Bog of Allen, was a peculiar choice; moving there made as little sense as walking out of Bellair had. Her new home was a suite of rooms in a hotel which was still being built when she chose them. The suite consisted of a bedroom, sitting-room, two bathrooms, a kitchenette and a large balcony overlooking the lake. How different from Powerscourt with its hundred rooms and vast gardens, except that at Palma au Lac, as in County Wicklow, Sheila had to do nothing for herself. The hotel staff cleaned and cooked and probably allowed her to order scrambled eggs whenever she wanted. She had the entire suite painted pink, installed her thousands of books and stayed in her pink rooms for the best part of thirty years.

The arrangements for transferring Sheila and her financial assets from Ireland to Switzerland were made by Peter Hetherington of the London-based chartered accountancy firm, Rawlinson & Hunter. He was to become her mainstay for the rest of her life, listed as her next of kin on the information page of her diaries. She was a clamorous and demanding client and Peter Hetherington travelled to her pink hotel suite four or five times a year to see her. He found her intriguing and admired her financial acumen, especially when she acquired a second fortune by making a timely investment in gold. She told him that Claude had advised her always to own property or gold, and now she had no property. He enjoyed her outrageous flattery, fully aware that she was never less than charming because he was so useful to her. It had been years since Pat had felt the warmth of that charm, but after that harsh ultimatum to leave Bellair, Sheila settled enough money on him to buy another house. He spent a miserable eighteen months in rented houses until Grania had a bungalow, Tara Beg, built for him, nestled in fields below the Hill of Tara, in Meath. She installed a married couple to look after him and he was comfortable enough, although he never stopped talking about Powerscourt. CB, when told of these surprising new arrangements, wrote tactfully to Sheila, 'I think the change of climate will do you good.'

And it seemed to. Living in two rooms gave her an unshackled feeling. 'Abrupt liberty is a great comfort,' Sheila wrote towards the end of her life in her third and final memoir, *Ladder to the Loft*, and the move to Palma au Lac was shockingly abrupt. Her mysterious and debilitating ailments were suddenly cured and she enjoyed a new sprightliness. Instead of reclining in pink bed jackets and travelling in ambulances, she went out riding and rowed boats on the lake. And at the end of this first year of liberty came a blessed relief: on 19 December, in a London nursing home, Ethel died of colon cancer at the age of eighty-four. She had made the final draft of her will two years before, leaving her silver christening mug and framed family tree to her great-nephew, John Nutting, and the bulk of her estate to various academic institutions for the setting up of the 'Mrs Claude Beddington Prizes'. Her collection of signed portraits and photographs, her 'Gallery of the Great', was left to the Over-Seas League (now the Royal Over-Seas League) which does not seem to have received it. She stated in her will, 'I declare that I have not given legacies either to my daughter the Viscountess Powerscourt or to her children because said daughter and her children are already adequately provided for.' Claude's money had indeed kept both his widow and their only surviving child in great comfort.

Ethel's funeral, or non-funeral, arrangements were nearly identical to the ones that Sheila made in her own will almost thirty years later. Both mother and daughter donated their bodies to medical science and both insisted that there was to be no funeral or memorial service of any kind. It's hard to believe that Sheila's wishes were inspired by the mother she hated, but she was her mother's daughter in more ways than one: in her coldness towards her husband, her humiliation of her children, her sudden terminations of friendships and her love of literature. Ethel was the more appealing character, buoyant where Sheila was easily cast down, and cheerfully sociable where Sheila often preferred solitude. She was also ridiculously full of herself; her *Who's Who* entry listed among her recreations, 'Launching young artists, helping underdogs, working for lost causes [and] conversation in four languages.' Unlike Sheila, who wore her neediness on her sleeve, Ethel never asked for sympathy.

One of Sheila's favourite books was George Moore's autobiography,

Hail and Farewell; she once told John Hayward that it was 'a mass of inaccuracies, and yet artistically so true that it gives the most just picture there is of Ireland'. And now she followed the advice that Moore gave in his book: 'It is the plain duty of every Irishman to disassociate himself from all memories of Ireland – Ireland being a fatal disease, fatal to Englishman and doubly fatal to Irishmen.' But settled in Palma au Lac, Sheila could never disassociate herself from Ireland. She wrote on the back page of one of her diaries, only a few years after leaving the country:

> No Escape from Ireland
> Ireland's in the way
> Somehow always Ireland
> Ireland Everywhere
> Some Ireland Ireland
> Ireland
> Here & There
> Occasionally & Always
> Ireland
> All Over Wherever you go
> Never Without Ireland
> Salute Ireland, She's Everywhere
> What do we always find? Ireland
> You can't lose Ireland
> Ireland can't be lost
> A Part of Everything is Ireland.

She wrote some of her loveliest poems about Ireland – 'Clonmacnois', 'Brigid', 'View', 'In a Dublin Museum', 'Any Weekday in a Small Irish Town' – in a hotel beside a lake in Switzerland; one more Irish exile having home thoughts from abroad.

15. LA CONTESSA

'A diary is an inadvertent self-portrait.'
Elizabeth Bowen

It looked like an exciting discovery when, ten years after Sheila's death, Peter Hetherington found a secret compartment in the pine-wood writing desk left to him in Sheila's will. The compartment contained Sheila's diaries for most of the years she spent in Palma au Lac, records of her drug-taking, illnesses, financial outlays and 'to-do' lists. By the time Peter found the diaries, I had started to write this memoir, so he sent the diaries to Grania, who sent them to me. Yet, although it was interesting to learn Sheila's dress size, what she paid for lunch in a Locarno restaurant and how often she had her hair done, the diaries shed little light; reading them felt like squinting through yet another of the smokescreens with which Sheila deliberately fogged her life. The 'true' lies found in her letters and memoirs are more revealing.

Her first full year of 'abrupt liberty', 1964, began with a hip operation carried out in the private wing of the Middlesex Hospital in London. This was 'brilliantly done', Sheila told her son Guy twenty-five years later, although it didn't prevent difficulties in walking as she got older. She loved being in bed, even a post-operative one, and during her stay at the Middlesex her diary records her visitors, among them Margaret Rawlings and the wonderfully-named Miss Tambourine, who came in to type Sheila's letters. In *Sun Too Fast*, she also claimed Ivon Brabazon as one of her hospital visitors. His heart 'was in such a bad way that each time he turned up, the bitter February wind, which caught him between taxi and hospital door, had forced him to take nitro-glycerine and rest in the porter's lodge before going any further'. These visits existed only in Sheila's imagination, although Ivon had longed to make them. He wrote to her in hospital, 'I am still Dicky or I would have come to see you. Getting better slowly though. Hope leg getting stronger. Will come round very soon. Love from Ivon.' It would be April before they would meet again, for the last time, two months before Ivon's death. By March, according to her diary, Sheila was swimming in the private pool of the White House, a block of luxury apartments near Regent's Park, getting her hair done in her room at the Hyde Park hotel in Knightsbridge and inviting people to lunch in the hotel's Grill Room, among them her son Guy, living in America since 1960, Peter Hetherington and Harry d'Avigdor Goldsmid. She hired a wheelchair, however, when she went to a lecture given by the biologist Julian Huxley at the Royal Anthropological Institute. In April, Ivon really did visit her; he came to have lunch with her twice and it was perhaps on that last occasion, 15 April, that he had to take nitro-glycerine upon getting out of the taxi. Miss Tambourine continued to be kept busy.

This was the month that Sheila's fifth collection, *The Leaves Darken*, her first book of poetry for ten years, was published by Weidenfeld & Nicolson. Her diary lists an appointment with her publisher to sign advance copies, but it is crossed through and there is no other mention of the book. She was ambivalent about these poems, written during those lost years of unhappiness and drug addiction, and brusquely rejected by Dennis Cohen and John Hayward. She later rejected many of the poems herself when making the selection for her final *Collected Poems* towards the end of her life and when, years after its publication, Grania found a copy of *The Leaves Darken* in a Dublin bookshop, Sheila said, 'You should never have been able to find that. I didn't like that book at all.' She thought of herself as an objectivist poet and would have liked Anne Fogarty's description of her work as 'reticent, probing, impersonal and non-declamatory'. The poems in *The Leaves Darken* don't fit this appraisal and are the most hauntingly personal that she wrote. They are among her best but it's clear why she didn't think so; they come dangerously close to personal revelation.

These lines from 'Cartography' are far from the 'etched suggestiveness' admired by Fogarty:

No light can gauge
Hollows and sudden gaps, or chart
Those devious reefs
And unsure soundings of one person's heart.

In this collection, but removed from later ones, was 'You Who Pass By', a skewed homage to the epitaph which W.B. Yeats had written for his gravestone:

Cast a cold eye
On life, on death.
Horseman, pass by!

Sheila's version is a defiant rebuttal of this stony instruction: 'Shout for public joy; weep common plight/Before death's personal and iron bite.' It is one of the very few poems filed in her archive, typed out on a tiny fragment of paper.

She had never allowed a photograph of herself on the back-flap of her books when she was young and pretty. Contrarily, at the age of fifty-eight, and looking much older, she did. *The Leaves Darken* carried a picture of a woman whose deadened eyes stare out beyond the camera. The mouth is thin; the hair, in spite of its frequent styling, looks uncared for. Autobiographical details also appeared for the first time. The poet 'attempted – always in secret – to train herself to write because of opposition and difficulties'. She was 'attached to a well-known library whose collection of Chinese makimonos she helps to grade'. In spite of this intriguing information, or perhaps because John Hayward was no longer interested in promoting her work, it made little impact. John Hayward's review of a previous collection, written for the *Spectator* at the time when he was Sheila's poetry editor, was quoted on the dust jacket of the new one: 'She knows, for she has observed things closely, what she is talking about; her thought is never woolly, her sensibility never vague.' Sheila sent him an advance copy and received a thank-you letter signed 'Your affectionate friend, John', although by this time he had stopped being affectionate or friendly. John Betjeman told her that his favourite poem in the collection was 'Sea at Dalkey', which wasn't enough to save it from being rejected for the last *Collected Poems*. Monk Gibbon, a more steadfast admirer, wrote that Sheila's poetry reminded him of the Indian belief that 'whereby everything that comes into being is also subsequently dismantled and destroyed'. And indeed *The Leaves Darken* is full of crumbling empires, mishandled love affairs and the cruel, unstoppable flow of time, as shown by the poem 'On Being of One's Time': 'That plain-faced clock whose stare/Is a big cheat ...'

Back at Palma au Lac, later in the spring, Sheila bought herself a new Triumph 2000. She had been taught to drive as a young woman by Tom Salmon, the steward at Bellair since her grandparents' time, who took her out in the Mulock motorcar, 'a high square thing with a lot of brass on it'. She was a clumsy driver, apt to crash gears, and, since she had always employed a chauffeur, without much driving practice. Only a day after her return to Switzerland, she had an accident in the Triumph, resulting in a broken rib and collarbone. She required an immediate operation: not the best way to recover from her recent hip replacement. Her friend and Powerscourt neighbour, the composer Ina Boyle, sent her the cheering news that Fred Hanna's, one of Dublin's most famous bookshops, had given *The Leaves Darken* a window-display. In June, a well-wisher not named in her diary, sent her bunches of Powerscourt sweet peas. And there was another reminder of Ireland, when Margaret Rawlings read Sheila's very Irish poem, 'On Looking Down a Street', at the World Book Fair, held in London on 8 June.

The move to Switzerland had improved her relationship with Grania, because it was impossible at long distance for Sheila to constantly control and correct; to issue bossy instructions and ruthless public put-downs. And for once, she gave her daughter exactly what she wanted. On Peter Hetherington's advice, for taxation purposes, Sheila divested herself of all her Irish possessions and gave Grania Camillaun Island, off Ballycurrin, where Claude, years before, had planned to build a house. Only the island had been left in Claude's hands and Sheila remembered it from childhood as 'a forest-like picnic place of shade and midges'. By the end of the Second World War, its trees had been cut down for firewood and 'stumps showed everywhere like bleached bones'. But bare and bleak though it was, Grania loved the island and immediately sought planning permission to build a house on it.

Although still in pain from her injuries, Sheila went back to Ireland to buy a horse, Zodiac, a 5-year-old chestnut gelding. He was shipped to Switzerland and Sheila began riding him regularly, the first time in years that she had been on horseback. Her diary entry for 8 September 1964, reads 'No barbiturate for one week,' obviously a record. She arranged furniture and shopped for clothes in Locarno's boutiques, which were much smarter than Dublin's shabby department stores. In spite of Locarno's attractions, Sheila never felt that it was home. Once its novelty had worn off, it became 'a deadly uninspiring place'. She had been living there for ten years when she wrote a poem called 'A Melancholy Love', which described Dublin as 'the only city that has lodged/Sadly in my bones'. Still, she enjoyed riding Zodiac in the woods and getting Italian lessons. CB was concerned about the riding because of Sheila's reconstructed hip. 'It might be dangerous in a thunderstorm to have so much metal in your system,' he wrote to her, and suggested that Zodiac could be made into juicy steaks. She was proving to the world that she could live without Pat and the worn-out privileges of the Ascendancy, although she never quite let go of them, always introducing herself as 'Lady Powerscourt of Ireland'. The hotel staff called her La Contessa, which was equally acceptable.

And then came her second car accident, hardly more than a year after the first one, and this time far more serious. On 17 February 1965, Sheila had been taking three English visitors to the hotel on a scenic drive. She described what happened in a letter to her son Guy: 'A 19-year-old Italian workman in a fast Ford came tearing round a blind mountain corner and pushed me ... back in a somersault over the precipice, killing one of my passengers and injuring two other of my passengers and myself ... That is, cracked vertebra, torn muscles, cracked ribs, broken collar-bone, head-injuries.' No blame attached to Sheila over the accident but in the days before it happened, she had taken several does of 'chloro'; her reactions could have been muzzy. Peter Hetherington succeeded in keeping the incident out of the newspapers. She was in a plaster cast for a month and was scarcely out of it, and suffering from diverticulitis, an inflammation of the gut lining, when she was riding Zodiac again. At the end of April, she took a mountain driving test, not before time.

In June, she went to London as usual and then on to Dublin to lunch with CB who, that February, had celebrated his ninetieth birthday. That summer was the first of many that she spent in Bermuda, where she had more or less contentedly sat out the war. From 1965 onwards, she rented a cottage at Pink Beach, Smith's Parish. The Pink Beach Club and Cottage Colony offered, it claimed, 'luxurious living and cuisine par excellence', as well as the chance of underwater swimming, which soothed Sheila's by now very battered body. In 1965 both John Hayward and T.S.

Eliot died, but neither event is mentioned in her diary. Nor is there any reference to her writing. It is only, two years later, when a diary entry reads, 'CORRECT TYPESCRIPT', that it becomes clear that between the hair appointments, lunch parties and fittings for jodhpurs, she was working on both a new poetry collection and a new prose work. Writing was such a complicated secret that she could not even report on it in the pages of a diary, which nobody else was likely to see.

For the whole of 1966, there are no references to her writing. She went to an animals' benediction service at the church of San Antonio, helped to haul up and bail out her dinghy and, on 23 April, mystifyingly reminded herself to 'Take tortoises to Jeremy – etc.' In May, she treated Grania and Heck to a fortnight in Bermuda and went to stay with them at Ringlestown over Christmas, her first Christmas in Ireland since she had stopped living there. The day after a 'big family Xmas lunch', she transferred herself and her thirty pieces of luggage to the Intercontinental Hotel in Dublin, to everyone's relief. Sheila was an impossible houseguest. Her suitcases filled the hall and she stood helplessly at the top of the stairs, beseeching 'someone' to help her unpack, sort out her clothes, and post her letters. The children's governess, Connie Blatch, who came to her aid, gained the nickname 'Someone' from then on. At the back of her diary for 1967, she wrote:

> Things without all remedy
> Should be
> Without regard: what's done is done.

This was advice to herself that she never took; remorse shadowed her late poetry and the memoir she wrote near the end of her life. Meanwhile, she starting putting her literary affairs in order. It began to dawn on Harry d'Avigdor Goldsmid that although Sheila's output was small, her demands on his time as literary executor were enormous. Without meaning to, he had become an indispensable 'someone', one of those who Sheila was prepared to put to any amount of trouble. There was this mixture of pathos and iron will in Sheila that made her a superb manipulator, something about her that made the 'someones' open-hearted. Perhaps they discovered that carrying out her wishes gave them a better opinion of themselves. Harry was himself a busy man: the first Conservative MP for many years, as well as president of the Jewish Colonization Association. His duties on Sheila's behalf can hardly have been insignificant additions to his workload.

Sheila issued Harry with a list of instructions and stipulated: 'With the unlikely possibility in mind that my work might interest someone in the future, I leave my small literary remains in your care.' She claimed that all her work was out of print, although this can't have been true of *The Leaves Darken*, and laid down rules for possible re-issues. Harry then found himself in possession of a blue suitcase, whose contents would go whizzing about between London and Switzerland, causing organizational chaos as Sheila corrected and re-corrected already published work. Harry often found himself pressed into service in the cause of literature. He was a close friend of Anthony Powell, who relied on his advice when it came to charting the career of Powell's villainous protagonist, Kenneth Widmerpool, in *A Dance to the Music of Time*. It was Harry's idea to give Widmerpool a job in industry at Donners-Brebner and to involve him in the murky post-war East–West barter trade. Harry's contributions to Powell's great work were so significant that Powell joked that some people would claim that Harry was responsible for it, creating the basis for a future Bacon/Shakespeare controversy.

Claridge's hotel in Brook Street, just across the road from the house in Grosvenor Street where Sheila had once acted as her father's hostess, became her London base. For the next twenty years, she occupied Room 633 for a few weeks in early summer and then for a few more on her return from Bermuda at the end of August. Bruno Rotti, the restaurant manager of the hotel for much of that time, remembers Sheila as a rather lonely figure who lunched frugally off grilled fish and half a bottle of wine at lunchtime and had supper in her room. She gave this impression of apartness, something between a dowager and a waif, which made the hotel's staff regard her with a mixture of pity and fear. In spite of her slight frame – she weighed only seven and a half stone – and her round of visits to doctors when she was in London, she was robust enough to make ambitious travel plans. In 1967, she wrote to her son Guy that she hoped to travel to Tokyo and Kyoto the following year for a world conference of archaeologists and anthropologists after her usual Bermuda holiday, and proposed that they might meet in California before she flew to Japan. The Japan trip didn't come off but she reported to Harry, in April 1968, that she was jumping her beloved thoroughbred in the privacy of a private open-air manège, rather than in competitions. 'Even so, it's dead against all my doctors' orders. Fat lot I care,' she bragged. This also featured in her diary, so appears to be true.

Sheila's blue suitcase began to take over Harry's life. After Sheila had sent him two copies of the corrected version of *Real People* – nine months after she had promised to, since she was now working up to eleven hours a day on the new prose book – she asked him to take the suitcase to Claridge's to await her arrival. She proposed to leave the suitcase at Barclays Bank at West Halkin Street while she was in Bermuda, retrieve it on her way back, take it to Locarno and then send it back to him again. Feeling that this behaviour could be regarded as tiresome, she offered Harry a handsome present, the Goncourt brothers' unexpurgated journals, 'about ten or fifteen vols. Paper-bound. Please send one line to say: Goncourt "Yes" "(or "No")'. Harry's response is not known. She also told him that she would be spending Christmas and New Year in Barbados, 'What luck I have in that swimming in tropical waters proves the only thing that helps my constant pain.' Having been previously told about her energetic riding, Harry must have been understandably confused about her state of health.

During Sheila's visits to London, Mervyn and Wendy and their two children, Anthony and Julia, often came to see her at Claridge's, so perhaps she didn't notice that their marriage was deteriorating. At one point, Wendy and the children were living in a squalid flat with an outside lavatory in south London, until they were rescued by Pat, who took them back to Ireland until the family could be settled at a new address in Wimbledon Park Road. By 1969, Sheila realized that her daughter-in-law was struggling to cope on her own and began to give her financial help, paying for the children's tonsil operations and, with uncharacteristic tact and delicacy, arranging a monthly allowance so that Anthony and Julia 'could go riding'. The decline of the Wingfields' marriage was never mentioned. But knowing that the deception could not last for ever, Sheila began to change her will, making bequests directly to Wendy and the children. Peter Hetherington's assistant, Philip Prettejohn went to Claridge's with a codicil for Sheila to sign and found that she wanted to go on talking to him long after their business was concluded.

Her life seemed like that of any rich, coddled middle-aged woman with too much time on her hands. During that Christmas in Barbados, she had a course of vitamin B injections, was fitted for new clothes, had her hair done – although she now wore a postiche, she had her own hair, as well as the hairpiece, styled once a week – and spent a lot of time at the smart Coconut Creek Club at St James's. But she was also working hard on the new prose book, noting down remembered conversations or, more likely, making them up. That summer Grania and Heck took her to visit the house which, after three years of wrangling over planning permission, they had built on Camillaun Island. It was a simple, wooden structure on concrete blocks and Sheila found fault with everything. During her stay, Heck chopped more firewood than he had ever done in his life, just to get out of the house and away from his mother-in-law's carping. In spite of her complaints, it's clear that she missed living in Ireland terribly; even after Peter Hetherington had explained the advantages of being a tax-exile, she wrote plaintively in her diary, 'WHY all detachment self from Ireland?' questioning her own contrary decision to leave.

That autumn, back in Switzerland, she came down with colds, chills and bouts of flu, perhaps brought on by the damp, cold weather or because the book she had been working on was almost finished. As we have seen, whenever her work was at the stage when other people, publishers and critics, over whom she had no control, were about to judge it, she retreated into ill-health. The previous Christmas, she had socialized gaudily in Barbados but this one saw her in bed at Palma au Lac, 'rest COLITIS/DIVERTICULITIS pm. 2 x MEXASE' is the diary entry for Christmas Day. In the evening she rang her doctor. Chronic colitis is associated with stress and there wasn't much that the doctor, dragged away from his Christmas dinner, could do. The New Year began badly. On a cold February night, she fell out of bed, had a violent attack of nausea and was sent to the Clinica St Agnesa in an ambulance. She stayed there for three weeks having blood transfusions, glucose and vitamin D. Although she went to Bermuda, as usual, that summer, she was warned not to swim or overexert herself. The sun and sea made her feel better and she was fully recovered when she came back to London in the autumn. In spite of Bruno Rotti's memories of her as a solitudinous old lady, in 1970, Sheila, at the age of sixty-four, entered into the spirit of Swinging London. She saw the film *The Boys in the Band*, about a group of gay men and, more daringly, that showpiece of the new permissiveness, *Oh! Calcutta*; a review featuring nudity and bad language, at the Roundhouse, as well as the Kirov Ballet at the Royal Festival Hall. In a more grandmotherly role, she entertained Anthony and Julia to tea at Claridge's, ordering 'marmite sandw., egg sandw., choc. cake, milk, Indian tea'.

Having made her escape from the unbookish Big House, she fell in with the London literary set during her twice-yearly visits to that city. Cecil Day-Lewis, who would soon become England's Poet Laureate, visited her at Claridge's, as did Sacheverell Sitwell, Rebecca West, and Cecil Woodham-Smith. West, who had a soft spot for writers whose work she admired but who were not in the public eye, thought of Sheila as a sister, although, just as Ottoline Morrell had done, she took on the role of substitute mother. West and Sheila had much in common; both were prolific letter-writers, both drove themselves into states of exhaustion. In her collection of essays on 'outsider women', Rosemary Dinnage wrote of Rebecca West, 'as someone whose pattern was to do battle and then collapse with an illness', a pattern familiar to Sheila. Cecil Woodham-Smith didn't claim sisterhood with Sheila but she ended her letters with 'Bless you and a thousand loves.' The two older and more successful writers acted as literary advisers to the rather neglected poet who, after a lifetime of seclusion, appeared to be clueless about the book industry. West told Sheila not to join PEN, as it would not be useful to her and Cecil Woodham-Smith introduced her to her publisher, Roger Machell of Hamish Hamilton, in the hope that he might accept Sheila's new prose book, now called *Sun Too Fast*. He turned it down, 'and quite rightly, I do now see', Sheila wrote to Harry, 'because it was a new form (neither proper diary, nor proper autobiography, nor proper any known category) which did not stand up in its own right'. She started to revise it.

Over Christmas, in her pink apartment at Palma au Lac, again suffering from colitis, she finished the revisions, at least for the time being, and also noted in her diary that 'poetry came back'. In June, from Claridge's, she sent Harry the corrected typescript, asking him, if he disliked the book, to put her 'in touch with a reputable literary agent who may in time manage to peddle it to someone who is blind to its defects'. But, if Harry thought that the book had merits, 'all I pray is that you submit it for me to a publisher you know and approve of'. She told him that she knew that publishers prefer the known and familiar, but:

> If I've produced something new and strange, that was my intention. For this is an exact reflection of how I really am — or rather, of how the six or seven people in me truly are. Each poem of mine is different from the others. A new form of factual prose writing is imperative for me. It is the only thing that makes the navvy's work worthwhile.

Then came the demands and conditions. She would object to having to pay for publication: 'I'd take this as a real insult. Any prose of mine must be a commercial proposition. *Real People* was. With illustrations too.' *Sun*

Too Fast must be illustrated to demonstrate the theme running through it, 'i.e. the astonishing persistence of prehistoric symbolic designs'. The letter ends, 'This book is my swan-song, and perhaps the only justification for having tried to be a poet. If you succeed, I shall be happier than I can say. A million thanks. I never take your goodness and patience for granted.'

Harry took this new and unasked-for role of unofficial literary agent very seriously. He wrote to Jocelyn (Jock) Gibb at Collins, trying to reconcile Sheila's demands with the requirements of commercial book publishing:

> I have read the book which is certainly interesting though not in the usual run of autobiography. Is this something you would be able to consider? For your guidance, I would say that she was willing to pay for the publication of her verse but considers it *infra dig* to pay for prose (why I don't know). I wonder, however, how it would appeal to you to take this on the basis that you had recourse to her if it did not sell a sufficient number of copies.

These gentlemanly negotiations on Sheila's behalf were to continue for the next three years, during which Harry learnt that being Sheila's literary executor involved rather more than being put in charge of a blue suitcase.

By the beginning of that year, plans for the publication of *Sun Too Fast* were proceeding at a polite pace. Before he had even read the typescript, Gibb suggested to Harry that Michael Balfour of the Garnstone Press, who also ran the small publishing house, Geoffrey Bles, might be prepared to accept it, warning, 'I think the method you suggest of what we call in the publishing world giving a "guarantee against loss" is a good one in the circumstances; although of course it might well be able to stand on its feet.' Once Jock Gibb had read the book, however, he became more enthusiastic. He wrote to Harry again:

> If you and the author are prepared to be a little patient, which I am sure you will, my guess is that there is quite a good chance of publication taking place, particularly if you were prepared to put up (privately, I know, and not with her knowledge) a few hundred pounds to lay off part of the risk ... I hope Michael Balfour will arrive at the same conclusion as I have done. In arriving at it I must be honest and say that I started reading the book with every kind of prejudice against it.

Harry then proved himself to be a man of guile as well as generosity. He wrote to Sheila at Claridge's, 'I think you will be pleased to see the enclosed copy of a letter I have had from Jock Gibb about your book.' But the enclosed letter can't have been a copy of the original, since Harry kept

Sheila in the dark about the 'guarantee against loss' and shielded her from Jock Gibb's initial reaction. It was November before Harry and Michael Balfour met and reached an agreement. Harry then wrote to Sheila more candidly, saying that Balfour was keen to do the book, wanted to sell it at a reasonable £3, so as not to inhibit sales and would therefore need a subsidy. He told her:

> The amount he mentions is £600, which may be a bit stiff and which I think might come down with a bit of bargaining, but as I was not sure whether you were willing to pay anything at all I did not indulge in it. If you do decide on a figure with him, I should be very pleased to pay half of it as I should like to see the book out. Will you let me know your views?

Sheila suggested a subsidy of £500 to Michael Balfour and ended her letter to Harry, 'Your offer to pay half is so hugely kind and generous that I cannot thank you enough. Typical of you. Words really fail me.' What doesn't seem to have astonished her was that, in these negotiations, the sum discussed was the fee that should be paid to the publisher by the author rather than the other way around. On 24 January 1973, Sheila met Michael Balfour for the first time, and handed over the typescript which she had again revised extensively. Balfour insisted that she publish the book under the name of Sheila Powerscourt rather than Wingfield and that she include a chapter on her mother. The first condition was to ensure publicity and the second to make the book more interesting. He was right on both counts. Sheila's recollections of her mother are the most interesting sections of the book. After the meeting at Claridge's, Sheila wrote to Harry, favourably comparing her new publisher with Dennis Cohen of the Cresset Press, 'who didn't even have one commercial traveller'. From now on, in the course of several 'swan-songs', of which *Sun Too Fast* was the first, these comparisons would always be made, the current publisher approved of, then vilified and, at times, threatened with lawsuits.

The day after her meeting with Michael Balfour, Sheila flew to Ireland for the funeral of Tom Salmon, the Bellair farm bailiff who had worked for the family for sixty years. Tom died in extreme old age and had been, Sheila wrote to Harry, 'one of my oldest friends'. She described him in *Sun Too Fast* as an orderly, diplomatic man who calmed her anxieties with 'Lookut, it's a thing of nothing.' Her presence at his funeral was welcomed as was the wreath she sent, inscribed simply 'Sheila'. This was not the case at the next funeral she attended in Ireland. For the past two years, Pat had been living with Caroline 'Sam' Pike at Tara Beg. Always a heavy smoker; he suffered from emphysema and was aware that, like his father and grandfather, he would probably die in his sixties. It was rare for Pat to insist on anything, but his dislike of his wife was so strong that he had made Grania promise that she would not allow Sheila attend his funeral. But, when he died, on 3 April 1973, and Sheila insisted on coming, Grania couldn't fight against her mother's cold rectitude. Cecil Woodham-Smith wrote Sheila an awkward letter of condolence, saying, 'I am sure you behaved, as indeed you always do, angelically always.' Pat would have been amused.

Sheila did not enter Pat's death or the date of his funeral in her diary. But on 7 April, two days before she left Switzerland for Dublin, she wrote, 'Send for black coat.' The most important thing about her husband's funeral was that she should be appropriately turned out. On the day of the funeral, Sheila, rather cool-heartedly, had lunch with Peter Hetherington at the Shelbourne Hotel before arriving at Enniskerry church for the service. Pat had wanted to be cremated and, since there wasn't then a crematorium in the Republic, his body was driven to Roselawn cemetery in Belfast. In 1973, the Troubles were at their worst; the car was stopped at checkpoints and Grania, jittery with nerves and grief, broke into hysterical giggles while explaining her mission to the soldiers guarding the border crossing. Mervyn, wrapped in a fur coat, slept in the back seat beside his estranged wife. After that bizarre journey, the burial of Pat's ashes in the graveyard at Powerscourt was equally strange. In what had been the final resting place of generations of Wingfields, that small graveyard with 'brambles and tipped headstones', which Sheila had described in 'Darkness', Pat's remains were interred, courtesy of the Slazengers. Pat was the first Lord Powerscourt not to have been living on the estate at the time of his death. That sad fact was Sheila's fault and her presence at his graveside was unwelcome and resented. Gwen Slazenger hospitably offered drinks to those attending the funeral but the Langrishes were so distraught that they left immediately after the burial. The difference between the funerals of Pat, the 9th Lord Powerscourt, and that of his father, Mervyn, was marked. Mervyn's death had called for public homage, ranked Boy Scouts, dignified orations. Pat, Mervyn's heir, had seen it as both a duty and a privilege to take over Powerscourt and had devoted his life to the estate, only to die in a bungalow.

'I felt no grief,' Sheila wrote to Rebecca West after Pat's funeral. She returned to Palma au Lac and began the annual ritual of putting away her winter clothes. Widowhood was a relief; a much easier social position than that of separated wife. Determined to break out of the persistent obscurity of the last decade, she began to concentrate on polishing her literary reputation, putting in a lot of time discussing promotional material for *Sun Too Fast* with her publishers. In August, in Bermuda, she noted 'Patsy Wilson = G [Garnstone] Press takes over.' She was taking a lot of Valium but there were fewer complaints about her health. On Christmas Day, at Palma au Lac, she attended the hotel's Christmas Gala and, two days later, went for a four-mile walk in the afternoon, which she completed in fifty-five minutes. Not surprisingly, the following day's diary entry is 'BED! (TWO STICKS).' That walk may have been overdoing things, but for once there was no recurrence of the chronic colitis which usually accompanied her Christmases at Palma au Lac. Her doctor was able to enjoy Christmas Day, undisturbed by a telephone summons from La Contessa.

16. AN UNRELIABLE MEMOIR

'Whom need one fight but God? Others I can deceive.'
From 'Patriarchs', by Sheila Wingfield

'**M**emoirs,' the novelist Joyce Carol Oates once wrote, 'are not lives, but texts alluding to lives. The technique of memoir resembles that of fiction: selection, distillation, dramatization … Memories are notoriously unreliable, particularly in individuals prone to mythmaking and the settling of old scores, which may be all of us.' Sheila herself described her second memoir, *Sun Too Fast*, as 'a highly deceptive book', superficially a chronicle of what turned out to be, in her own eyes, her last year of health – September 1953 to September 1954 – but 'underneath an examination of all kinds of themes'. Marred 'by misprints and written at gun-point', the book was deceptive in another way, not admitted to by its author. In her desire to fit events into her self-imposed time span of that one year, she altered dates, or ignored them if they didn't fit into her pattern, for example, 'Other recollections of Sissinghurst have fused together and are impossible to separate.' Since she almost certainly kept a diary during the period in question, her recollections could have been easily unfused. Then there are the outright lies, such as Yeats saying, 'I wouldn't help a young poet if he were starving in the gutter,' when, in truth, he had given Sheila every encouragement at the beginning of her career, and she had taken advantage of his kindness.

And how can one believe her anecdote about the time she was at the hairdresser's, reading 'a cheap woman's magazine', and came across a letter to the editor written by Ethel: 'I'm filthy rich. My husband used to collect Rolls-Royces as other men collect stamps. Ethel (Mrs Claude) Beddington.' Even if Ethel had been eccentric enough to have written it, it would hardly have been printed. One of the book's themes, which Sheila mentioned in her letter to Cynthia Cawley on 5 January 1975, was 'love, and its opposite, treachery'. Treachery was personified by Ethel, the villainess at the heart of the memoir, introduced with the chilling sentence: 'My chief objection to the theory of an afterlife is the prospect of meeting my mother.' Sheila's lacerating portrait of the heartless beauty with her unwashed blue-black hair is so compelling as to make her beloved heroes – Claude, Ivon and CB, those men of brainy vigour – seem faint and papery. The three men emerge as almost indistinguishable, and somewhat implausible, in their brilliant careers, loveable eccentricities and firmness of character. This is because, unlike Ethel, they are never fully revealed. Claude's Jewish background, an essential part of him, isn't mentioned, neither is the predatory, unspecifically sexual element of her relationships with Ivon and CB. She insists that her friendships with both men were based simply on mutual admiration.

Pat, the man she was married to for more than forty years, is only a smudgy shadow in the memoir; the impression is given that during her years at Powerscourt, Sheila ran the place single-handedly. The estate and its history is described with happy relish: the portraits of generations of Powerscourts over the staircase; how George IV narrowly escaped drowning in the waterfall; dawn breaking over Juggy's Pond, 'nature untampered with, and no moral judgments'. And not just Powerscourt but the entire island of Ireland is the object of her affection: the Little Sisters of the Poor, the Royal Dublin Society and even that scourge of the Ascendancy, Eamon de Valera. Readers, learning from the back of the dust jacket that the memoirist 'now lives in Locarno, Switzerland', may have wondered why. Unlike *Real People*, *Sun Too Fast* isn't a selfless biography; Sheila is at its centre, surviving Ethel's grotesque torments, airing her own provocative views on religion, archaeology and the time/space continuum. This Sheila is a jaunty, insouciant, independent solo traveller, pursuing her varied interests; vibrant and slightly reckless, a woman whom you couldn't imagine vetoing her daughter's choice of a Catholic bridesmaid or constantly worrying about what people will think of her. The memoir is beautifully written, its opinions interesting, but vague and undisciplined in its lack of chronology.

Two weeks before publication, Sheila cancelled its distribution because there were so many errors in the printing. Too late for the *TLS*, which published a favourable review two months before the book was in the shops at the end of May. A more critical piece, by Patricia Hutchins, pointing out various inaccuracies, which were corrected in the final version, was published in *The Irish Times*. Harry broke the news to Sheila about the premature *TLS* review. He had just lost his parliamentary seat and been told that he had clogged arteries. Begging him to follow his doctor's advice and eat more sensibly, Sheila told him, 'I speak as one who has to obey, very strictly, three different diets at the same time.' She wrote plaintively to Terence de Vere White, the *Irish Times* literary editor, apologizing not only for the uncorrected copy of *Sun Too Fast* but for having kept her distance in the past:

> Dear Mr de Vere White,
> (Or couldn't it after all these years be Terence and Sheila?)
> I can't tell you how sad and frustrating it was for me never to be able to enjoy the friendship of people in the purely literary world: poor Pat, an arch-philistine, completely forbade it early in our marriage, and for love of him I obeyed.

She also told him that she was forced to write *Sun Too Fast* as 'Powerscourt' – 'This is the last persona under which I wanted to appear' – and asked very charmingly if he would read the corrected version of the memoir. It was mean of her to blame the 'arch-philistine' for her previous lack of friendship towards de Vere White, a man whom Pat would very much have enjoyed knowing. The literary editor and author was himself an Anglo-Irishman, a descendant of twelfth-century mayors of Limerick.

Reluctant though she may have been to write under it, the name Powerscourt, associated with a magnificent estate and a notable dynasty, meant that Sheila's latest memoir was given attention. Installed at Claridge's, she gave interviews to the BBC's *PM Report*, to Radio London and to the *Evening Standard* feature writer, Valerie Jenkins who, under her married name, Valerie Grove, was to become a columnist for *The Times* and biographer of Dodie Smith. Her interview with Sheila was for a series called *Where I Was Young* and Sheila was photographed outside 33 Grosvenor Street. Sheila repeated the stories of her childhood which she had told in both memoirs and gave some questionable advice to book collectors: books should be protected with face cream and a thick coating of boat varnish: 'It keeps them in perfect condition and they look so good.' Valerie Jenkins found her interviewee, 'a little mad'.

A new author's photograph appeared on the jacket of *Sun Too Fast*. The obvious postiche is cut in a gamine fringe at the front and tied at the back with a ribbon. Sheila wears a dark waistcoat over a white blouse with a floaty pussycat-bow at the neck. If the effect is of an elderly schoolgirl, the *Evening Standard* photograph, by Arthur Jones, is even less flattering. This time, her blouse has a cascade of frills down the front and the postiche seems to have slipped. 'Article with awful photograph in *E. Standard*,' Sheila wrote truthfully in her diary. Seldom could anyone have spent more time and money on her appearance with such unglamorous results. As a young woman, she had looked wonderful in sports clothes and simple styles; as she got older, her outfits got fussier and she chose clothes which Claude would never have allowed her to wear.

Always generous with invitations to her family to stay at Claridge's, she had Heck and Grania and Miranda put up at the hotel to celebrate Miranda's confirmation in May 1974. Since the death of his father in January, Heck had inherited the title, but he and Grania felt anything but self-confident aristocrats as they endured a weekend of mortification and embarrassment, the price often paid by those on the receiving end of Sheila's lavish hospitality. The limousine Sheila hired to take her family to a cinema in Soho couldn't get around corners; she insisted on speaking Italian to waiters; she threatened a barman with the sack after he repeatedly failed to make the perfect dry martini. These martinis were delivered to Heck and Grania in their rooms, before dinner, and no sooner tasted when the phone rang with instructions from Sheila that they were not to be drunk since they had not been mixed properly. They were remixed four times, and Heck, who had disobeyed Sheila's orders not to drink earlier versions, went down to dinner slightly drunk.

Sheila's son Guy came to London that summer, to have an operation on his nose at the London Clinic and to be fussed over by his mother. Guy was 'always the most cheerful person at table! But this is his natural courage', Sheila wrote to Cynthia Cawley. She loved this tall, good-looking son of hers who had triumphed over his deafness but, as usual, her way of expressing love was through control. She paid for his medical care and didn't let him forget it. As always, on her London visits, she entertained her literary friends, finally part of their enviable, well-regarded world, thanks to the extensive coverage of *Sun Too Fast*. Her health was good, her career rekindled, so, characteristically, just when she was at her liveliest, Sheila began to brood on death.

In a 'Letter of Wishes', to Peter Hetherington, she set out her burial instructions. These, uncannily, were almost identical to those listed in Ethel's will, which Sheila was unlikely to have read. Like her mother, Sheila initially wanted to be cremated with the utmost privacy: 'I wish absolutely that no religious ceremony be held … at the place of cremation. I would also wish absolutely that no relatives or friends whatever attend the cremation.' Should she die in Bermuda or Switzerland, her ashes were to be airmailed 'without any urn' to Peter Hetherington in London. He would then arrange for them to be scattered on Bellair hill where, as a child, she had picked primroses every Easter. The curt death notices to appear in *The Times* and *The Daily Telegraph* were to read: 'Sheila, widow of 9th Viscount Powerscourt (Sheila Wingfield, poet) aged … Private cremation has already taken place.' At odds with this lack of ceremony, was another instruction in the letter. Sheila requested, according to arrangements that she had already made with the Meath Diocesan Registry, that a commemorative Mural Tablet be erected in Liss (Kilnegarenagh) church, where Irish Grandma had once chosen the hymns and played them sturdily on Sunday mornings. The plaque was to have Sheila's name and the dates of her birth and death above a quotation from Micah, which she had copied out in capital letters in her 1974 diary: WHAT DOES THE LORD REQUIRE OF THEE BUT TO DO JUSTLY AND TO LOVE MERCY, AND TO WALK HUMBLY WITH THY GOD.

As she usually resorted to capital letters when she thought that something was important, it is surprising that her entry for 3 November, although far from undramatic, is in lower case: 'Powerscourt burnt to ground.' Sheila was not exaggerating. At Ringlestown, Heck and Grania heard the news on the radio, drove straight there and saw the house in flames. Their first reaction was relief that Pat hadn't lived to see his life's work destroyed in a few hours. *The Irish Times* called the fire, 'the greatest architectural disaster in Éire for many years', while Desmond FitzGerald, the Knight of Glin, thought the loss of the Saloon, modelled on an Egyptian hall, 'a major tragedy for Irish architecture'. Gwen and Ralph Slazenger had decided to open the house to the public. They held a lunch party beforehand to show off the newly-decorated rooms and a fire was lit in the seldom-used morning-room, setting its chimney alight. The fire brigade, thinking that they had put out the fire, left, but too soon. Early the next morning, an electric bell rang faintly in the Slazengers' bedroom, alerting them to danger. The top floor was now ablaze and before the voluntary fire services from Bray, Greystones and Rathdrum could rush back to the scene, the roof was destroyed, leaving the ruined house open to the skies. Not everything was lost: Gwen Slazenger managed to snatch from the flames the 7th Lord Powerscourt's three-volume collection of plans for the house. The local civil defence volunteers saved the east wing. Most of its contents, spanning five generations of acquisitive Powerscourts, survived, as did much of the contents of the armoury.

Sheila blamed the Slazengers. Two years after the fire, in a letter to the historian Leslie Rowse, she told him that 'the new people', had burnt down Powerscourt and all its treasures 'by sheer carelessness', and because they no longer had footmen but 'only a couple of housemaids or so, to look after it all. Ineffectual and rather sad'. The following year, she repeated the charge in another letter: '[Powerscourt] Now, alas, all ashes, due to the new people's ignorance of Georgian brick chimneys sixty-foot-high and with no flue linings.' But what could you expect of those so unused to gracious living that they didn't have a footman to their name. She returned to this theme in her poetry:

> Domes and domesticity, entire
> As stallions, but now
> Burnt to the ground.

are lines from 'View', a poem in *Her Storms* (1977).

The Irish Times' reporting of the Powerscourt fire referred to the coincidence that 'The 10th Viscount is married to Mr Slazenger's daughter, Wendy.' Five days later, that restive marriage was officially ended. For a long time, Wendy had been involved with a school teacher, Ray Watson, and was expecting his baby; her divorce from Mervyn couldn't be put off any longer. Sheila's diary went straight into capital letters. 'M DIVORCED BY WENDY' registers her shock at the end of a marriage which, from the start, she had predicted would be difficult. Wendy continued to be part of her life, and her diary. Her entry for 14 December records the fact of Wendy's remarriage, and then, sadly, for 27 December, 'W's child stillborn.' Even in those jolting times, she went on writing what she recorded as 'NEW VERSE'.

These new poems, to her delight, came at the rate of one a day. She planned to publish them in a new 'Selected', which would also include poems going back to the beginning of her career. In May 1975, during her annual early summer visit to London, George and Paddy Fraser were invited to lunch at Claridge's, to find that it was not a free one: Sheila wanted George to act as her literary agent and help her get the book into print as Harry was now too ill to take on this demanding job. George agreed to write a preface for a new collection but, pleading lack of time to do any editing, suggested that Isobel Armstrong, a young colleague of his at the University of Leicester, and herself a poet, might be able to help. Two days after that lunch, Mervyn, now Lord Powerscourt, came to Claridge's to have drinks and dinner with his mother. Of her three children, he had been the most regular visitor. He had flown to Switzerland to comfort her after her car accident and brought his estranged wife and children to see her in London, acting out a game of happy families for Sheila's benefit. If he had been a bit disappointing academically, he made up for it in wit and charm and a love of racing cars which reminded Sheila of her dead brother, Guy. Looking forward to Mervyn's visit, she had her hair done in the afternoon. Before the evening was out, her diary spluttered into red-inked capitals: 'HATEFUL SHOUTING VILIFICATION from M – after 20 mins. made him leave.'

Whatever happened between them, Mervyn's exit from her life was final and her relationship with him became the subject for two disturbing poems by a poet who was rarely this confessional. In 'Pitchforks' (1977) she wrote,

> I know Hell is to feel
> A mother's son,
> The white-necked boy,
> Grown and pointing those tines
> To pierce my head
> Then rip me apart.

'Hazards' (1983) lists three nasty events: Aeschylus, killed by an eagle, who dropped a tortoise on his head; Euripides, ripped to pieces by a pack of hounds, and the 90-year-old Sophocles taken to court by his son. The poem concludes, 'Eagle, son, or savage hounds:/Which was the worst? I know.' Wendy was a more soothing presence than Mervyn. Sheila invited her and her new husband for dinner at Claridge's that June, an occasion providing its own drama, as Wendy recalls. Sheila ordered a bottle of wine and, having been told that Ray had recently attended a wine tasting in Bordeaux, asked him to taste it. It was the most expensive wine he had sampled, and delicious. Sheila tasted it and spat it out. 'Iron filings,' she screeched and summoned the waiter. 'My guest is a wine expert,' she shouted, 'being a perfect gentleman he accepted it.' Wendy and Ray calmly let her rant for some minutes; when she was satisfied that everyone realized that she called the shots, she behaved herself for the rest of the evening.

George Fraser wrote to Isobel Armstrong, in the autumn of 1975, suggesting that it might interest her to help Sheila put a new poetry collection together. He told her that Sheila hadn't written any poetry for some years but had recently had a rebirth in which intense, small poems had come to her. Isobel Armstrong had three children, one of them a baby, and was also caring for a teenage nephew. She was reluctant to take on what sounded like a demanding job: 'I thought I was going to get involved with someone very imperious and be cast in the role of a servant.' But Sheila didn't give up; she sent Isobel her previous collections and, although Isobel didn't like *Beat Drum, Beat Heart*, she loved the early work. 'I thought that she was probably a great poet. So, perhaps against my own instincts, I suggested that I send her a list of the poems I liked best.' Sheila wanted more than that. She thought that the poems needed revision and that Isobel was the person to guide her. On 13 December, she travelled to Leicester to meet Isobel at the Holiday Inn and persuade her to come to Switzerland. It was a major manoeuvre for Isobel to arrange for her children to be looked after so that she could get to the meeting. Sitting among the packets of Coffee-Mate and plastic cutlery, Sheila presented an extraordinary sight, as Isobel recalls.

> With her wig and make-up, she looked as if she'd been constructed out of something. I could see that she wasn't well and needed to rest and her courage in coming all that way touched me. I had a sense of someone who was deeply lonely. The intensity of her creativity attracted me – there was something wonderful about it.

At a subsequent meeting the following day at the Frasers' house, Sheila persuaded a hesitant Isobel to spend two or three days at Palma au Lac during the next Easter vacation, while her husband looked after the children. All through the winter, Sheila telephoned Isobel constantly, to keep her to her promise. In spite of some bad bruising from a fall on wet, icy roads in February, she typed out her new poems on an electric typewriter and organized them into folders. She counted the days until Isobel's arrival.

March 26th 1976, is recorded in Sheila's diary as 'Isobel's weekend'. Isobel was installed in Sheila's hotel; her room had a balcony overlooking the lake, which she found overwhelmingly glamorous. She soon had her first experience of Sheila's unpredictable temper. A fruit basket in Isobel's room had been sheathed in coloured cellophane and tied with a satin bow. Sheila proclaimed the wrapping to be vulgar, tore at it with her talon-like nails and shouted at the waiter responsible. Isobel noticed that her hostess always seemed to have a glass of *blanc de blanc* in her hand, which she explained was for her constant pain. When she approved of Isobel's Biba trouser suit and a black fur coat by remarking, 'You look so nice; I was expecting you to come in frayed jeans,' Isobel decided to match her for rudeness and from that point they got on well. Between work on the poems there were confidences, among them the story of Sheila's hellish marriage, how animal passion faded, to be replaced by Pat's constant disapproval of her work and his refusal to let her mix with other writers. The work itself was exhausting. When Isobel remarked that the final line of a poem seemed to fade away, she was made to supply alternatives, Sheila claiming, 'I can't think of anything.' They scribbled on the actual published text and Isobel had to suggest revisions on the spur of the moment. 'I thought her poems were her own business and that I shouldn't have been there. And she was so domineering.' Distressed and exhausted, Isobel got flu just as she was about to leave. Sheila made the staff cover the bathroom floor with towels for Isobel to lie on. When she was well enough to travel, she was sent off with lots of fruit and full of resentment. The alarming weekend forced Isobel to come of age, and, as she puts it, 'not to be so biddable'.

In London, later in the spring, Sheila went to Cecil Woodham-Smith's eightieth birthday at the Travellers' Club and gave several literary lunch and dinner parties at Claridge's. These were formal, well-planned occasions; impromptu visits rattled her, as can be deduced from her diary entry for Saturday, 15 May. '4.15 Miranda and two friends turned up to see me unexpectedly. Was in bed. Ordered tea on my bill for them downstairs.' Miranda knew perfectly well that her grandmother wasn't somebody you called on without prior warning and predicted correctly that, when she arrived at Claridge's with two school friends, Sheila wouldn't come down but would invite them to gorge themselves in the hotel lounge. How wilfully self-imposed Sheila's loneliness was; she often said that Miranda was her favourite granddaughter but, because the visit hadn't been prearranged, she couldn't ask the girl to come up and see her for a few minutes. A week after that visit, on 23 May, Sheila was seventy. Celebrations were muted; she seems to have gone to the Duveen Gallery at the British Museum and to the National Gallery by herself before seeing Cecil Woodham-Smith in the evening. When she went to Bermuda in July, she gave a dinner party for eight at the Pink Beach Club House, providing a menu that seems at odds with the club's boast of 'cuisine par excellence'. Even in the culinary-uninspired 1970s, prawn cocktail, Campbell's consommé with sherry, steak with mushroom sauce and peas, and poached apples and baked Alaska for dessert, were banal choices. Sheila had lived in Ireland at a time when it was hard to order anything other than overcooked meat and watery vegetables, which had perhaps blunted her appetite. Apart from that bottle of aromatic, golden wine which she had drunk in Italy on her honeymoon, she seemed generally indifferent to food and drink.

It was around this time that Leslie Rowse became a frequent correspondent. Her first letter to him, on 1 July 1976, was to point out that in his autobiographical trilogy, *A Cornishman Abroad*, he was incorrect in describing the Powerscourt footmen as 'flunkeys in red plush wigs [and] white silk stockings', when, in fact, they wore bottle-green tail coats and black trousers. She beguilingly pleaded forgiveness for daring to correct him, 'revered historian that you are'. Rowse, a man not averse to titles and pedigrees and gossip about great houses, replied and their correspondence continued for many years. Since he was the proudest of Cornishmen, Sheila paraded her own Cornish antecedents: one of Irish Grandma's forbears was Stephen Braddon, the MP for Bossiney in the mid-1600s. She asked for more forgiveness, this time for her megalomania, 'most dull to anyone but a Cornish addict', which, for the purposes of this correspondence, she had now become.

Sheila had always been rich, so it didn't occur to her that displaying her wealth in front of other writers – the Claridge's lunches, the hired cars, the comings and goings of hairstylists and dressmakers – distracted from the impression she wished to give of being a serious literary figure. Shortly before her death in 2003, the poet Kathleen Raine described Sheila to me as 'an aristocratic lady who dabbled in poetry', although, during Sheila's lifetime, Raine had reviewed her work glowingly: 'She is a true poet with that intelligence of feeling that is woman's authentic contribution to knowledge.' That impression of Sheila Wingfield had, in the end, been submerged by memories of Lady Powerscourt, who, for all her courting of writers, belonged to another, lusher world.

Perhaps Claude had persuaded his daughter that money could buy anything, including love and a literary reputation. She shocked George Fraser by suggesting to him that she should offer to pay Oxford University Press, who were considering publishing her new poems. Fraser warned her, 'Professional poets have to be very careful about subsidizing their own work.' She took no notice and after spending Christmas at Ringlestown, had lunch with Liam Miller of the Dolmen Press at the Shelbourne Hotel in Dublin. They discussed the possibility of Dolmen publishing her new collection. Sheila would provide a 'guarantee against loss', that euphemism for what was, in effect, vanity publishing. When the book was published by Dolmen the following year, it was so well-reviewed that Sheila could probably have found a publisher who would have paid her, rather than the other way round.

17. A POETIC REVIVAL

'... I must, like him, with all force possible
Try out my tongue again.'
From 'Waking', by Sheila Wingfield

'It seems that, in every generation, some worthy poets suffer neglect: probably because they are too true to themselves to ape fashionable modes.'
Review of *Her Storms* in *The Scotsman*, 11 March 1978

Spending the icy winter of 1977 in Switzerland, Sheila put herself and
her clothes in order. She had new swimsuits fitted, her wigs were
reworked and a new, blue one bought. An exercise bike and a walking
machine were set up on the balcony. Cecil Woodham-Smith had died in
March but Rebecca West, then aged eighty-five, was as lively as ever, still
writing books and articles, having a dress designed by the Japanese couturier Yuki and acquiring a new mink coat. She and Sheila, in their
impeccable but alarming wigs, as they lunched in Claridge's, had similar
experiences to share: their partly Anglo-Irish ancestry and a lifelong
feeling of displacement; an isolated childhood and the resulting resilience.
Both of them were hurt by distressing relationships with their sons; West's
son, Anthony West, continually accused her of doing whatever she could
to hurt him. The two elderly women looked after each other; Sheila
always arranged for a car to take Rebecca from her flat in Kingston House
to Claridge's, and back again, while Rebecca always offered encouragement in this careerist phase of Sheila's life.

Harry d'Avigdor Goldsmid, her patient and protective literary adviser, had died the year before but Sheila, who could now call on other writers for advice, even if she seldom took it, began to manage her own affairs with relish. She put up her new publisher, Liam Miller, at Claridge's, so that they could discuss the December publication of the new poetry collection. They decided to publish the poems in two volumes, to appear simultaneously. *Her Storms: Selected Poems 1938–1977*, would have George Fraser's preface, while *Admissions*, a slimmer book, would contain work from 1974 to 1977. Dolmen Press was to publish the books in Ireland, John Calder in England. Sheila agreed to pay her publishers £4,620 in three instalments, although Peter Hetherington foresaw that they might ask for more, 'in view of the expenses and attendances'. And also, perhaps, in view of the anxiety caused by taking on an author who had withdrawn copies of her previous book almost on the eve of publication.

These attendances could be fraught. At a meeting on 10 November, something that John Calder said, or did, resulted in a diary entry: 'BLACK RAGE.' The books that resulted from this odd publishing arrangement, however, were beautiful editions with simple cream and olive-green dust jackets. The epigraph for *Her Storms* is again taken from Quarles's *Emblèmes*, this time words from St Augustine: 'Behold, the world is full of trouble, yet beloved: what if it were a pleasing world? How would'st thou delight in her calms, that canst so well endure her storms?' There is a fulsome acknowledgment: 'No words can adequately thank Dr Isobel Armstrong of Leicester University for selecting what she considered worthwhile from five previous books of verse and one, new, unpublished collection. I have submitted to her draconian judgment with happiness and gratitude.' Isobel, remembering Sheila's arrogance and rudeness during that unpleasant Easter weekend, was not mollified. A few weeks before publication, Sheila wrote to Leslie Rowse, 'I've just had my swan-song produced. Devilish price; but I thought I'd spend cash on good production rather than on lack of sales of tatty paperbacks.' Then, having asked him for his opinion of her two memoirs, which she had previously sent him, she made another demand: 'And I hope you won't think I'm taking advantage of your overly generous remarks to send you the enclosed, do please forgive me. Kindness always results in exploitation. But naturally, you needn't pay the slightest heed to such outrageous behaviour!' The 'enclosed' were promotional flyers for the latest swan-songs, which she evidently expected Rowse to distribute among his friends.

Her Storms and *Admissions* were well received. The poet's own comparison of her new-found voice with the revived Lazarus, in her poem 'Waking', was taken up by her reviewers. 'Between 1938 and the mid-1950s Sheila Wingfield, Viscountess Powerscourt, was one of the leading poets of her generation,' Kathleen Raine wrote, in the aforementioned review in *Country Life*, as though doubting that her readers would have heard of Sheila. George Fraser admitted as much in his preface: 'There are, I suppose, many readers today who have never heard of Sheila Wingfield's work generally.' This was true of the anonymous reviewer in *The Scotsman*, who said that he had heard of Sheila Wingfield only in the last month. Brendan Kennelly, in a Christmas Day edition of the *Sunday Independent*, didn't mention the poet's obscurity but approved of the way she expressed 'quiet, even reticent emotions'. In *The Times*, Robert Nye described a poet who 'is perhaps about to be discovered again'. As much as the poetry itself – 'her work has an uncommon but essential quality of necessity' – he approved very much of Sheila's lack of limelight:

> Here is a poet who has not spent all her spare time in a BBC studio, who is hardly represented in any of the anthologies, who has probably never given a public reading nor won a literary prize – in short, a poet who has not played the dangerous game with Fame which so many twentieth-century poets assume to be necessary to their careers ... She has simply pursued a life-long vocation of writing poems.

This echoed George Fraser's preface, which stated that 'It was her fate, and in some ways a lucky fate, to be a natural poet and to live quite outside the literary world.'

Sheila emerged from these heartening reviews as not only Lazarus-like but the poetic equivalent of Norma Desmond, the anti-heroine of Billy Wilder's *Sunset Boulevard*, although Sheila's comeback was more successful. On the day that she read Robert Nye's review, she gave a rare admission of her feelings in her diary, '*Times* Review: shock – but pleasant one – for system!' In the first of many letters to Nye, she wrote to him at once, admitting that she knew it was bad form for a reviewee to write to a reviewer. She thanked him effusively for praising her 'swan-song', for which she hoped to reward him by giving him 'the best luncheon and wines you've ever had'. In spite of her tendency to point out other people's mistakes, she didn't put him right about the few errors in his review; she had in fact, been quite widely anthologized and had been awarded the

Poetry Book Society Choice in 1954. Instead, she encouraged him in his belief that she was a literary isolate. She poured out the story of her fight against the obstacles that stood in her way: the beloved but unliterary father, the philistine husband, the crowded schedule that allowed her to read and write only in the hours of darkness. She told of her joy, since the death of the philistine, in getting to know other poets and then, for added pathos, mentioned her constant pain, 'from a bungled operation' in 1954: 'No cure. Must be endured.' This was the latest variation of the self-portrait that she had been presenting for forty years, which had first surfaced when she told Ottoline Morrell how she hid in her bedroom, copying out pages of literary criticism, when she was supposed to be entertaining her father's guests.

Realizing that the letter to Robert Nye made her sound unhinged, she hastily sent a follow-up: 'You must have thought me drunk. It was a wholly crazy and ill-conceived scribble.' She pleaded for forgiveness and assured him that her 'gratitude is and always will be – endless'. Robert Nye soon found that he had become a 'someone' and, for the next few years, devoted much time to keeping Sheila's flame burning bright, involving himself in a melodrama of lost manuscripts, frantic telegrams from Palma au Lac, and complicated revisions of poems, all followed by grovelling apologies from Sheila for the trouble she was causing him, although she went on causing it. She also went on writing to him, sometimes twice a week, page after page of her version of her life history, a chronicle of self-sacrifice and courage: 'Almost no sleep; for fifteen years when entertaining for my father on his grouse moor, or for my husband at Powerscourt.' Although she ended one letter, 'That's quite enough about my futile self,' a further instalment of The Trials of Sheila Wingfield soon followed. Among Nye's many assignments as prolific poet, novelist and literary critic, he chose poetry for publication in *The Scotsman*. As his correspondence with Sheila got underway, he asked her if she would like to submit some poems. Insisting that he tell her honestly if they weren't 'up to snuff', she sent him three poems in February 1978, followed by corrected versions of all three and a letter asking for his opinion of her alterations.

Sheila was determined on further recognition. She wrote to Christina Foyle, the redoubtable proprietor of Foyles bookshop in London, suggesting that one of Ms Foyle's celebrated literary luncheons be given in her honour. She received a tactful but non-specific reply about the luncheon and a promise that Sheila's books would be put in the window. When, five

months after publication, the *TLS* still hadn't reviewed the two poetry collections, Sheila put some pressure on the journal's editor, John Gross,
through his friend Francis Wyndham. Francis was a distant cousin of hers
and a journalist on *The Sunday Times* magazine, whose offices were in the
same building as the *TLS*. A review duly appeared on 2 June. Francis,
thus, became a 'someone', in his case a reluctant one, since he was not part
of the poetry establishment, nor wished to be. He began to dread Sheila's
invitations as they always involved his being asked to use an influence
which he didn't possess. The *TLS* review by Douglas Sealy, like so many
others, praised not only the poems but the modesty of their begetter: 'She
never makes a parade of learning and she never shouts.' On the day the
review appeared, Sheila drew Leslie Rowse's attention to it: 'Forgive this
lapse in taste in mentioning it.' Her kindly correspondent went out and
bought copies of both books.

The Scotsman had still not published the poems it had accepted and
Sheila, who, very unprofessionally, hadn't made copies, now wanted them
back. She asked Robert Nye to retrieve them because Martin Amis, the
new literary editor of the *New Statesman*, had asked to see them. Then she
sent Robert Nye a telegram, asking him to leave two of the four submis-
sions with *The Scotsman*. She sent him another letter, after *The Scotsman*
printed one of the poems, 'Keeping House', at the end of May, unfortunately inserting a full stop, 'which made it either more modern, or else a
nonsense, according to one's point of view'. After Nye sent back the other
poems, she insensitively informed him, 'This action of mine, as you know,
is merely because my own intellectual friends are more likely to read this
journal [*New Statesman*] than the very highly thought-of *Scotsman*.' He
can't have felt too concerned when the *New Statesman* rejected the poems.
When Sheila then sent them to the *TLS*, they were returned to her, as
Times Newspapers, to which the *TLS* belonged, was about to face a long
shutdown. Nye hadn't heard the last of the matter. In July 1979, he
received a clamorous postcard from Bermuda: Sheila couldn't remember
where she had last sent the poems, or even their titles – 'I forget all when
on holiday.' She thought she might have given them to Kathleen Raine for
a 'small magazine', whose name she couldn't remember either. (It was
Temenos, which was launched in 1980.) She wanted Nye to list the titles of
her poems, and, having asked this favour, accused him, none too subtly, of
having sold review copies of her latest books. 'I wonder how and where
you rid yourself of them. Most rude of me to ask! So I ask with apologies.'

She had gone too far; this time, he didn't reply. This brought more apologies. 'I feel I've been truly horrid-minded all along, vis-à-vis yourself; and that the least I can do is send you two brand new copies from Liam Miller.' Enclosed with the letter, written from Claridge's in September, were two stick-on labels, to be put in the books when they arrived. One label was inscribed, 'For Robert, my rediscoverer, with endless gratitude, from Sheila Wingfield', and the other, 'Robert Nye, with affection and deepest gratitude, from Sheila'. In case this did not make up for her exasperating incompetence over the poems and her bad manners, she mentioned that her chronic pain was worse than usual – 'tho' this excuses nothing' – and that she was 'mostly in bed from this and that (one is not seventy-three, with a life-total of fifty-two operations for nothing)'. Nye didn't give her up 'as a bad lot', as Sheila feared he might have done after a lengthy silence on his part. For, although the mood of her letters veered from the peremptory to the ingratiating and although she was infatuated with her own myth, she had the professional charmer's way of tailoring her letters to their recipients, offering congratulations whenever they had a book published, which she would then buy and discuss in further letters, making every flattered recipient feel like the sole object of her affection.

She told interesting stories too. Learning that Robert Nye was travelling to Dublin, she instructed him to look out for Chapelizod, an ugly village on the main road but, supposedly, the place from where Isolde had sailed down the Liffey to meet King Mark. Leslie Rowse was fascinated by Swift, as well as by great estates, but may not have known, until Sheila wrote him a letter about it, that Swift had written his *Directions to Servants* while staying at Powerscourt. She didn't take this much trouble just for her famous friends. When Atalanta (Atty) Langrishe, the most artistic of her granddaughters, was studying for her A-levels, Sheila sent her an encouraging letter, 'You may be the genius the world is waiting for', and copied out for her an 1843 account by Mrs John Simon, of a meeting with J.M.W. Turner in a railway carriage. Atty had visited the Turner exhibition in London with her grandmother and noticed that Sheila was overcome with emotion as she looked at the paintings. It made her wonder whether the move to Palma au Lac was made because Turner had loved and painted Switzerland. It seemed as good a reason as any; nothing else about her country of exile seemed to have much appeal. London was where she was happiest, snug in Room 633 at Claridge's, which she described to Leslie Rowse as 'antique', but home-like in the familiarity of its sticking drawers and leaking taps, and spacious enough for her to store the large amount of luggage that always accompanied her on even the shortest journeys. 'And the staff are a lot of nannies to me. Rather necessary as I'm invalidish.'

She was well enough in 1979 to spend her birthday at the Blake exhibition at the Tate with Kathleen Raine. This friendship was not of the kind that Sheila usually formed with other women writers; it is unlikely that the scrupulous Dr Raine would think of Sheila as a sister or take her under a protective wing. Raine was Blake's disciple, sharing his belief that 'One power alone makes a poet – imagination, the divine vision.' Like Sheila, she had known as a child that poetry was her vocation, although this was really all they had in common; Kathleen's values were spiritual and she dabbled in the occult. In 1991, she rejected the honour which the Royal Society of Literature wished to bestow on her, that of Companion of Literature, because she felt that Blake would not have approved. The tragedy of her life was that she had fallen in love at first sight with the homosexual writer Gavin Maxwell, who was unable to fall in love with her, although they formed a tense and difficult friendship. While Kathleen was staying with Maxwell at Sandaig, his isolated home on the west coast of Scotland, during one stormy night they had a bitter row. Kathleen ran through the gale to the rowan tree beside the house, held its trunk and shouted, 'Let Gavin suffer in this place, as I am suffering now!' Her curse had alarming results; Maxwell suffered a spate of misfortunes, the first being the death of his semi-tame otter, Mijbil, hero of Maxwell's popular book, *Ring of Bright Water*. A miserable marriage and a fire which destroyed Sandaig followed. Kathleen Raine never forgave herself for this descent of the furies on the man she loved.

Although Raine later dismissed Sheila as a lady dabbler, she must once have held her in some regard or she would not have visited the Blake exhibition in her company, an outing that Raine would have considered a holy pilgrimage. During that year, she introduced Sheila to Valerie Eliot, widow of the poet, who, after lunch at Claridge's, wrote Sheila a postcard saying that her friendship was the most delightful thing that happened to her in 1979. Sheila, invalidish or not, entertained her Wingfield grandchildren, went to the opera with her godson, Guy Beddington, and decided to stay in London over Christmas in the hope of seeing Leslie Rowse, although a postal strike made it impossible to fix a meeting. Even though the former restaurant manager at Claridge's holds in his memory the picture of a woman who was frail and lonely, this wasn't always the case; Sheila entertained more in London, in her old age, than she had ever done at Powerscourt. Her 1979 diary entries are sparse, suggesting other distractions. But, from October onwards, the entries are more frequent, often consisting of the one word 'WRITE'. She was preparing another swan-song.

18. A FRIGHTENED CREATURE

'Each year
I'm more afraid. Is this the due seed of Age,
And Age's right?'
From 'A Frightened Creature', by Sheila Wingfield

In 1980, at the age of seventy-four, Sheila found romance. The man who visited her frequently at Palma au Lac, pursued her to London, telephoned her twice a day and showed her photographs of China, is referred to in her diaries only by the Greek letter 'phi'. Having a new secret probably thrilled her as much as having a new suitor. Her diaries, until now rather mundane, become fascinatingly encoded. From his frequent appearances in Palma au Lac, Phi must have lived nearby. He also had enough time and money to follow her to London, where he stayed, in the spring of 1980, at 'CH', which could stand for Claridge's hotel, except that he telephoned Sheila there so often that it seems more likely that he was somewhere else. Phi was a scholarly gentleman; he arrived for lunch at Palma au Lac to show Sheila 'a Japanese bk', to discuss the Synoptic Gospels or to work on translations with her. On one occasion he came to discuss Sheila's finances, a meeting that she didn't reveal to Peter Hetherington, her financial adviser, who, since 1980, was listed at the front of her yearly diary as 'next of kin'. Possibly Phi was married since, at Christmas, his telephone calls stopped and resumed only when the holidays were over, the universal behaviour of straying husbands.

This clandestine relationship made life more interesting, but Sheila was not so much in the mood for love as for recognition. In her old age, and at last an established member of London's literary set, she discovered the drawbacks of belonging to a group: the rivalries and competitiveness among its members; the disappointment when, having pleased the critics, someone else's work pleases them even more. Sheila's two 1977 poetry collections had received excellent reviews but they didn't sell particularly well, or bring publishers to her door. Although she was fond of Rebecca West, it was galling when she was one of the twenty writers promoted in the Book Marketing Council's Best of British campaign in 1981, much to West's surprise since she, like Sheila, felt that her books had been ignored for years. Sheila sought encouragement from every quarter. In reply to one of her demands, Douglas Matthews, the Deputy Librarian of the London Library, which Sheila had applied to rejoin, wrote wryly, 'I shall certainly do what I can to advance your claims to recognition and praise.' He also promised to have a word with the editor of the *TLS*, should Sheila have any publishable short verse available.

She was convinced that the Poetry Society and arts programming at the BBC were controlled by 'what appears to be a mild Mafia (but deadly to one's career)', which was against her. 'Lord how they [the literary establishment] loathe me and I'm jolly well against the wall,' she wrote to Leslie Rowse. And more pitifully:

> If ONLY I could cease being obscure, as a writer ... but I'm not scribbling to someone as rightly famous as yourself to complain that merit, by itself, has made so little mark that I have never seen Sheila Wingfield mentioned when any, or every other living poet is being discussed ... never anthologized. Never called (or ordered) to take place in the ranks.

She was exaggerating, as before, since her shorter poems were quite frequently anthologized, but her work should definitely have received more attention than it did. Lacking patronage in England, she decided to try to find an American publisher for her current swan-song, her *Collected Poems*, whose contents were being typed up by Valerie Eliot's secretary. 'I feel America alone might perhaps look at it; the future, if there is a future for our globe, may find me again,' she wrote wistfully to Robert Nye.

In the spring of 1980, after Phi had left London, Sheila invited Francis Wyndham and Valerie Eliot to dinner at the Café Royal. Francis was surprised to see the two women dissolve into girlish giggles because Leslie Rowse, a constant correspondent of Sheila's but one whom she had never met, had finally invited her to visit him in Cornwall. The historian had once issued a similar invitation to Elizabeth Bowen, somewhat hesitantly, since he recorded in his diary, 'I have never aspired to such heights as to entertain a lady before.' In the end, neither lady was able to accept the invitation, perhaps somewhat to Rowse's relief. Soon after that dinner, and after three years of correspondence, Sheila and Rowse met for the first time. They got on wonderfully well. According to John Betjeman's biographer, Bevis Hillier, the historian was 'infinitely flatterable', and Sheila was an arch-flatterer, as well as an interesting woman who was impressively rich and titled. Rowse, no mean flatterer himself, in his letters to Sheila showed an appreciation of her rank. Referring meanly to Elizabeth Bowen, who had been a close friend of his and whom Sheila insisted disliked her, he wrote, 'You and Powerscourt must have given her an acute inferiority complex – your beauty and that palace confronting an Irish squireen.' What a wily compliment and just what Sheila wanted to hear. but it was far from the truth. It was Sheila who felt inferior to the handsome and successful Bowen, whose life at Bowen's Court had indeed been enviable. In that elegantly plain, eighteenth-century house in County Cork, Bowen had run an easy-going salon, entertaining housefuls of writers such as Iris Murdoch, Virginia Woolf and Cyril Connolly, while in London, she had been a leading figure in the capital's literary life.

Rowse's letters to Sheila dropped names endlessly: from the scandalous socialite, Margaret, Duchess of Argyll to the upright politician, Quintin Hogg. He knew everybody, and a life spent travelling around the globe to deliver lectures and to launch books meant that he moved in the widest social circles. In 1926, as a very young, recently elected Oxford Fellow, he had greatly admired Ottoline Morrell, and wrote in his diary, 'The people she knows, and has known – a step down when it comes to inviting me.' The admiration was mutual; Ottoline described Leslie Rowse to Bertrand Russell as 'a wonderful young man, the son of a stonemason in Cornwall … P[hilip] and I were enchanted with him.' Rowse and Sheila shared the same literary interests and perhaps recognized in each other that peculiar loneliness which stems from having joined a world into which they were not born. Leslie Rowse, the working-class grammar school boy from Tregonissey, who became a Fellow of All Souls College, Oxford, and a member of the Athenaeum, understood that sense of duality felt by an Anglo-Irish peeress, whose grandfather was born Alfred Henry Moses.

The difference between Leslie Rowse and Sheila Powerscourt was that the former never made a secret of his origins. He thought that it was quite marvellous that he, the son of a poor, almost illiterate Cornish china-clay worker, had, via his own brilliance and a scholarship to St Austell Grammar School, become a distinguished Elizabethan scholar and one of the most prolific and best-loved authors of his day. Sheila, on the other hand, had been excessively cagey about her ancestry, as about much else. In the flyleaf of her diaries, she gave her religion as 'between C. of E. and agnosticism'. Her children had never been curious about her background. They had grown up without knowing any of their grandparents and, whereas the Powerscourt side of the family was familiar from the ancestral portraits on the wall, the Beddingtons had not been in evidence. Even if Sheila's children had read the evasive account of their mother's childhood in *Real People*, which they probably hadn't, they wouldn't have learnt much. Then, in the 1980s, something that her son Mervyn said to his younger brother made Guy aware that he might have Jewish ancestry. In all innocence, since there seemed nothing shameful about the question, Guy asked Sheila whether this was true. The secret that should never have been a secret was out in the open; Sheila reacted with hysterical outrage.

An increasingly agitated series of letters, heavy with capital letters and emphatic underlinings, winged their way from Palma au Lac to Guy's home in Applegate, California. Sheila accused Mervyn, whom she had not seen since the traumatic evening at Claridge's, of lying when he told his younger brother that she was Jewish, just because he wanted to get back at her and cause trouble. She concocted a dubious Beddington family history from which all traces of Judaism had been erased in the seventeenth century. Her only acknowledged Jewish forebear, as described in an early poem, 'Origins' (1949), was a pedlar from Colmar in Alsace-Lorraine. He, she told Guy, once established in London, 'assimilated completely [underlined twice] with the Protestants'. The Beddingtons had not been Jewish 'in any way or form', for several generations, something that might have surprised Claude's father Alfred, that pillar of the Jewish community. 'As "Jewishness" had been passed by, so many centuries ago; *never* did I take part (nor did my father) in any Jewish ritual. Never. Because I was in no way at all Jewish.'

To steer Guy away from further investigation of the Beddingtons, she gave him an elaborate and glorified account of the Mulock side of her family. 'My grandpa Mulock was head commissioner of the Central

Provinces, which was about the size of France.' Her reaction to Guy's enquiries reeks of snobbery on the part of an insecure woman who was fond of being addressed as 'La Contessa'. But that wasn't the whole story; fear had a part in it too. In the 1980s the world seemed to be becoming a more dangerous place. IRA bombs in London, a neo-Nazi revival in West Germany, a country to which Guy, having taught himself German, sometimes travelled on behalf of institutions for the deaf, and some red-neck posturing in California, where he lived. 'There is a lot of neo-fascism around now, particularly in S. California. So I send you this note, darling Guy. Alas that Hitlerism is no longer dead. It revives, and that's a bad thing for the world.' The note, headed 'KEEP THIS' now merged the ancestral pedlar with a Spanish diplomat, who had come to England from Spain, where he had been a favourite of King Ferdinand and Queen Isabel '(not Isabella, as is taught wrongly)', who had given him 'an extremely important diplomatic and financial post at Court. And also looked after him marvellously. (So that [underlined twice] ancestor cannot have been Jewish or he would have been killed or expelled by Ferdinand, who did this to all Jews in his kingdom) – and indeed she was so loved by my father's family that all the female descendants were called Isabel. I well remember my father's mother, who I called "Grandma Bel". So no Jewish blood there.'

There are holes in this story. 'Grandma Bel' was a Beddington only by marriage, so would not have followed that family's tradition of being named in homage to the Jew-expelling Spanish queen, even if such a tradition had existed. Sheila's paternal grandmother, born Isabel Lindo Alexander in 1841, was almost certainly Jewish, since it would have been unthinkable for her husband, Alfred Henry Beddington (né Moses), that zealous founder of synagogues and benefactor of Jewish charities, to have married a Gentile. Unlike her Mulock grandfather, Alfred Henry is not mentioned by Sheila in her letters to Guy, and neither is the fact that his son, Sheila's father, was enrolled in the Jewish house of his public school. And what a terrible alibi she chose in Isabel of Spain. That heartless monarch, who brought in the Inquisition and expelled Jews and Muslims from the Iberian peninsular, is not a patroness whom anyone would want to boast about. It was not that Sheila herself was anti-Semitic, as she was at pains to point out. Claude had 'always taught me to be proud of the achievements of the Jewish race: philosophy, medicine, etc. in which they were (and, still are) outstanding'. As for her father's religious beliefs, 'I was brought up to believe there was a God. But that human beings could not fathom his nature. This I still believe.'

Like the 'literary scum' story, she repeated the bogus account of her ancestry to Guy so many times that perhaps she came to believe it, although the lies she told did nothing to dissolve her terrors. In one letter, again marked 'KEEP THIS', she wrote, 'If ever you choose to live where neo-Nazism is beginning to take hold, all the better for you that you know the truth of your origins.' (That you are Protestant through and through, is what she meant.) The kindest interpretation of all these panicky denials is that they were protective lies to shield her son from the perceived dangers of a fascist revival. She never talked about the concentration camps and they are seldom mentioned in her poetry, one exception being in the 'Tailor' section of *God's Nature, A Guessing Game*:

> ... and a vast
> Final heap that wastes
> And heaves at Dachau, nearly
> Dead.

She was haunted by the camps, however, but could never openly acknowledge it. It wasn't just Guy who had to be careful; the murder attempt on Pope John Paul II, in May 1981, made her anxious about the safety of anyone who was in the public eye. Writing to her granddaughter Atty, to congratulate her on getting into the City and Guilds of London Art School, she had a bad case of the jitters: 'I fear for P.[rince] Charles's wedding and am sure they'd prefer a registry office in some unexpected part of London.'

The duality which she acknowledged was of being 'Bally Ard in my bones and full of love for England'; not that of being half Anglo-Jewish and half Anglo-Irish. A dual heritage can affect people in different ways. It can impart a double helping of connectedness, or can impose a sense of being an impostor, always in a precarious position and belonging nowhere. This describes Sheila's case; she was a self-written woman in every sense and had successfully made the journey from Grandma Bel's ugly parlour to the splendours of Powerscourt, but she didn't have the self-confidence to understand that once you've reinvented yourself, that is who you are. This was the reason behind her jittery snobbery, that concerned 'What will people think of *me*?' And this was the reason for the distraught distancing of herself from her background. Her denials seem particularly puzzling, since her Beddington ancestry was an open, if largely forgotten, secret. When Sheila was young, both Bethel Solomons and Signe Toksvig looked on her, approvingly, as Jewish. Later, in 1977, Francis King, in a reference to *Sun Too Fast*, with no intention of malice, described Sheila as the daughter of a Jewish businessman, who had made a fortune in Abdulla Cigarettes. Sheila was profoundly upset by this reference. She wrote to Rebecca West, 'Of course my darling pa wouldn't have touched "making tobacco" with a barge-pole, had he known what we know now.' She hated to see Claude described as a Jew, as well as a businessman. In her own memoirs, 'the Colonel of the Yeomanry Regiment' was something of a gentleman of leisure: gardener, fine shot, fisherman. In those feverish letters to Guy, the Beddingtons 'were a very wealthy upper-middle-class lot of merchants, as I said. (This does not [underlined] mean merchant = shopkeeper as in American usage). As I said, it means an import–export business or firm, on a large and wealthy scale.'

She described her fear, but not the cause of it, in a late poem, 'A Frightened Creature', in which she thinks that a constant state of terror is one of the necessary nuisances of old age. And old age was making itself felt. She was beginning to have more falls, not only on the icy winter roads of Palma au Lac – 'this comatose village which lacks all mental stimuli', as she described it to Rebecca West – but at other times of year and in other places. A diet of booze and drugs made her wobbly; she once had to apologize to West after a lunch at which she had been in the throes of 'drug-induced dottiness'. Although she followed, or said she did, the various diets prescribed by her various doctors, she didn't obey instructions not to drink, as a daily allowance of 'light wine' was 'the only thing that helps my old incurable chronic pain'. The constant attentions of Phi didn't improve her balance, although their discussions on Italian literature and scientific tests lightened her spirits. It was getting more difficult for her to travel to Bermuda, or to enjoy that beloved island once she got there. In 1981, hurricanes made it impossible to go swimming, the friends she had made at the Pink Beach Club over so many sociable summers were dying off and the local taxi drivers had become thuggish. During that holiday, she lost a gold bracelet, which was found only after a frantic police search had been undertaken and a reward handed over.

What kept her going was the latest swan-song. In Locarno, she had met a retired publisher, Robert Knittel, and, at his suggestion, sent her last two poetry books and Robert Nye's rapturous review of them to Roger Straus, head of the American publisher, Farrar, Straus & Giroux. She assured him that a trust fund was available 'to deal with this special situation, so that the publisher cannot lose'. By now, she was resigned to subsidizing her books, although she told Robert Nye that she hardly ever touched the trust fund since 'it's a shameworthy kind of thing to have to use if needed'. Roger Straus accepted Sheila's proposition and suggested that *Collected Poems* be published by his subsidiary, Hill & Wang. This threw Sheila into a frenzy. In that same letter to Robert Nye, she made a frantic appeal: 'Who is to write a foreword? Who is to hurl out any truly rotten pieces?' Robert resisted her strident neediness; he still had memories of that crisis of missing manuscripts and frantic postcards, when he had offered to publish some of Sheila's poetry in *The Scotsman*. Sheila had no choice but to edit the poems herself. To do the typing, she brought over a secretary from London to work seven-hour daily stints for £8 an hour, for a whole week in November. That Christmas, as always when she was about to have a book published, she was in great pain.

On 27 May 1982, Gwen and Ralph Slazenger celebrated twenty-one years at Powerscourt. Since the fire, eight years before, they had been living in the east wing, the only part of the house that had not been gutted. It had taken them a long time to recover from the shock of seeing the eighteenth-century architectural masterpiece go up in flames, but now they were ready to restore it. They set up the Powerscourt House Study Group, a voluntary organization whose members included Desmond FitzGerald, Nicholas Robinson, co-founder and former chairman of the Irish Architectural Archive and Professor Alistair Rowan, Head of the Department of Fine Arts at University College, Dublin. The house could never be restored to its original beauty but the Study Group hoped to raise enough money to replace the roof and find some beneficial use for what remained of the building, perhaps as a resource for architectural students. None of this interested Sheila. She had a refreshing ability, rare among septuagenarians, of not clinging to the past; what mattered to her were her health, her appearance and her career. Her hairdresser constantly restyled her wigs; in bitter January weather, she 'walked' a mile on her machine on the hotel balcony and tried to wean herself off codeine; 'NO COD' is a frequent diary entry during the winter of 1982, although, in February, she was in such bad pain that she had to have Valium injections.

Collected Poems was still some way from publication when she got embroiled in messy confrontations with Hill & Wang. This was entirely predictable, as predictable as the fact that her last publisher, Dolmen, was now thoroughly out of favour. She engaged an expensive (£100 an hour) literary solicitor to do battle on her behalf, but Hill & Wang weren't impressed. When Sheila enquired about an English distributor, they languidly admitted that they didn't have one and were trying to find an English co-publisher, something that hadn't been discussed beforehand. In April, still in Palma au Lac, she had another fall, cracking two ribs and breaking her arm. This delayed her departure to her London haven, Room 633 at Claridge's. She had insisted that Hill & Wang send the galley proofs to Bermuda but, when they got there – 'Galleys here (!!!)' – she contrarily cabled the publisher to say, 'Cannot, will not, correct till back in Locarno.' In November, she did make the final corrections. New wigs and a new, pink day dress were fitted, so that Sheila could lunch with Phi who brought photographs of China to show her. She told Grania that she had found someone who took care of her and thought she was marvellous and then never mentioned him again. Like the ancestral Spanish pedlar, her attentive suitor remained a man of mystery.

19. MISS WINGFIELD GETS HER WAY

'This creaking kind of ugly gargle is my swan-song. For it's all gone
from me now. Kaput.'
Letter from Sheila Wingfield to Robert Nye, 4 November 1983

'Good luck; use your life to some purpose, and make us all happy,'
Sheila wrote to her 20-year-old granddaughter, Atty, in 1983. She
was certainly being purposeful herself; a matter, she felt, for self-congrat-
ulation. Her diary entry for 28 January of that same year, reads, 'EXCEL-
LENT RESULT OF UTTER FIRMNESS WITH WANG BY TELEX.' In
this communication, she voiced her disapproval of her publishers' proposed blurb for *Collected Poems* – 'am mailing my version which insist
must replace yours' – demanded further sets of proofs, as the previous
ones had been full of misprints, and reminded them that 'surely these
demands only fair as I stand all costs'. This resulted in a meek telex from
Hill & Wang. An English co-publisher had been found: Alan Clodd of
Enitharmon Press, who Sheila coerced into joining her in battle against
the American side of the operation. 'Please beat fire with fire and be
tough. The bill is mine,' Sheila urged him.

There shouldn't really have been any problems with the proofs: there
was only one new section, 'Cockatrice and Basilisk', containing twenty-
two poems. The rest of the contents, drawn from previous collections, had
been scrupulously edited by Isobel Armstrong only six years previously.
But Sheila insisted on correcting previously corrected proofs, adding to
the cost, slowing down the printing process and, no doubt, exasperating

her publishers. 'Maddening delays, enormous expense, difficulties end-less,' she wrote to the always sympathetic Robert Nye. Sheila added to the enormous expense by taking out advertisements for the book in the *Poetry Review* and the *TLS*, and was only deterred from buying space in *The Sunday Times* because of the price.

The draft of the blurb, which she had insisted on rewriting, was melo-dramatic, repeating the story of her lifelong struggle to become a poet, but, this time, in the language of a Victorian novelette. 'Instead of heading for Cambridge, into which she had passed at fifteen, she was morally forced to become surrogate hostess. Gone was the imaginary garret; gone all possibility of meeting fellow workers able to help her overwhelming ambition.' And, concerning her marriage: 'A promise was wrenched from her that never, in her husband's lifetime, was she to fuss over writing or associate with literary people.' For all their compliance with their pay-master poet, Hill & Wang managed to tone the blurb down a bit in the published version, but it still presented Pat as a philistine who kept his wife in friendless isolation: 'When she married, she found her husband liked farming and nothing else; he extracted a promise from her that while he lived she should never associate with literary people.' Admit-tedly, 'extracted' is a little less censorious than 'wrenched'.

Collected Poems, fronted by the preface which George Fraser had orig-inally written for *Her Storms*, and reprinted with the permission of his widow, was due to be published towards the end of the year. All through 1983, although she admitted to Robert Nye, 'I can only write what nobody wants to read,' Sheila went on a campaign of relentless self-promotion. Nearly half a century before, Signe Toksvig had attributed Sheila's eager-ness to be published and reviewed to the young poet's naiveté. At the age of seventy-seven, she was as keen as ever to publish and be reviewed, and still hustled for recognition as unsophisticatedly as she had done at the beginning of her career. Sending Robert Nye an advance copy of the new book, she wrote what she acknowledged to be a 'begging letter for help so badly needed by a helpless writer in a strange land. But as your UK sup-port did such marvels, I don't, I'm certain, need to ask for more than that. (Should contents be worthwhile, needless to say.)'

Alan Clodd was asked to send an advance copy to Francis Wyndham, with this further request:

> Could you I wonder, be excessively kind and ask him to have a word with the
> *TLS* editor to see if there's any chance of a good review of a whole page – as it's

my swan-song, and the *TLS* did lose something like 21 submitted poems of mine during the Times strike. It would make the most handsome of amends – provided my work deserves it. I think they did it for Seamus Heaney and it made him at once. If you have a photo, it would (or might) help.

The photograph, used on the back-flap of *Collected Poems*, would not have seemed like an attractive proposition to the *TLS* or anyone else. Sheila's hairpiece is crooked and her paleness and dark, glittery eyes make her look drugged or deranged. She had sent Hill & Wang another photograph which would have been a better choice, as it showed a smiling Sheila with short, natural-looking hair, wearing a silk, flower-printed dress, in her sitting-room at Palma au Lac. On the back of the photograph, Sheila wrote: 'Suggestion = delete the "rich" element by trimming curtains on left of photo and half curtains (vertically 1/2) on right. This to avoid what looks snobbish or rich.' A belated realization that her supposed enemy, the poetry establishment, might see such trappings as floor-length silk curtains as the sign of a lady dabbler.

A week after Sheila was installed at Claridge's, Rebecca West died (on 15 March 1983) but Sheila doesn't mention this in her diary and she does not seem to have attended her friend's funeral or thanksgiving service. During her last few years, West, until then robust and hard-working, had become too ill to receive visitors. On West's ninetieth birthday, in the December before she died, Sheila had sent her a telegram, 'Among millions I send you my love,' on which Rebecca's secretary had noted, 'No address so cannot thank.' Once again, Sheila invited her grandson, Anthony Wingfield, to stay at Claridge's during her spring visit to London. He was now at Bath Technical College studying graphic design and Sheila was proud of his artistic talent, as she was of Atty's. She hadn't allowed Grania to go to art school, but Sheila isn't the first woman to be better at being a grandmother than a mother. The annual journey to Bermuda had become too tiring, although Sheila missed the island very much. In one of her last poems 'All But Gone From Bermuda', she mourns its bright birds – ground-doves, chick-of-the-village, longtail, goldfinches – 'O my lost loves'. For the first time, she spent the summer at the Dolder Grand Hotel, Zurich, 'a discreet refuge for the discerning built in 1899', according to the brochure, and close to woods, where she walked when the weather was cool enough during that hot August. When she returned to Palma au Lac, Grania and Atty came to stay with her for five days before going on holiday to Venice, a trip paid for by Sheila, although by no means lavishly.

Collected Poems 1938–1983 was published in November, without any celebration on the author's part, except for a lunch date with Phi, who arrived at the hotel with his interminable photographs of China. This is his very last appearance in Sheila's diary. That year, 1983, was a year of losses: Rebecca West, Bermuda and now her furtive suitor. At the beginning of December, she was back in Claridge's; she had hoped to see Leslie Rowse during her stay but he didn't get in touch. London was no longer her safe haven; on 17 December an IRA bomb exploded outside Harrods, killing six people and injuring ninety. Sheila, who sometimes bought clothes from the store's Model Dresses Department, might have been among those lunchtime shoppers in Knightsbridge, buying Christmas presents. The IRA now terrified her as much as the neo-Nazis and she tried, unsuccessfully, to persuade Grania and Heck to leave Ireland. On Christmas Day, she went for a walk in Green Park, which resulted in a pain in her hip that left her bedridden for two days and requiring an X-ray at the London clinic.

Having paid such a high emotional and financial price to get *Collected Poems* published, she was bound to be disappointed by the coverage it received. Robert Nye, always a fan, praised her in *The Times*, but was given only thirty lines to do so, which Sheila, gloomily miscounting, insisted were ten. Peter Porter, in *The Observer*, liked the poems too, but mentioned them almost as an afterthought in a poetry roundup: 'Lastly, a *Collected Poems* worth acquiring.' The publishing details were missing from the column's stand-first. 'No title, author, price, nothing,' Sheila wailed to Peter Hetherington, adding, 'am in the depths'. She had to wait until the following summer for most of the reviews, since, during that traditional lull in the publishing calendar, minority interests such as poetry are more likely to be given an airing. The *TLS*, far from giving her a whole page to herself, included *Collected Poems* in a half-page review, by William Scammell, of three recent collections. He was dismissive of *Beat Drum, Beat Heart* – 'the modernist gestures are little more than mannerisms' – but conceded that, at her best, 'Wingfield can be powerfully herself'. David Wright, in *The Sunday Telegraph*, praised the poems a trifle condescendingly: 'Finally, Enitharmon Press, which has an honourable record of printing excellent but overlooked poets, is to be congratulated on bringing out Sheila Wingfield's *Collected Poems*.'

The strangest review was by Peter Levi in the *Spectator* on 5 May 1984, which linked Sheila's collection with *Collected Poems 1912–1944* by H.D.

(the American poet, Hilda Doolittle). Describing the poets as 'these two ladies, both famous in their time, and both serious and able, but now rather forgotten', he determinedly found similarities between them where few existed. H.D. (1886–1961) had been a literary bohemian, a friend of D.H. Lawrence and Ezra Pound, who once sneered at her, 'You are a poem but your poem's nought.' With her husband, Richard Aldington (1892–1962), H.D. was associated with the Imagist periodical, *The Egoist*. Levi acknowledged that Sheila's life had been rather different, since she had lived in 'a schloss with pepper-pot turrets', a curious description of Powerscourt. And, whereas, 'in youth, H.D. looked precious but beautiful', Sheila had looked 'zany but intriguing'. The one similarity between the two poets, not mentioned in the review, is that both had published a long, meditative poem in 1946 – H.D.'s *Trilogy* and Sheila's *Beat Drum, Beat Heart*. Could Levi have got the 'ladies' mixed up? The young Sheila had been impassively beautiful and about as zany as the Powerscourt butler. Levi's description of Sheila's poems, 'they spit and crackle like holly', is perfect but then he makes a strange admission: 'I am now ashamed that thirty years ago I was ashamed of liking her poems so much.'

None of the reviewers paid much attention to the new poems in the last section of the book which are some of the best poetic expressions of regret ever written. Remorse had always been one of Sheila's favourite subjects. An earlier poem, 'One's Due', has these uneasy lines:

> Chances of good aborted
> When my tongue was too quick
> Or my heart too slow,
> The lost moment,
> Unmeant betrayals from sheer
> Inadvertence or stupidity –
> Huge or trifling,
> These too call for the pit.

She returned to this desolate theme in some of her last poems. In 'We Were Bright Beings': 'The hot reminders/Of what's gone, the cold revulsion/From what's done', and, in 'No Instructions', the last poem in *Collected Poems*: 'We die the moment that we start to learn/Just what we are, just where to turn.' A fine and honest epitaph.

'*Collected Poems* has not taken off and now never will,' Sheila wrote sadly and somewhat prematurely, to Robert Nye in February 1984. But this wasn't the sole cause of her downheartedness; she was more than usually worried about her health until, a few days after that letter, she was able to tell Nye that, 'Today the doctor has pronounced me fit of what I feared, so the old outlook has changed.' So much so that she felt able to appoint a new literary executor. On the advice of Rosie d'Avigdor-Goldsmid, she chose David Pryce-Jones, a young writer with impeccable literary connections, being the son of Alan Pryce-Jones, *TLS* editor from 1949 to 1959. Sheila told Peter Hetherington, 'David Pryce-Jones has come up trumps. He's a charmer, a hard worker, and is doing all this for me because of Harry d'Avigdor-Goldsmid's widow Rosie; he being a great friend of them both, the same as myself.'

David and his wife Clarissa spent part of the year in their house in Florence, which made it convenient for them to visit Palma au Lac en route, which they did in the middle of April, 1984. They dined with Sheila and stayed overnight at the hotel. Sheila got herself up for them, wearing the short black wig which suited her best and a long black skirt. Over drinks in her room, where an attentive nurse was on hand, David noticed that her papers were chaotic – a sign of trouble to come – but dinner in the hotel's restaurant was delicious. Much as Isobel Armstrong had been, he was struck by Sheila's wistfulness. She told him that she was very lonely but that there were one or two people who came to have tea with her. Rosie had led the Pryce-Joneses to expect an invalid, boasting of having had eighty operations but Sheila, in spite of the hovering nurse, did not seem to be in any kind of physical decline.

In fact, there had been a dramatic improvement in her health. Her 'brilliant orthopaedic surgeon,' had given her some pink pills which not only restored her circulation, but cured the chronic pain which she had endured for most of her life. 'Worth waiting thirty years in agony, as I have, to feel the difference,' she wrote to Guy during that miraculously pain-free summer. That 'thirty years' was a variable figure; sometimes she claimed that the pain began earlier, in the 1940s, or more often, in 1954, 'the last year of health', due to a botched operation in Dublin, which had left her with a rare and incurable condition that she could never quite bring herself to name. As we have seen, the pain was real enough. At the very end of Sheila's life, the doctor attending her came to exactly the same conclusion as her very first doctor had: there was no doubt of her suffering but no evident physical cause.

That summer, with renewed energy, she was her old controlling self.

She had read a travel book, *Blue Highways: A Journey into America*, by William Least Heat-Moon and was convinced that Guy should write something similar, 'You could make a fortune.' Grania came to Palma au Lac, for what was by now a yearly visit. When she expressed interest in a box of family photographs in Sheila's apartment, Sheila removed all pictures of Pat overnight. Anticipating this, Grania had already filched a photograph of Pat in sailing gear, possibly the one taken on that carefree pre-war cruise on *Cachelot*. At the end of June, Sheila returned to the Dolder Grand Hotel for two months. It was not a successful holiday: the effect of the pink pills had worn off and Sheila, gulping painkillers, was again convinced that she had a fatal disease. She made a note to call her London doctor, to 'ask to tell me the truth', but didn't record whether she made the call, or what he told her. Back in Palma au Lac, the diary entry for 11 October is 'ALL EVENING FELT SURE I WAS DYING' but, in spite of the alarming capital letters, this terror seems to have been confined to a single evening.

On 24 and 25 September, the sale took place at Powerscourt of the remaining contents of the house – paintings, furniture, silver, sculpture and the collection of arms and armour – which, as Desmond FitzGerald wrote in an introductory essay in the lavish sale catalogue, was 'evidence not only of the frequently turbulent history of the estate but, later, of a family of collectors whose enthusiasm for gathering interesting and exotic weapons and armour has spanned at least five generations'. Although the 1974 fire had destroyed whole roomfuls of objects, there was enough left to make up 732 lots, much of which had been stored in cellars and out-buildings at the time of the fire. FitzGerald was the representative in Ireland of Christie's, who conducted the sale. His sparkling catalogue essay focused almost entirely on the generations of Wingfields who had lived at Powerscourt, from the Elizabethan Sir Richard Wingfield, to Pat, the 9th Viscount, the last Wingfield to live in that great house. FitzGerald paid a generous tribute to Sheila, whose sketch of the 8th Viscount in *Real People*, he judged, 'cannot be bettered'.

The sale of the Wingfield portraits, as well as the family's former possessions, from salt cellars to 'stained and holed' tablecloths, obliterated the last traces of the Wingfields' possession of Powerscourt. Portraits of recent Viscounts were sold in adjacent lots. There were three portraits of that profligate collector of Italian bronzes and French furniture, the 7th Viscount, one of them by Walter Osborne, as well as a bust of him in Carrara marble. His son Mervyn is represented by two portraits, one of them as a young man, in 1901, looking understandably worried at the debts he is about to inherit and the second, painted in 1922, in the uniform of an Irish Deputy Lieutenant, with the sash, star and cloak of the Order of St Patrick. Lewis Strange Wingfield's set of eight murals, representing scenes from the poems of Thomas Moore, which Sheila had removed from the Saloon years before it was destroyed by fire, was sold for £1,500.

Gwen Slazenger withdrew from sale a portrait of Pat, wearing a sports jacket and accompanied by a spaniel, painted by Robertson Craig in 1951, and gave it to Grania. The Lavery portrait of Sheila, painted at the time of her engagement, was sold for £3,200, exceeding its estimated price, to the owner of a nearby Big House. He bought it because of the fame of the artist; he had never known the sitter. Among other paintings sold was 'Farm Buildings' by Kenneth Webb, which CB had given to Sheila years before. Grania bid successfully for a set of eight late-George III oak hall chairs, whose fluted backs carried the Powerscourt crest, and gave two to each of her children. The sale of objects that she had grown up with did not upset her. Her childhood in that lovely house had not been happy; she preferred being a visitor welcomed by the Slazengers, who were always as delighted to see her as her own mother had never been. Sheila did not mention the sale in her diary and may not even have known about it. Visits to Ireland, like those to Bermuda, were too complicated; she did not attend the wedding, in Trim, of her eldest granddaughter, Miranda, in October. All through the autumn, she worked hard on yet another swan-song, this time in prose.

20. LAST THINGS

'But cottage Death, huge fisted, wrings
The sheet out when it pleases her, intent,
Intent on other things.'
From 'Village Seasons', by Sheila Wingfield

In Sheila's eightieth year, writing was as painful as it had always been. 'RE-STARTING BOOK brings all the "inner trembling" back,' she wrote in her diary on 6 May 1985, complaining that her feet were 'boiling' and her legs 'simmering'. To cool her hot limbs, she took large doses of morphine, which she insisted was 'non-addictable'. A Dr Papa recommended sibellium, lots of walking, and, like many of his disregarded predecessors, advised her to stop drinking. Perhaps because of all the medication she was taking, she began to have nightmares. In spite of pain and sleeplessness, she still went for walks, visited the shops and exercised on her balcony, as well as working on the book which was the cause of the 'inner trembling'. This was her final memoir and, as it turned out, her real swan-song, to be called *Ladder to the Loft*.

She stopped writing those long letters, full of flattery and self-pity and wheedling demands, to people she knew only through her correspondence, such as Robert Nye and Leslie Rowse, but when her sister-in-law, Dar Wright, whom Sheila had not seen for years, got in touch in September 1985, Sheila responded with apparent delight: 'To feel in touch again warmed the old heart. For I can never forget your marvellous kindness – particularly when we came back, Pat and I, after the war.' This was either insincerity taken to a masterly level, or Sheila had forgotten that prickly post-war reunion with the Wrights in Derbyshire, when the air had been thick with mutual disapproval. In her letters, Dar, rather insensitively, presented herself as the family matriarch, living among her own children and grandchildren and in close contact with Sheila's, including Mervyn and his second wife, Pauline, whom he had married in 1979, and Sheila's favourite grandson, Anthony.

If Sheila was hurt, she hid her feelings under swathes of graciousness: 'Am so glad you are living among your own; there is surely nothing like it … So glad you saw Mervyn and wife,' even though Sheila herself doesn't 'even know his London address and [has] never seen Pauline'. Her trump cards are her other two children: 'Grania I consider superb in what she's achieved in life … Guy's a star (in my opinion) … he attended some high-level conference in Hamburg on deaf people's futures and opened the whole thing with a speech in perfect German.' When, after both Dar and Sheila were dead, Grania read these letters for the first time, she could hardly believe that Sheila had admired her so much. During her lifetime, Sheila never made any of her children feel that they were anything other than disappointing. Grania never made the journey to Palma au Lac without worrying that Sheila would find fault with something: Grania's clothes, or the choice she made from the menu, or her sightseeing plans. And all the time, Sheila, it seemed, had considered her daughter 'superb'.

Dar, inevitably, was given a full description of her sister-in-law's state of health, but Sheila described her pains in jokey, jaunty tones, perhaps to convey to Dar that she was not to be pitied in spite of illness and isolation: 'My legs have gone from me, and there's poor circulation in feet, hands and alas head: in other words sclerosis of the extremities.' A recent operation to find out what was wrong had revealed nothing and hadn't 'taken a feather' out of her. She commiserated with Dar on the Powerscourt fire: 'Poor you, that fabulous carpet,' which is a bit rich since it was her fault that Dar's childhood home had to be sold to the Slazengers, whom Sheila, as usual, disparaged. On 23 July 1986, Dar's granddaughter, Sarah Ferguson married HRH Prince Andrew, Duke of York and Dar wrote excitedly to Sheila that she had hobnobbed with the King of Greece and the Archbishop of Canterbury at the wedding reception. Dar's bustling life can only have made Sheila feel that there was something dismantled about her own. Congratulating Dar on acquiring a royal grandson-in-law, she wrote that she herself was now bedridden, 'occasionally being lifted out and put in a wheelchair to go a few yards'. She rarely let her guard down, but now she told Dar, referring to the long distance, in every sense, between herself and her family, 'I feel as if there are great holes in what I know.'

At the beginning of September 1985, David and Clarissa Pryce-Jones visited Sheila on their way to Florence. Arriving unexpectedly early at the hotel, they found Sheila very agitated. Later, a nurse explained that she hadn't got her wig on when they were announced. Sheila calmed down sufficiently to ask favours: she wanted David to take Claude's medals to be cleaned; she needed suggestions as to who should publish her latest memoir, all previous publishers being out of favour. David suggested the Cygnet Press (how apt for a swan-song) a small publishing company which produced beautifully-bound small editions. It was understood that Sheila would pay the costs of publication. That autumn, Grania spent a week at Palma au Lac; it wasn't always convenient for her to leave Ireland but she visited Sheila as often as she could, concerned that her mother seemed always to be falling out of bed, in spite of round the clock nursing, but knowing better than to question her living arrangements.

Guy wrote regularly. He continued to be interested in his background but his attention was now on the non-Beddington side of the family and Sheila gladly provided potted biographies of Wingfields and Mulocks, those uncomplicated and uncontroversial Anglo-Irish men and women. In these, Pat's Aunt Clare and her husband, Lord Templemore were 'dear people', while his uncle, the Hon. Maurice Wingfield, was 'a distinguished general in the British Army in the 1914–18 War and came back – into the War Office in London for Hitler's war. A very good and fine man.' Sheila's own aunt, Enid Nutting, was, 'a superb woman [whom] I adored'. Pat was not included in this list of the good and great: 'Dad was in my eyes a most uncaring father, who never took any pains with his children.'

'Mom', as she now signed her letters to her younger son, liked hearing about his life in Applegate, California: 'I'm so glad you have a bird bath and are going to hang a hummingbird feeder.' She never stopped giving him advice: he was to wear a signet ring only on his little finger, to avoid vulgarity; he was to use Calgon, 'THE water-softener for washing-machines or whatever, in any country.' She apologized for his lonely childhood at Bellair and Powerscourt, 'where I could find no youngster to play with you. It made me so sad, and still does'. She knew as well as Guy did that both estates had been full of children but, since their parents had been Sheila's employees, she hadn't let Guy play with them. She loved Guy but she couldn't stop trying to control him. She vetoed his idea of moving to Europe: 'If you want my own personal view, this is pessimistic. All Europe seems to be on the verge of war and other disturbances.' She reminded him that she managed the purse strings, 'I am, and always have been the person who pays out the cash for you,' and told him bluntly to 'scrub out any idea of not sticking to Applegate'.

During the late 1980s, she began to fret about money, recording in her diary the tips she gave the hotel staff. Not that she tightened her belt; there was no cutting back on manicures, pedicures and massages and her apartment was frequently redecorated. She employed a secretary to type her letters and the diary entry for 21 July 1986 is: 'BIJOUTIER POUR BAGUES [jeweller for rings].' She still gave wonderful presents; for Christmas 1986, she sent David Pryce-Jones a case of Lafon-Rochet 1975 from Berry Bros & Rudd. But life in the hotel where she had lived for more than a quarter of a century, was becoming more expensive as she got older and frailer; there were the round the clock nurses and the room opposite her own which had to be rented for them. Mindful of the expensive mishandling of *Collected Poems*, she kept an eye on the cost of producing *Ladder to the Loft* and told Simon Rendall, who ran the Cygnet Press, that the book was to be budgeted at £2000. Wary of telling the prudent Peter Hetherington that she was about to finance the publication of yet another swan-song, she craftily broke the news to his personal secretary, Diane Colls, in February 1987: 'Before you faint at the news, let me quickly add that I am expecting £1750 from the National Library of Ireland, to whom Bertram Rota sent four of my letters from Yeats, so the expense will hardly be shattering.' She needn't have worried; Peter replied soothingly, 'There is no need to feel concern at the cost,' since there was still 'a comfortable amount' in the bank.

Sheila was selling more than her letters from Yeats. What was offered to the National Library of Ireland through John Byrne of Bertram Rota, the antiquarian bookseller based in Covent Garden, was her entire archive, including the box of photographs which Grania had noticed on a visit to Switzerland. Bertram Rota described Sheila as having 'a high if limited reputation', and her archive as 'while small in extent [was] rich in quality and interest'. True enough; there were no manuscripts or diaries but it did contain Ivon's love-letters, a framed watercolour portrait of CB and Ottoline Morrell's cobwebby encouragements to her young friend.

The National Library paid £2500, which, once Bertram Rota's commission had been paid, almost covered the cost of producing *Ladder to the Loft*, published in December 1987.

This final memoir, 'a reflective and discursive essay of forty pages, bound in marble paper wrappers', as described by the Cygnet Press, is the testament of a secret reading girl. Most of those forty pages are rhapsodic listings of the books read by the memoirist during her long lifetime. The pain felt by her childhood self is still sharp in its depiction of that pig-tailed little girl, who had been denied access to the parental bookshelves. She can't stop marvelling at how well-read she is, considering her early difficulties. There are regretful hints that the memoir she once had in mind was something more personal than this sketchy collection of literary anecdotes and nimble-minded philosophizing: 'Old age recalls, at each step, more and more moments of having been unkind ... Causing rents that can never mend.' The concluding sentence is the wistful 'Nothing is now left.' What might once have been there is not explained and the book is little more than a tour of 'my doll's house library in my doll's house drawing-room'. A non-life in miniature. Predictably, there was a falling-out with the publisher. 'Simon Rendall NBG [no bloody good]' grumbled her diary entry for 14 May 1987, comparing the hapless man with Mr Wang of Hill & Wang, who, inevitably, had also found himself in her black books. At one stage, she wanted to withhold part of the payment to Cygnet because of a few misprints which she herself had failed to spot at proof stage, but was deflected from this course by Peter Hetherington: 'The consequent altercation would put a strain on you and the end result would be we should still pay in full.'

Ladder to the Loft received only one mention, in the very idiosyncratic 'Diary' by Peter Levi in the *Spectator* (10 February 1988), which was quite as eccentric as his review of *Collected Poems* had been. Referring to the memoir as 'the most beautiful of last year's pamphlets to handle, and one of the most rereadable', he concluded, 'Literature is life, as she [Sheila Wingfield] points out, and her decorum is her own and it is lasting, being concrete and fastidious, like the mind of Edward Lear.' In the same piece, he described Roy Fuller as 'the only great poet to have shown interest in earwigs'. Despite this, Levi's praise went to Sheila's head. Two years later, she wrote to Peter Hetherington, 'I ought to boast that the greatest literary critic raved about the pamphlet in *The Observer* [sic] ... The piece began with "This is how English should be written"!' (It didn't.) The point of her letter to Peter was to ask for his help: 'Could you ever, dear Peter, think of writing to Mr Rendall and suggesting that the book be done again.' Peter managed to avoid carrying out this request, which, almost certainly, would have led to further altercation.

While Sheila had been working on *Ladder to the Loft*, there had been an exciting distraction. Anne Roper, an RTÉ producer and an admirer of Sheila's poetry, came to Palma au Lac to interview Sheila about her life and work, with a view to making a documentary programme about her. Anne Roper arrived on 12 April 1987, to find the 81-year-old poet, 'last great chatelaine of Enniskerry's grandest home ... armed with a fortifying brandy to ward off interview jitters'. Here was a new audience for all the old lies: Sheila's acceptance by Cambridge, aged fifteen; the vile behaviour of W.B. Yeats and, naturally, the promise that her philistine husband extracted from her to avoid literary people. This interview, conducted over two days, saw the light of day only in 1997, five years after Sheila's death. It appeared in the *Sunday Independent*, to coincide with the opening of Powerscourt House to the public.

The last year that Sheila kept a diary was 1987. The final instalment is filled with lists of past illnesses, real and imagined: 'Cancer '85, Osteoporosis '86, Arteriosclerosis '85/'86', and her nurses' rotas. In the autumn, severe cystitis returned and her eyes became inflamed so that they looked 'like ripe tomatoes'. November 3rd was 'my nightmare day', but she doesn't say why. She seemed lucid enough, although she did sign one letter to Guy, 'Your ever-loving Grandma.' She had written in *Ladder to the Loft*, 'Abrupt liberty is a great comfort. No need for worry about the Grand National, the Boat Race or the Derby; no fret and despondency after reading gardening articles in English Sunday newspapers.' But increasing frailty made the liberty of Palma au Lac less comfortable. 'I never know where any of you are,' she complained miserably to Grania, on one of her daughter's visits. She had broken her hip falling out of bed; she imagined that everyone was stealing from her. By the spring of 1991, Grania decided that the time had come to take Sheila back to Ireland. With Miranda's help, she embarked on a complicated operation, which involved tussles with Sheila's nursing agency, an air ambulance, a doctor's certificate, and the hotel's hall porter hurriedly changing the locks on the doors of the pink-painted apartment, to safeguard Sheila's books and furniture and the drawers full of cashmere sweaters.

Sheila was taken to St Vincent's hospital in Dublin. From the window of her room, she could see the Sugarloaf mountain, just as she had at Powerscourt. This delighted her: 'O look, there's a view I know so well.' It was discovered that, this time, she *was* suffering from cancer. The disease progresses slowly in the old and the hospital couldn't keep her there for any length of time. With trepidation, Grania moved her mother to the Woodlands Nursing Home outside Navan, near to where she and Heck lived. She dreaded Sheila performing as 'La Contessa', making scenes and behaving with devastating rudeness. But, to her family's surprise, Sheila was a model resident, grateful and appreciative towards the staff. Heck, the son-in-law she had always loved, came to see her every day. As Sheila became more confused, she mistook him for the gardener and told him off because the grounds were untidy. She still suffered from the chronic pain which defied diagnosis and was not connected to her cancer. Her death, on 8 January 1992, was caused by pneumonia.

In one of her most powerful poems, 'Darkness', she had written about her eventual burial in the Powerscourt family graveyard:

> Let me predict my funeral weather
> Biting at black coats,
> With the new box – cave dark and cupboard thick –
> Brought to a lurching halt …

She had changed her mind about her funeral since then, first wishing to have her ashes scattered over Bellair hill, and then deciding instead to donate her body to medical science. 'I think it is important to be unselfish in death as well as in life, if one can be,' she wrote sanctimoniously to Guy, in 1988, telling him of this decision. Since making it, she had carried cards in four different languages to make sure that it would be implemented. Accordingly, her body was taken from Woodlands to the Anatomy Department of the Royal College of Surgeons at 123 St Stephen's Green in Dublin, unattended by any mourner. She had stipulated the wording of the death announcements which were to appear in *The Irish Times*, *The Times*, *The Daily Telegraph* and *The Royal Gazette*, Bermuda. In them, she was styled, 'Viscountess Powerscourt, daughter of the late Lt Col Claude Beddington and widow of the 9th Viscount'. The announcements ended, 'Funeral has taken place. No letters please.' Under the terms of the Anatomy Act of 1832, remains donated for medical research must be buried or cremated after three years. Again, in accordance with Sheila's wishes, her next of kin were not informed when her remains were taken by the undertakers, Corrigan & Sons, to be buried in the Royal College of Surgeons' plot at Glasnevin Cemetery, without the presence of a minister. Burial in this plot is anonymous; those brought there lie beneath a central Celtic cross and a headstone inscribed, 'The Dublin Medical Colleges. Here lie those who have assisted us in the study of man. Pray, O traveller, for their souls that they rest in the peace of God.'

The obituaries which appeared in the English and Irish newspapers listed the impressive early admirers of her work – Yeats, Stephens, Raine – and repeated, unquestioningly, her account of Pat's marital ban on the literary life. Only the obituary which appeared, anonymously, in *The Annual Obituary* for 1992, a yearbook published by the St James Press, was modified in its praise: 'During the later 1930s and 1940s, Sheila Wingfield had a reputation in London literary circles as an aristocratic dabbler in poetry, but her gifts were genuine, if not overpowering.' It also mentioned that some critics regarded *Beat Drum, Beat Heart* as 'a lengthy ramble in search of a subject, confused in its oscillation between the private and the public, and unconvincing in its manipulation of irony'. There was a problem with what had been intended as Sheila's lasting memorial: the plaque in Liss (Kilnegaragh) church, near Bellair. Some years before her death, she had indicated where this tablet was to be placed and had obtained permission for this placement. Foreseeing, correctly, that Liss church, which was in a bad state of repair, might have disintegrated by the time she died, she had told Peter Hetherington that 'the Church of Ireland at Clara would fit the bill,' Clara being five miles away from Liss. There was some doubt as to whether the plaque should be erected on the wall of a church where Sheila never worshipped, and it has yet to find a home. Perhaps this was the price to be paid for labelling yourself a 'liberal' agnostic, as Sheila did in her later diaries. But although she rarely attended church, and had never, as she shrilly insisted to Guy, seen the inside of a synagogue, she was acutely responsive to religion and biblical scholarship, subjects which she referred to frequently in her poetry. She may not have walked humbly with her God, as the verse from Micah on her plaque required her to do, but notions of godliness absorbed her nonetheless.

21. AFTERWARDS

'Stupendous,
Most loving,
Ineffable poetry.'
From 'Rose and Creed', by Sheila Wingfield

In Sheila's archive is a manila folder filled with small scraps of paper on which she scribbled various notes and queries: 'Great painters show madness and deep, exact thought.' 'G. Gershwin's *Rhapsody in Blue* and *Porgy and Bess* – why is this oddly called a folk-opera and *Carmen* is not?' 'Habit = subconscious memory leading to survival.' 'Every national anthem is too long.' 'It was optimistic of Sir Thos Browne to hold that "there is a kind of Triumvirate in our Soul of Affection, Faith and Reason".' On one scrap, typewritten rather than scrawled, is this untitled poem:

> Her quill
> You may be sure,
> Wrote steadily, with good command
> And ease,
> Forceful,
> Unimportant words.

This wasn't her view of her own work. She knew that she was a good poet and that her words were forceful and important. Lack of recognition during her lifetime made her bitterly angry and while it probably wasn't true, as she claimed, that the 'poetry establishment' hated her, it certainly didn't give her the attention she deserved. Noting her expensive clothes, jewellery and her use of Claridge's as a home from home, it probably decided that she had little need of help. She was aware of this too but, unwisely, did nothing to dispel the impression of being 'an aristocratic dabbler', as an unkind obituarist put it. But there are signs that she is emerging from that all-enveloping obscurity which Anne Fogarty predicted to be her fate. Fogarty herself is one contemporary admirer; Alex Davis of University College, Cork, is another. His essay, '"Wilds to Alter, Forms to Build": The Writings of Sheila Wingfield', discusses at erudite and entertaining length the poet's 'tangential relationship with high modernism', a relationship which Sheila would probably have denied. She always insisted that since she was not allowed to meet with other poets, she never heard about any poetic movement until it had ended. She thought of herself as *sui generis,* without literary antecedents or influences. Recently, as well as coming to the attention of Deryn Rees-Jones, who included Sheila's work in *Modern Women Poets*, Sheila has also found a place in the best-selling, international poetry anthology, *Staying Alive*, subtitled 'real poems for unreal times', which includes two of her poems, 'Lazarus' and 'A Bird'.

Just as Sheila may find a new readership, the Big House is having something of a revival. Powerscourt, now run by the third generation of Slazengers to live there, is being energetically restored, the building work funded by various enterprises – a light-filled cafeteria and fashionable boutiques on the ground floor; a larger and more ambitious garden centre than the one Pat had opened in 1971. Its forty-four acres of gardens are open all year round and attract 250,000 visitors annually. There is a golf course and a beauty salon and Ireland's first Ritz-Carlton hotel is being built on the estate, as part of a very luxurious resort. Owners of other Irish historic houses have become equally entrepreneurial; they hold rock concerts in the grounds, install zoos and theme parks, rent out wings. But there have been many casualties; the last few years have seen the sale of the Farnham estate in Cavan, owned by the Maxwell family since the late 1600s; Carriglas Manor outside Longford, owned by the Lefroy family from the early nineteenth century and Lissadell House, in County Sligo, the home of the Gore-Booths, made famous in Yeats's poem 'In Memory of Eva Gore-Booth and Con Markiewicz'.

In 2002 the Department of the Environment, Heritage and Local Government, and the Irish Georgian Society commissioned historian Terence

Dooley, to write a report on the state of the Irish Big House. This was published as *A Future for Irish Historic Houses* and, although its findings were bleak – of the 1500 houses of national importance in 1900, only thirty remain – it suggested remedies, such as a heritage trust and tax concessions, to keep these precious buildings in good repair. As a result of this report, in September 2005 the Irish government announced the establishment of an Irish Heritage Trust, partly modelled on the British National Trust, to acquire and safeguard historic buildings and property. Owners of stately homes would be able to stay on in them, free of charge, but transfer ownership to the trust, which will take over the running costs and open the houses to the public. The government is to provide up to €5.5 million in funding to the first endowment scheme established by the new trust.

As a sign that the Big House should not be regarded as a celebration of landlordism, Taoiseach Bertie Ahern referred to the new measures in a speech to mark the opening of the third Annual Historic Houses of Ireland conference in Maynooth on 9 September 2005. Reflecting that the Big House had been ignored for too long, he went on to say, 'If we want to gain a fully rounded understanding of the past, it is critical that we not let these repositories of our social, cultural and architectural history slip from our grasp.' Had this conciliatory tone been taken forty years sooner, Pat Wingfield might not have ended his days in a modern bungalow. On a more optimistic note, Pat's daughter, Grania Langrishe, now widowed and in late middle-age, has achieved her ambition to become an artist; her vivid watercolour illustrations enliven Niall Mac Coitir's books, *Irish Trees: Myths, Legends and Folklore* (2004) and *Irish Wild Plants: Myths, Legends and Folklore* (2006).

I started to write this biography because I liked Sheila Wingfield's poetry so much; it was so crackly-fresh, taut and simple compared to the humid bathos of much of the poetry written by women in the twentieth century. I became fascinated by this neglected poet's skewed and strangely divided life, admired her beauty and the indomitable way she tried to shape her own circumstances in the face of parental disapproval and marital indifference. In our own times, when women writers receive every kind of encouragement, it is easy to forget earlier struggles. Edith Somerville, co-author with her cousin Violet Martin, of the Irish RM series, described her family's reaction to her writing: 'When not actually reviled, we were treated with much the same disapproving sufferance that is shown to an outside dog that sneaks into the house on a wet day.' That more or less describes Sheila's situation. To get what she wanted, in the face of such disapproval, Sheila made her family suffer but she was the one who suffered the most, for stubbornly fulfilling her childhood ambition to become a poet.

The biographer, Iris Origo, believed that, 'the only tribute that a biographer can pay to his [or her] subject [is] to tell (in so far as is possible) the truth about him [or her]'. When the subject of a biography has gone to great pains to conceal the truth, as Sheila did, trying to dig it up feels more like an exposé or an attempt to catch her out, to be one of those 'posthumous exploiters', whom Henry James complained about. The lies Sheila told reveal a truth of sorts; this woman, so determinedly deracinated that she denied her own ancestry, so involved in the false manoeuvres of trying to reconcile her two incompatible selves that she made herself ill, was tragically self-revealing. I hope very much that recent attention will result in her work being republished and that people will start reading her poems again, although perhaps this is a process that can't be hurried. W.H. Auden was once asked why the poet Stanley Kunitz did not have the following he deserved. He replied, 'It's strange, but give him time. A hundred years or so. He's a patient man.' And Robert Lowell, at the height of his own fame, wrote to the then less celebrated Elizabeth Bishop, 'Anyone who builds on rock as you do, can take her time – let the world come to you.' There is always time to discover a good poet.

A SELECTION OF SHEILA WINGFIELD'S POETRY

From *Poems* (1938)

Winter
The tree still bends over the lake,
And I try to recall our love,
Our love which had a thousand leaves.

A Bird
Unexplained
In the salt meadow
Lay the dead bird.
The wind
Was fluttering its wings.

Odysseus Dying
I think Odysseus, as he dies, forgets
Which was Calypso, which Penelope,
Only remembering the wind that sets
Off Mimas, and how endlessly
His eyes were stung with brine;
Argos a puppy, leaping happily;
And his old Father digging round a vine.

From *Beat Drum, Beat Heart* (1946)
[From **Part Four: Women at Peace**]

There's a small hill on the Bog of Allen
With jackdaws and beeches and a square house.
The maids are by the fire. They sew and speak
Of a cousin, or how to help the niece,
Or will Dolan sell, or of the boy
One of them went with (as she bites a thread),
Or else the time long back when they found
An empty can of tea and some sandwiches
Wrapped up in a *Freeman's Journal*, and left
By the ambush there must have been at the gates
(And the mistress in bed seeing on the wall
The flash of the fired barracks across the way);
And will her great-grandchildren, they wonder,
Take after their da?
      It's to be hoped they will,
Thinks their mother (keeper of all things
Who has watched her children sleep) who now watches them
With their father making a garden bonfire.
He's grinning and swearing under his breath
And tearing his coat and telling them how to help.
Screaming, happy in doing something,
And bringing the wrong sticks, they'll now and again
Take fright at the blaze, run away to her, then
Forget and dash back to add more. She looks
At their napes, at the back of their knees, and sighs:
How to guard them from danger, from fear,
For ever? The dogs go off to sniff and to hunt
On their own. Smoke tingles and eddies
Through sparks of laughter, gusts of seriousness
That are insubstantial and flickering
To anyone else – but to her, solid
As each farm building in the yard.

Leaf upon earth, and loam under the frame,
And pear, espaliered, nailed across a wall;

The chatter of small-territoried birds,
Or a staked plant that where it blooms will fall;
The fly crawling up a stem it hugs;
Beetles that drag their carapace, alone,
Intent, through thickest grass where groundbees drone;
A swan that dents her breast against an edge
Of lake, her feet now softly on the ooze
And now her bill nudging in roots of sedge –
These are my kin (she well might cry), their labours
Are my days and reasoning: as strong
And logical as schoolmen after long
Disorder, wreckage and dark anarchy.

We will now do the linen. The weight of it, lifted out of
    deep drawers
    And cool to the touch, and the warm smell when it's taken
    Out of the airing cupboard, give me a pride
That any woman has felt who's putting a room to rights,
    Scrubbing as if herself were being scrubbed,
    Scouring as if her soul were being scoured,
Straightening up and sorting as if in her own mind.
    (My helper, bending her neck, shows tendrils of hair
    That surely her friend, who has his bicycle propped
This instant against the ivied wall, admires. Let him wait.)

                        How good
To spice and flavour well; to walk the dim and white
    And dairy-smelling passages; to look
On harbours, as in Boston, when the fishermen are home
    (Their boats are *Evie II* and *Maria Soccorsa*
    With dories slung on the pilot-house roof, the snow
Filling them) – to be safe, and have enough for the fire.
    Or beside other quays where in markets, we women,
    Scarf-faced and red-fingered, must sell fish:
This is also good, the mist mingling with our breath
    In gossip and curses, to rid us of old shames
    And old mistakes that make us groan at night.

From *A Cloud Across the Sun* (1949)

Ireland

This is the country
That has no desolation, no empty feel
(The pagan kings are always there)
In ruined abbey, ruined farmhouse,
Slab of cromlech, or a wheel
Travelling a bog road
Through Calary's too quiet air.

Origins

I

Thinness of music far away –
Repeated thuds, a few high notes,
Are all one hears – how well this teases
Memory, angers the brain.
Towards me in the same way floats
A sense of forbears long ago
Distressing as that distant playing:
For it can never be made clear,
What did our predecessors fear?
How did they sleep? When did they smile?
Were they uneasy in their souls?

2

A wind blows along the quays.
Rigging slats. Hawsers creak.
Here they stumble: in big hands
Smaller hands that pinch and tweak;
Coming from the barest mountain
Or a quiet of flat lands
To cities smoking in the dusk,
To pestilence and grime that's both
On water and the merchant-desk:
These ancestors, these falling leaves
That as they rot make green my growth.

3

Before them – pedlar, diplomat,
Landlord, peasant – these talk low,
Whistle, curse, stamp their feet;
That one greasy as his hat,
This one laughing from conceit.
All mine. As for the women: some
Have a scent of melancholy sedge,
Or laurels in wet woods; others
Rock slowly on high balconies
Under a charring sun; and some
Are rags along a gutter's edge.

4

Could quick, varied contradiction
Of a mood or thought derive from difference
Of fancies they were racked with – could
It stem from their belief in arches
Made of angels' wings, from fret
Of learning, or from schemes sad
As rain falling from winter larches?
And some ghastly call of wit
Come from where there was a joke
Before a murder – now where flit
Jackdaws in the ivied tower?

5

Beyond such silting up, such tracts
Of time and back to paradisal
Leaves: this moist and sheltering sight
Of the great garden, dense, entire
With fruit all year, and flying lizards
Settling in the tree of life,
Wings folded; and the sweet thorn-apple
Sharpening minds into a knife –
This land which none need go from, past
The distant, guardian sword of fire
That wavers to the left and right.

6

However vast and ancient are these
Epochs, all of them seem mirrored
In my temper, which can feel
Walled in, or else defenceless, eager
And thrusting like armies, soft as sand,
Cast down like cities; never still
But moving on to a new land
Or climate, all in a few hours –
Contracted yet exact, as after
Rain the storm-filled sky lours
In the smallest rut. But if

7

There were an age yet earlier,
North of the dank Caucasian pass,
Before the everburning fields
And Tartarus the triple-moated
Town, and near the iron-throated
Mountain coughing brass and steel –
Then, as a woman, I have found
What we inherit in our blood,
From those bereaved by the first waste
And wailing for their menfolk drowned
In utter darkness of the flood.

Poisoned in Search of the Medicine of Immortality
When Hsüang Tsung, great emperor,
Giddy and ill, carried in a litter,
Saw the stars sway,

His conquests and his arguments
And powers, falling into fever with him,
Pulsed their lives away.

Bow to his shade. To be at rest
Is but a dog that sighs and settles: better
The unrelenting day.

On Looking Down a Street
My mind's disturbed as rooks in the air ...
May a thin-shouldered mountain hare
Or shy and meditative donkey,
Cat that gallops down an alley
And the squint-eyed, sandy dab,
Curlew, spider, vole and crab –
Creatures both severe and great
Or nimble as hens running under a gate –
Pray for me now. Lord, how I need
Their cleverness, their careful speed
Or power to be still, their sense,
Their pride and total innocence!
To keep from being fool or wretch
Till some hearse-horses trot this stretch.

From *A Kite's Dinner* (1954)

Venice Preserved
Under the tingling bongle-booming
Of St Mark's, the pigeon-whirring,
Death-black shade and seablown hopes,
Light must dance and ripple. Copes
Of gold speak to the sun out loud
As crocus-mitres pierce a crowd
Policed where choirboys formulate
With shy and swaying, shuffling gait,
A ceremony old as dreams.
O fond Evangelist: here gleams
His silvered, sleeping effigy
To dazzle hearts; then, dry and grey,
Skull and legbones under glass
Joggle at shoulder level, pass
Old men and Mickey Mouse balloons
While jew's-harps buzz and plainchant swoons
And postcard sellers, touts and pimps
Keep up their trade. A woman limps,

Pulls her black shawl, and with a tear,
Sees the slow walkers disappear,
Then puts thick fingers on her mouth
To kiss the whole warm, saintly South.

To lipping sounds of water, dark
As dissolution, we embark
Among these stones that weep in grandeur
For such hovels; for the slur
Of palaces whose bricks are cracked
From old decay or greed and racked
By ills; and for a poverty
That dreads a winter. Now, most gently,
We are shivering in moonlight
As if lovesick, while the night
Reveals each column, balustrade,
Dome and doorway. Unafraid
Of placards for some brand of gin
Where steamer-wash comes nosing in,
Or trash, or shabby songs: all merge,
Uplifted like a bridge's surge.
In her unbroken dignity
This trollop crumbles; painted, easy,
Filled with power to exploit
Prodigious charms and still adroit
In voice and beauty – she cajoles
Fine, votive answers from our souls.

From *The Leaves Darken* (1964)

Darkness

And what will mitigate my life's long fault,
   I beg you, if authority's black stuffs
   Should fail to reconcile me
   To the final blindfold?
   Cassock and mortar-board
   Are under the same burden,

Suffer the same problem, as ourselves;
While conscience comes at night and stings
The darkness: much as Carthage, ploughed under,
Was then sown with salt.
A conjuror's cloak; the Queen of Spades
With her poor migraine face: these
Are for innocence: it waits agog,
For flourishes of fireworks to exalt
A pitchblack sky. Later,
Incredible beliefs, the greatest things
Given to the soul, are only
Metaphors or hints
Taken from lovers when they meet
Bemused, in gardens,
Among mooncast shadows
Denser than a vault.
Let me predict my funeral weather
Biting at black coats,
With the new box – cave dark and cupboard thick –
Brought to a lurching halt
Near brambles and tipped headstones in the family
Burial ground, and flurryings
Of shocked and interrupted jackdaws ...
With so much still unlearned, ignored;
So many moments of compassion skimped
By me or lost; this private graveyard seems
An apt memorial, with its church a ruin,
And its quiet cracked
By the quick clatter of black wings
In crude assault.

When Moore Field Was All Grazed

When Moore field was all grazed
And Finnesburie ploughed,
People were fiery, clever, glum or crazed;
Hard knuckled; and proud
Liars; and well-phrased.

The Leaves Darken
If a child's tale were sung
To kings and the tired spearmen;
Or if Outer Isles, fog-blind,
Are found only by raven
Croaks; or a new housing scheme should geld
Some king-cup creek;
If Menelaus hung
His head in Egypt
After war was done,
While gnats, then flies, sipped
His blood by night and blistering sun
Until those bony temples held
Ideas that were quite brittle, hollow, weak;
As an old parrot tears a rind
From sugary belief –
So, juices of the year
Dry into blacker leaf
And darker fear.

From *Her Storms* (1977)

Brigid
Brigid, once
Protector of poets;

Patron of Kildare
Where nowadays foxhounds

Keep muzzles down to the scent
While bullocks fatten;

Worshipped by Romans
Under Severus in York;

Protector from domestic fires
In Ireland

And now its own saint;

Lady, I bow to your diversity.

Pitchforks

Pitchforks tossing the dead
Like mice in stable straw,
So people thought,
Had prongs that went through
Gullet and heart.

I know Hell is to feel
A mother's son,
The white-necked boy,
Grown and pointing those tines
To pierce my head
Then rip me apart.

View

At the sea's edge, near Bray
In County Wicklow,
From a lonely
Field for dumping rubbish,
Water and air seemed shining, pearly,
Still. No sound.
Gulls rode the gentlest swell
Of this small estuary.

Nearby in Rocky Valley
Among small concrete homes
Fenced round with wire,
One could smell
Bracken and a few sheep, and see
Both copper domes of Powerscourt
Rising over the haze, far off.
Domes and domesticity, entire

As stallions, but now
Burnt to the ground.

A Melancholy Love
Part elegant and partly slum,
Skies cleaned by rain,
Plum-blue hills for a background:
Dublin, of course.
The only city that has lodged
Sadly in my bones.

In a Dublin Museum
No clue
About the use or name
Of these few
Bronze Age things,
Rare
And in gold,
Too wide for finger-rings.
Till some old epic came
To light, which told
Of a king's
Daughter: how she slid them on to hold
The tail ends of her plaited hair.

From *Admissions* (1977)

Any Weekday in a Small Irish Town
A rusty, nagging morning.
By the pub's
Front door, now shut,
An ass-cart waits and waits.
This scrap of donkey
Wearing blinkers cracked, old,
Askew, blocking one eye,

Has also a string
Bridle pulled on crookedly
And tight enough to smother:
You can see where it rubs.

At dusk, cornerboys
So shy
And full of silent hates,
Get lanced by rain and cold.
They stand beside
The factory gates
Before the shift goes off,
Scowling at each other.
Girls hurry out
Together, giggling by.
And still the donkey waits.

Sparrow

Slim, chic and pale,
This young sparrow looks, pecks, looks.
His beak and my thumbnail
Are made of the same stuff,
Spin with the same atoms.
How can I understand,
While my finger turns a bookleaf,
That for him seeds and quick sips
Of water are enough?

The Oath

Hand to hand, foot to foot,
Knee to knee, breast to breast
In darkness: a masonic rite.
Would that all lovers
Kept their oath so well.

From *Cockatrice and Basilisk* (1983)

We Were Bright Beings

We were bright beings
Made of wave and plunging light.
In a surprise of seas we sauntered
Who now dry our scaly nets
Over the rocks.

The hot reminders
Of what's gone, the cold revulsion
From what's done:
O lucky wave. O lucky leaf
Where autumn woods must smoulder
Till put out by rain
And pigeons clip the empty air.

Hazards

Among the hazards that infect the world,
Tough Aeschylus, who'd fought
In Persian wars,
Died when an eagle – as we know –
Thought his head, shining-bald,
A stone. And dropped
That tortoise on it from a height.

Bitter for Sophocles
At ninety, when his son
Hauled him to court
To prove him both incapable and imbecile.
Father recited from his new,
Unplayed *Oedipus at Colónus*.
Suit dismissed.

Or take Euripides, guest
Of that cultivated man,
King Archelaus of Macedonia –

Ripped into pieces by a pack
Of hunting-dogs.
Eagle, son or savage hounds:
Which was the worst? I know.

A Frightened Creature

I

Clearly, I take delight
In any smattering
About poor, cold
Antigone;
Zeus as an infant, bawling
In his Cretan cave;
Teiresias; or crossroads ruled by Hecate
At midnight.
But, when these come into my home
Or I near theirs,
I know considerable fear.
Legends brimming with wonder
Pain us like a wound – more so than some big
Chronicle of actuality.

2

Out of a tome
Giving the stories, names leap free.
Characters, in force, have faces shining
From their grief; from exultation; fright
Or lack
Of it: such as Hippolytus, young prig,
Who dares
To manage without love.
Here I step back –
I made a blunder:
Blind Teiresias the seer,
This womaned-man, has cheeks so grave
And furrowed, they reflect
No light.

3

Each year
I'm more afraid. Is this the due seed of Age,
And Age's right?

No Instructions

To give quite freely or else hold,
To be amazed, or bold:

How can we judge? Connect
Our body's bias, dogma, sect?

Once, Dr Dee's high-polished coal
Played mirror. We have quasar or black hole

For marvel. Not a thing
Is understood. And, ripening,

We die the moment that we start to learn
Just what we are, just where to turn.

NOTES

(p.x) Elizabeth Dorothea Cole Bowen (1899–1973). Anglo-Irish novelist, memoirist and short story writer. Born in Dublin, spent much of her childhood in family home, Bowen's Court, in County Cork. Awarded CBE in 1948.

(p.x) Edith Somerville (1858–1949) and Violet Martin (1862–1915), who wrote under the name Martin Ross. Cousins, they collaborated on many books, set mainly in Ireland, where both women lived. Their most famous work, a collection of stories, *Some Experiences of an Irish RM*, was published in 1899.

(p.xi) Dr Kathleen Jessie Raine (1908–2003). Poet. Born in Ilford, Essex. Educated County High School, Ilford; Girton College, Cambridge. Awarded Queen's Gold Medal for Poetry, 1992.

(p.xv) Stevie (Florence Margaret) Smith (1902–1971). Poet and novelist. Born in Hull and brought up in Palmers Green, north London. Author of three novels but more widely recognized for her verse and spiky drawings which accompanied them. Her best known collection is *Not Waving but Drowning* (1957). Her *Collected Poems* appeared in 1975.

(p.xvi) George Sutherland Fraser (1915–1980). Journalist, editor and critic. Born in Glasgow. Educated at St Andrews University. Lecturer, University of Leicester 1959–1979. Associated with the Apocalyptic Movement in poetry.

(p.9) Information on the Westmorland and Cumberland Yeomanry from research by Colin Bardgett, Penrith, Cumbria.

(p.11) Cecil Sharpe (1859–1924). English folk music collector and editor. Transcribed 4977 tunes. His work influenced a school of English composers, including Vaughan Williams and Holst.

(p.17) Sir George Robey (1869–1954). Born George Edward Wade. Dubbed 'The Prime Minister of Mirth', he was the most famous comedian of his day.

(p.17) Albert Sammons (1886–1957). Critics called this fine violinist 'The English Kreisler'.

(p.19) At least two of these bequests are still in existence: the Mrs Claude Beddington English Literature Prize and the Mrs Claude Beddington Modern Languages Prize, each worth £100, are awarded annually by Oxford University.

(p.19) Ethel M. Dell (1881–1939). Born in London. Once-popular novelist of exotic escapism. Her most famous novel, *The Way of an Eagle*, was published in 1912.

(p.19) Ella Wheeler Wilcox (1850–1919). American poet born in Wisconsin. Wrote popular collections of slightly steamy, sentimental verse with titles such as *Poems of Passion*, as well as novels.

(p.39) In *Twilight of the Ascendancy*, Mark Bence-Jones writes, 'The total number of Irish country houses burnt between 1920 and 1923 was not more than about 200, and when the Troubles started there would have been at least 2000 country houses in Ireland.'

(p.41) Lady Diana Cooper née Manners: Viscountess Norwich (1892–1986). Literary hostess and muse. Married historian and diplomat Alfred Duff Cooper in 1919. She wrote three volumes of memoirs and the account of her visit to Powerscourt is in the first volume, *The Rainbow Comes and Goes* (Rupert Hart-Davis 1958).

(p.47) Seumas O'Sullivan (1879–1958). Poet and editor. Born in Dublin. Founded *The Dublin Magazine* in 1923 and edited it until he died. His *Collected Poems* was published in 1940.

(p.50) Lydia Lopokova: Lady Keynes (1892–1981). Wife of the economist John Maynard Keynes (1883–1946). Ethel Beddington's offensive letter to her is in Lady Keynes' archive at King's College, Cambridge.

(p.51) Francis Hackett (1883–1962); Signe Toksvig (1891–1983).

(p.55) Robert Nye. Poet, novelist and critic. After he reviewed Sheila's 1977 poetry collection, *Her Storms*, she bombarded him with letters. These are in his archive at Edinburgh University.

(p.55) Sir Alan Charles Laurence Whistler (1912–2000). Poet and glass engraver. His biography of his brother, Rex Whistler, *The Laughter and the Urn*, was published in 1985.

(p.59) Sylvia Plath (1932–1963). Poet and novelist. Born in Boston, Massachusetts. Married poet Ted Hughes in 1956. Her novel, *The Bell Jar*, was published in

1963; her first poetry collection, *The Colossus*, in 1960, followed by *Ariel*, 1965 and *Collected Poems*, 1981.

(p.61) William Monk Gibbon (1896–1987). Poet, memoirist, novelist, editor. Born in Dublin. Conor Cruise O'Brien's review of his book *The Masterpiece and the Man: Yeats as I Knew Him*, was published in *Writers and Politics Essays and Criticism* (Chatto & Windus 1965).

(p.62) The 'single poem of about 4000 lines', was *Beat Drum, Beat Heart*, published in 1946. The final version was 2000 lines.

(p.65) In *W.B. Yeats: A Life II The Arch-Poet 1915–1939*, R.F. Foster puts the matter more delicately, writing that 'WBY's affinity with Fascism (not National Socialism) was a matter of rhetorical style.'

(p.68) Elizabeth Bishop (1911–1979). Poet. Born in Worcester, Massachusetts. Her *Complete Poems 1927–1979* appeared in 1983, the same year as Sheila Wingfield's *Collected Poems 1938–1983*.

(p.69) The Macspaunday poets: C. Day-Lewis; W.H. Auden; Louis MacNeice; Stephen Spender.

(p.79) Elizabeth Smith (1797–1885), better known as Elizabeth Grant (her maiden name), of Rothiemurchus in Speyside, Scotland. Her *Memoirs of a Highland Lady* was published in 1898.

(p.86) Theodora Fitzgibbon (1916–1991). Born in London of Irish parents. Novelist, author of several cookbooks, weekly cookery columnist for *The Irish Times*. Wrote a memoir, *Love Lies A Loss* (Century 1985).

(p.86) Joseph Maunsell Hone (1882–1959). Born in Killiney, Dublin. Novelist, publisher, biographer of Yeats, *W.B. Yeats 1865–1939* (Macmillan 1942). President of Irish Academy of Letters, 1957.

(p.89) Molly Keane (1904–1996). Novelist. Born Mary Nesta Skrine in County Kildare. Her mother was Moira O'Neill, poet and recluse, author of *Songs of the Glens of Antrim*.

(p.92) Iris Origo (1902–1988). Historian and biographer. Married Marchese Antonio Origo in 1924. Her autobiography, *Images and Shadows*, was published in 1970.

(p.94) Beatrice Glenavy RHA, née Elvery (1883–1968). Designer and painter. Born in Dublin. Published a memoir, *Today We Will Only Gossip*, in 1964.

(p.101) Dr A.L. (Leslie) Rowse (1903–1997). Historian, autobiographer, biographer, poet and diarist. Born in Tregonissey, Cornwall.

(p.104) Sir Alfred Chester Beatty (1875–1968). Became a naturalised British citizen in 1933 but later settled in Ireland and became Ireland's first honorary citizen in 1957. His grandparents were Irish.

(p.105) The Folklore Society, founded in 1878, was one of the first organizations in the world devoted to the study of traditional culture. Dr Margaret Murray was its president 1953–1955. Born and brought up in India, she became Assistant Professor of Egyptology at University College, London in 1924. She wrote extensively on Egyptology and eastern Mediterranean archaeology, but became better known as an authority on fertility rites and witchcraft because of her books *The Witch-Cult in Western Europe* (1921), *The God of Witches* (1933) and *The Divine King in England* (1954). Her autobiography, *My First Hundred Years*, was published in 1963.

(p.108) Francis Quarles (1592–1644). Born near Romford, Essex. Educated Christ's College, Cambridge and Lincoln's Inn. *Emblèmes*, a book of short devotional poems, was published in 1635.

(p.112) The Poetry Book Society founded 1953. T.S. Eliot was a founder member. The society administers the T.S. Eliot Prize.

(p.116) Elizabeth Jennings (1926–2001). Poet. Born in Lincolnshire, educated at St Anne's College, Oxford. As well as several poetry collections, she published two volumes of prose.

(p.117) Sidney Arthur Kilworth Keyes (1922–1943). Poet. Born in Dartford, son of an army officer. Educated Tonbridge School and Oxford. His first poetry collection, *The Iron Laurel*, was published in 1942, the year he joined the army. *The Cruel Solstice* was published in 1943, after he went missing, presumed dead, in Tunisia. He was awarded the Hawthornden Prize posthumously, in 1945, for *Collected Poems*.

(p.117) *The Listener*: BBC weekly magazine (1929–1991). J.R. Ackerley (1896–1967), autobiographer and novelist, was the magazine's literary editor, 1935–1959.

(p.117) Hilary Corke (1921–2001). Poet, composer and critic. He didn't always defend Sheila's poetry. In 'The Bad Old Style: From Toreador to Sacred Cow', an article published in *Encounter* magazine in 1955, he wrote of her work, 'I feel (quite erroneously I dare say) that much of her verse has been composed in women's college libraries.' In the margin of the copy of this article pasted in her cuttings book, Sheila remarked, 'SW never near such a place!'

(p.118) Sir Herbert John Clifford Grierson (1866–1960). Born in Lerwick, Shetland. First Professor of English Literature at Aberdeen University, 1894–1915. Professor of Rhetoric and English Literature at Edinburgh University, 1915–1935. His biography of Sir Walter Scott was published in 1938.

(p.119) Cecil Day-Lewis (1904–1972). Poet. Wrote as C. Day-Lewis. Born in Ireland, son of a Church of Ireland minister. Educated at Sherborne and Wadham College, Oxford. A member of the Communist Party in his youth, he became part of the establishment as he grew older, a frequent broadcaster and committee man. Professor of Poetry at Oxford 1951–1956. Poet Laureate 1968.

(p.122) Sybil Connolly (1921–1998). Internationally recognized Dublin fashion designer, especially celebrated for her use of pleated Irish linen. She also designed decorative textiles and interiors.

(p.126) Donagh MacDonagh (1912–1968). Poet and dramatist. Son of Thomas MacDonagh, one of the leaders of the 1916 Easter Rising.

(p.126) (Esmé Stuart) Lennox Robinson (1886–1958). Dramatist and author. Manager and then director (1923–1958) of the Abbey Theatre, Dublin.

(p.129) Brian O'Nolan (1911–1966). Writer and civil servant. Born in Strabane in County Tyrone. Educated University College, Dublin. As Myles na gCopaleen, wrote the 'Cruiskeen Lawn' column for *The Irish Times*, 1947–1966. As Flann O'Brien, author of four novels, including *At Swim-Two-Birds* (1939).

(p.130) Nigel Nicolson MBE (1917–2004). Author, biographer. Director of Weidenfeld & Nicolson 1946–1992. Conservative MP for Bournemouth and Christchurch, 1952–1959. He inherited, and lived at, Sissinghurst Castle.

(p.151) Sir Sacheverell Sitwell (1897–1988). Poet and writer on architecture, art, literature and travel. Born in Wiltshire. Author of the monumental *British Architects and Craftsmen* (1945). Younger brother of Oswald and Edith.

(p.151) Rebecca West, pen name of Cicily Fairfield (1892–1983). Born in London. Novelist, critic, essayist, reporter. Awarded French Legion of Honour 1957. Awarded a DBE 1959.

(p.151) Cecil Woodham-Smith (1896–1976). Author and biographer. Born in Tenby, Wales. Her biographies combined high scholarship with readability, for example *Florence Nightingale* (1950). *The Reason Why* (1953) is a brilliant analysis of the Charge of the Light Brigade; *The Great Hunger 1845–1849* (1962), a moving account of the Irish Famine. Awarded a CBE 1977.

(p.151) International PEN is the only worldwide association of writers. Founded in London in 1921 by Mrs C.A. Dawson Scott. Its first president was John Galsworthy.

(p.158) Terence de Vere White (1912–1994). Born in Dublin. Author and literary editor of *The Irish Times*, 1961–1977. During his early legal career, he had once been instructed by a Mr O'Toole, whose ancestors had owned Powerscourt in very distant days, to take proceedings to evict Lord Powerscourt from the demesne, as he was an interloper whose ancestors had only owned the estate since the reign of Elizabeth I. The instruction seems to have been ignored.

(p.166) Liam Miller (1923–1987). Founded the Dolmen Press, Dublin 1951–1987 with his wife, Josephine.

(p.171) *Temenos* (the word means the sacred area around a temple) was in Kathleen Raine's words, 'a review devoted to the arts of the imagination'. Founded in 1981, it ran for thirteen issues. Raine's co-founders were Phillip Sherrard and Brian Keeble.

(p.172) J.M.W. Turner (1775–1851). English painter. First went to Switzerland in 1802 and from 1841, visited the country three times in three years. The dramatic scenery and weather effects of the Alps gave new meaning to his concept of the sublime.

(p.173) Gavin Maxwell (1914–1969). Scottish writer, traveller and conservationist. Educated Stowe and Hertford College, Oxford.

(p.178) Sheila's letters to Guy began in 1980 and continued for several years.

(p.179) Five hundred years after the Inquisition, Spain's bishops are trying to get Queen Isabella I of Castile, despite her obsession with religious and racial purity, beatified as a step towards canonization. (Report in *The Guardian* 4/3/2002.)

(p.187) Peter Levi (1931–2000). Poet, translator, classical scholar, travel writer, archaeologist. Born in Middlesex. Jesuit priest from 1964 until 1977, when he resigned from the priesthood. Professor of Poetry at Oxford 1984–2000.

(p.188) Sheila Wingfield's note to 'Origins' in *Collected Poems*:

> 'Trying to discover what origins I might have had on both sides of the family who were roughly contemporary in the sixteenth or seventeenth centuries, I came up with the following: (a) "landlord": a Cornishman, Stephen Braddon of Treworgey St Gennys, MP for Bossiney 1558–1565; (b) "peasant": an Irish cattle-raider successful enough to build himself a small and now demolished castle called Bally Ard in County Offaly in the centre of Ireland; (c) "diplomat": a Financial Governer and Adviser to Ferdinand and Isabel of Spain, and their lifelong friend; (d) "pedlar": a Jewish pedlar in the Alsatian town of Colmar (then French).'

SOURCES AND SELECT
BIBLIOGRAPHY

ARCHIVAL SOURCES
Lady Ottoline Morrell Papers, Harry Ransom Humanities Research Center at
the University of Texas at Austin.
A.L. Rowse Papers, University of Exeter.
Rebecca West Papers, McFarlin Library at the University of Tulsa.
Sheila Wingfield Papers, the National Library of Ireland.
W.B. Yeats Letters, Oxford University Press.
All newspaper comments were sourced at the British Library's Newspaper
Library, London.

BOOKS BY SHEILA WINGFIELD
Poetry: *Poems* (1938); *Beat Drum, Beat Heart* (1946); *A Cloud Across the Sun*
(1949); *A Kite's Dinner: Poems 1938–54* (1954); *The Leaves Darken* (1964); *Her
Storms* (1977); *Admission* (1977); *Collected Poems 1938–1983* (1983).
Prose: *Real People* (1952); *Sun Too Fast* (1974) as Sheila Powerscourt; *Ladder to
the Loft* (1987).

SELECTED SECONDARY SOURCES
Astley, Neil (ed.), *Staying Alive* (Northumberland 2002).
Barber, Michael, *Antony Powell: A Life* (London 2004).
Beddington, Claude, *We Sailed from Brixham* (London 1938).
Beddington, Mrs Claude, *All That I Have Met* (London 1929).
Bence-Jones, Mark, *A Guide to Irish Country Houses* (London 1978).
—*Twilight of the Ascendancy* (London 1987).
Betjeman, John and Geoffrey Taylor (eds), *English Love Poems* (London 1957).
Blackwood, Caroline, *In the Pink* (London 1987).
Bowen, Elizabeth, *Pictures and Conversations* (London 1974).

Bunbury, Turtle, *The Landed Gentry & Aristocracy of Co. Wicklow* (Dublin 2005).

Cooper, Diana, *The Rainbow Comes and Goes* (London 1958).

Davenport-Hines, Richard, *A Night at the Majestic* (London 2006).

Davis, Alex, ' "Wilds to Alter, Forms to Build": the writings of Sheila Wingfield' in *Irish University Review*, vol. 31 no. 2 (Dublin 2001).

Dinnage, Rosemary, *Alone! Alone!* (New York 2004).

Fallon, Brian, *An Age of Innocence: Irish Culture 1930–1960* (Dublin 1998).

Field Day Anthology of Irish Writing, vol. V (Cork 2002).

Findlater, Alex, *Findlaters* (Dublin 2001).

Fingall, Elizabeth, Countess of, *Seventy Years Young* (London 1937).

Flanagan, Thomas, *There You Are* (New York 2004).

Fogarty, Anne, 'Outside the mainstream: Irish women poets of the 1930s' in *Suitar na n-Aingeal*, no. 17, Spring 1999.

Foster, R.F., *The Irish Story* (London 2001).

—*W.B. Yeats: A Life II The Arch-Poet 1915–1939* (Oxford 2003).

Franzen, Jonathan, *How to be Alone* (New York 1995).

Fraser, Antonia (ed.), *The Pleasure of Reading* (London 1992).

Glenavy, Beatrice, *Today We Will Only Gossip* (London 1964).

Glendinning, Victoria, *Elizabeth Bowen: Portrait of a Writer* (London 1977).

—*The Life of Vita Sackville-West* (London 1983).

—*Rebecca West: A Life* (London 1987).

Grant, Elizabeth of Rothiemurchus, Patricia Pelly & Andrew Tod (eds), *The Highland Lady in Ireland* (Edinburgh 1991).

Hillier, Bevis, *John Betjeman: New Fame, New Love* (London 2002).

Holroyd, Michael, *Mosaic* (London 2004).

Keogh, Dermot, *Jews in Twentieth-Century Ireland* (Cork 1998).

Lamb, Richard, *War in Italy 1943–1945* (London 1993).

Larkin, Philip, *Required Writing* (London 1983).

Lee, Hermione, *Reading in Bed* (Oxford 1999).

Lewis, Gifford, *Somerville and Ross: The World of the Irish RM* (London 1985).

McBreen, Joan (ed.), *The White Page/An Bhileog Bhán: Twentieth-Century Irish Women Poets* (Clare 1999).

McConville, Michael, *Ascendancy to Oblivion* (London 1986).

McCoole, Sinead, *Hazel: A Life of Lady Lavery 1880–1935* (Dublin 1996).

McCormack, W.J., *Blood Kindred: W.B. Yeats, The Life, the Death, the Politics* (London 2005).

Murphy, Richard, *The Kick* (London 2002).

Nichol, John and Tony Rennell, *The Last Escape: The Untold Story of Allied Prisoners of War in Germany 1944–45* (London 2000).

O'Brien, Jacqueline and Desmond Guinness (eds), *Great Irish Houses and Castles* (London 1992).

O'Brien, Marie Cruise, *The Same Age as the State* (Dublin 2003).

Oates, Caroline and Juliette Wood (eds), *A Coven of Scholars: Margaret Murray and her Working Methods* (London 1998).

Ollard, Richard (ed.), *The Diaries of A.L. Rowse* (London 2003).

Origo, Iris, *Images and Shadows* (London 1970).

Packenham, Valerie, *The Big House in Ireland* (London 2000).

Pihl, Lis (ed.), *Signe Toksvig's Irish Diaries 1926–1937* (Dublin 1994).

Powell, Anthony, *A Dance to the Music of Time* (1951–1975).

Rees-Jones, Dery (ed.), *Modern Women Poets* (Northumberland 2005).

Reynolds, Lorna, '*The Last September*: Elizabeth Bowen's Paradise Lost', in *The Big House in Anglo-Irish Literature* (Dublin 1992).

Rivlin, Ray, *Shalom Ireland: A Social History of the Jews in Ireland* (Dublin 2003).

Seymour, Miranda, *Ottoline Morrell: Life on a Grand Scale* (London 1992).

Solomons, Bethel, *One Doctor in His Time* (London 1956).

Tóibín, Colm, *Lady Gregory's Toothbrush* (Dublin 2002).

Walshe, Eibhear (ed.), *Elizabeth Bowen Remembered: The Farahy Addresses* (Dublin 1998).

Wharton, Edith, *A Backward Glance* (New York 1934).

Wistrich, Robert S., *Anti-Semitism: The Longest Hatred* (London 1991).

Woolf, Virgina, *A Room of One's Own* (London 1929).

Wyndham, Violet, *The Sphinx and Her Circle* (London 1963).

Yeats, W.B., *Letters on Poetry to Dorothy Wellesley* (Oxford 1940).

INDEX

Abdulla & Co., 11, 181
Ackerley, J.R., 119, 130
Act of Union (1801), 41
Æ (George W. Russell), 38
Anglo-Irish, *see* Ascendancy
Anglo-Irish Treaty, 37
anthologies, 93, 119, 126–8, 176; of Irish
    literature, 126
anti-Semitism, *see* Jewishness
Apocalypse Movement, 92, 127
Armchair Science, 25
Armstrong, Isobel, 49–50, 162–4, 168, 184
army careers, 5–6, 69–76; 8th Hussars,
    36, 71; Irish Guards, 36, 41, 111
Ascendancy, 33–4, 35, 43, 65, 81, 103,
    120; 'Descendancy', 36–8, 81; *see also*
    Big House
Auden, W.H., 61, 203
Austin, Alfred, 8

Balfour, Michael, 152–3
Ballycumber post office, Co. Offaly, 80
Barbados, 149
Beatty, Sir Chester (CB), 104–5,
    111–12, 128, 140, 146, 157, 191;
    portrait, 195
Beddington, Alfred H. né Moses
    (Claude's father), 5, 10
Beddington, Bel (Claude's mother), 14,
    179
Beddington, Claude (1868–1940, Sheila's

father), 3–6, 16, 49; and Africa, 3, 5–6,
    45, 49; as father, 12–13, 14–15, 30, 104;
    eccentricities, 25; in First World War,
    13–14, 104; in Ireland, 13, 16, 33, 80;
    in Second World War, 69, 70–2; in
    Sun Too Fast, 27, 157; *We Sailed from
    Brixham*, 49, 109; will, 72
Beddington, (Frances) Ethel née Mulock
    (1879–1963, Sheila's mother), 4, 6–9;
    All That I Have Met, 3, 50, 102;
    omissions from, 8, 17, 21; appearance,
    9, 11, 12; character, 6, 125, 140;
    credibility of, 12, 17; cutting postcards,
    21–3, 47–8; country pursuits, 27–8, 29;
    does not attend sons' funerals, 21, 48;
    eccentricities, 157; as hostess, 14, 17;
    collection of Famous Persons, 11,
    50–1, 124–5, 140; as mother, 4, 12–14,
    20, 90; in *Sun Too Fast*, 11–12, 20, 23,
    153, 157; will, 19, 140
Beddington, Guy (1901–25, Sheila's
    brother), 11, 13, 16–17, 19–22, 91;
    medical treatment, 20–21
Beddington, Guy (Sheila's godson), 173
Beddington, Herbert (Claude's brother),
    10, 33
Beddington, Niall (1913–35, Sheila's
    brother), 12, 43, 48
Beddington, Zillah née Simon, 14–15
Beddington family, 4–5, 11, 13, 43, 44,
    178, 179–80

Beddington homes, Arkwright Lodge, London, 22; Ballycurrin House, Co. Galway, 16, 33; Bellair, *see* Wingfield homes; 8 Cornwall Terrace, London, 10, 14; 3; Grosvenor Square, London; 48 Grosvenor Square, London, 21, 125; 33; Grosvenor St, London, 23, 47, 158; Kirtling Towers, Newmarket, 5, 11; Milford-on-Sea, 11; Ower House, Co. Galway, 13; 26 Seymour St, London, 3, 11, 12–13, 50; Villa Yolanda, Ospedaletti, 20, 44, 98

Behan, Brendan, 33

Bell, The, 78

Benghazi, 74

Bermuda, 69–73, 77, 139, 146–7, 155, 181, 186

Betjeman, John, 78, 95, 101–2, 116, 144

Big House, 33, 34, 36, 89, 91, 108, 123, 135; burnings, 36, 37; as source of pride and embarrassment, 123–4, 201–2

Bishop, Elizabeth, 68, 203

Bloomsbury set, 53–5

boats, *Cachelot/Orca*, 48–9, 71–2, 109; *Odile II*, 48; *Samaria, The*, 70

Boer War, 5–6, 10

Bog of Allen, 6–7, 10–11, 77, 139, 206

bookishness, 56; disapproved of, 3–4, 11, 26, 150

Boot, Rosie (Lady Headfort), 33

Bord Fáilte, 124

Bowen, Elizabeth, 53, 116, 124; Bowen's Court, 135, 177; *Seven Winters*, 102; 'The Big House' quoted, 39, 41, 66

Boy Scouts, 45, 81, 88

Boyle, Ina, 145

Brabazon, J.T.C. (Ivon) Moore, 24–5, 29, 72, 74–5, 92, 195; as Lord Brabazon of Tara, 76–7, 142–3, 157

Braddon, Mary Elizabeth, 8, 50

Bray, Co. Wicklow, 85, 161

British Library, recording of Sheila, 137

broadcasts, 30, 65, 128, 158

Calder, John, 168

Cameron, Dr A.J., 57, 58

Cameroons, 49

cars and driving, 97, 145, 146, 162

Cassels, Richard, 39

cattle-breeding, 101, 108, 113, 119, 131–2, 137

Cawley, Cynthia, 81–2, 157, 159

CB, *see* Beatty, Sir Chester

Censorship of Publications Act, 51

Church of Ireland, 41

Civil War, Irish, 16, 33, 38, 86, 133

Clara, Co. Offaly, 199

Clarke, Austin, 65, 85

Clifton College, Bristol, 5

Clodd, Alan, 184–5

Cohen, Dennis, 95, 108, 130, 143, 153

Colmar, Alsace, 5, 178

Connolly, Cyril, 78, 177

Connolly, Sybil, 122

controlling people, 92, 145, 159, 162–3, 189–90, 195; Sheila's father 25, 30, 50

Corke, Hilary, 117–19

Cornally, Joe, 80

Cosgrave, W.T., 37, 41, 84

Costello, John, 87

Country Life, 72, 169

Craik, Mrs, *see* Mulock, Dinah

Cresset Press, The, 54, 56, 61, 85, 93, 95, 153; refuses her poems, 130

Cumann na mBan, 111

Cumann na nGaedheal, 111

Cygnet Press, 194–6

Cyprus, 49

Daily Mail, 37

Davie, Donald, 117, 127

d'Avigdor Goldsmid, Harry and Rosie, 83–4, 104, 131, 143, 147–9, 168, 169, 189

d'Avigdor Goldsmid family, 28, 46

Davis, Alex, 67, 85–6, 201

Day-Lewis, Cecil, 119, 150

De la Poer family, 39, 82

de Valera, Eamon, 37–8, 44, 51, 78, 87, 157

death duties, 84, 123

de la Mare, Walter, 62, 65, 67

Dell, Ethel M., 19

Desart Court, Co. Kilkenny, 84

Dickinson, Patrick, 116, 119
Dolder Grand Hotel, Zurich, 186, 190
Dolmen Press, 166, 168, 183
Doolittle, Hilda, 188
duality, 46, 85–6; ancestry, 32, 180;
    Anglo-Irish, 32–3, 79, 177; *see also*
    outsiders
Dublin, 40, 42; Archbishop of, 80, 120;
    Bailey pub, 120; Dublin Arts Club, 52;
    Dublin Horse Show, 33, 88, 103, 112,
    134; Fitzwilliam Square, 47; Gate
    Theatre, 47; Kildare Street Club, 43,
    65, 134; Merrion Square nursing
    home, 114; Rotunda Hospital, 47; St
    Vincent's Hospital, 197–8; Shelbourne
    Hotel, 154, 166; Switzers, 114; theatre,
    7, 47, 128; Viceregal Lodge, 33
Dublin Magazine, 47, 52, 117
Dunne, J.W., 25
Dunsany, Lord, *see* Plunkett, Edward
Durrow Abbey, Co. Offaly, 131, 134

Eliot, T.S., 54, 108, 112–13, 128, 147;
    'Burbank with a Baedeker: Bleistein
    with a Cigar', 31; his widow, Valerie,
    173, 176
Enitharmon Press, 184, 187
Enniskerry, Co. Wicklow, 35, 87, 112;
    church, 48, 154
escape, 107–8, 113–14, 150; for Ethel,
    10–11; for Grania, 89–90; for Pat, 75–6
Eton College, 36
Eucharistic Congress, 38
European tour, 97–8
Evening Herald, 43

Farrar, Straus & Giroux, New York, 182
Felix Hotel, Suffolk, 59–60
Ferguson, Lady Sarah, 122, 193
Fettes College, Edinburgh, 36
Fianna Fáil, 37–8
FitzGerald, Desmond, Knight of Glin,
    160, 182, 190
Fitzgibbon, Theodora, 86
Florence (dressmaker), 23–4
Fogarty, Anne, 68, 143, 201
folklore, 105

Folklore, 129
Foster, R.F., 36, 39, 102
Foyle, Christina, 170–1
France, 40, 97; Sheila's finishing school
    19, 20
Franzen, Jonathan, 4
Fraser, G.S. (George), 100, 102, 119, 125,
    127–8; his preface, 115, 168–9, 166,
    169, 185; and Paddy, 127, 162
funerals, 80–1, 140, 153–4, 198–9; not
    attended, 21, 28, 48, 125, 186; poems,
    117–19, 129, 138

Gaelic League, 84
Garnstone Press, 152, 155
Gathorne-Hardy, Robert, 56
Gayfield Press, 'Representative Irish
    Poets', 67
Germany, 21, 65, 75–6
Gibb, Jocelyn (Jock), 152–3
Gibbon, Monk, 61, 94–5, 144
Girl Guides, Irish, 44, 45, 88, 115; Chief
    Commissioner, 45, 84, 106, 111, 129
Glenavy, Beatrice, 94
Glendye, Kincardineshire, 29
Gogan, Liam, 92–3
Gogarty, Oliver St John, 61, 66
Goodman, Julian, 57
Goodman, Philip, 56
governesses and nannies, 4, 7, 12, 13, 17,
    73, 89, 147
government of Ireland, 37, 84–5
Grand Tour, 39, 40
Greece, 99, 106, 109–10, 193
Gregory, Augusta, Lady, 50
Gwynn SJ, Fr Aubrey, 108

Hackett, Francis, 51–3, 59, 67
Harvard College Library, recording of
    Sheila, 137
Hayward, John, 54, 56, 89, 92, 95, 101,
    105, 108–9, 122, 131, 141, 143, 144,
    146; and *A Kite's Dinner*, 108, 112–13;
    champions Sheila's work, 61, 65, 108,
    128, 130; 'Saul Henchman', 109
Headfort, 4th Marquess of (G.T.
    Taylour), 33, 75

Heaney, Seamus, 186
Hebrides, 48
Hetherington, Peter, 139, 142–3, 145,
    146, 149–50, 154, 168, 175, 187, 189,
    199; given Sheila's burial instructions,
    160; and *Ladder to the Loft*, 195–7
Hill & Wang, New York, 182–5, 196
Holbrook Hall, 74, 77, 78
homosexuality, 99, 109, 128, 173
Hone, Joseph, 51, 86–7, 108; *The Moores
    of Moore Hall*, 124
Horizon, 78
horses, 10–11, 28, 34, 38, 129, 145; Old
    Times, 28; Zodiac, 145–6; *see also*
    Dublin
Hudson, Stephen (Sydney Schiff), 9
hunting, 4–5, 32, 42, 129; Claude and
    Ethel, 9; Ethel, 27–9; Grania, 89;
    Sheila, 25, 27, 29, 31, 77, 100;
    Wendy, 134

Illustrated London News, 72
Irish Free State, 9, 16, 36, 41, 87, 133
Irish Grandma/Grandpa, *see* Mulock,
    Mrs Frank/Frank Berry
Irish Guards, 36, 41, 42, 111
Irish Heritage Trust, 202
Irish Literary Revival, 7, 50
Irish Times, The, 38, 74, 158; quoted
    36–7, 69, 82, 83, 85, 133, 160
Italy, 97–8, 138

Japan, 131, 148
Jenkins, Valerie, 158–9
Jennings, Elizabeth, 116, 127
Jerusalem, 42, 43–4, 85, 119
Jewishness, 4–5, 6, 84; anti-Semitism, 6,
    31, 64–5, 84–5, 99; denied, 178–81; in
    high society, 28, 31; philosemitism, 51;
    'Rosie Manash', 31; Zion Schools, 111
Joyce, James, 9, 59

Kallasagaram, Namo, 30, 48, 72
Kavanagh, Patrick, 38, 52, 78
Kennelly, Brendan, 169
Killadreenan, Co. Wicklow, 51, 52
Kilnegarenagh, *see* Liss church

King, Francis, 101, 106, 108, 109–10,
    111, 115, 119, 126–7, 181
Knittel, Robert, 181
Kunitz, Stanley, 203

Land Act (1923), 16, 36
Land Commission, 16, 36
Langrishe, Grania, see Wingfield,
    Grania
Langrishe, Hercules (Heck), 111–12,
    137, 147, 160, 187, 198; he succeeds to
    baronetcy, 159; marriage to Grania
    Wingfield, 119–22, 136–7, 154; their
    children, 137, 159; Atalanta (Atty),
    172, 180, 184, 186
Langrishe, Miranda, 159, 164–5, 191,
    197; visited by Sheila, 137, 147, 150
Larkin, Philip, 127–8
Lavery, Sir John, 42; and Lady Hazel, 9,
    44; portrait of Sheila, 42, 191
Lehmann, John, 54, 119, 129
Leverson, Ada, 8, 15
Levi, Peter, 187–8, 196
Libyan Arab Force, 73
Liss church, Co. Offaly, 10, 160, 199
Listener, The, 126, 130; review and
    letters, 117–19
Liverpool Royal Infirmary, 122–3
Locarno, Switzerland, 139, 142, 146,
    157, 181, 186–7, 201
London, 24; Café de Paris, 24; Café
    Royal, 176; Carlyle Mansions, 108;
    Claridge's Hotel, 23, 148–9, 158, 159,
    162, 164, 167, 172–3, 201; Empire
    Nursing Home, Vincent Square, 59;
    10 Gower Street, 54–6; Middlesex
    Hospital, 142–3;
London Magazine, 54, 129
Lopokova, Lydia, 50–1

McCarthy, Desmond, 53, 61, 65
MacDonald, J. Ramsay, 38
MacEntee, Sean, 64
McNaughton, Sarah, 50
MacNeice, Louis, 35
Macspaunday poets, 69,
Manners, Lady Diana, 41, 42

Marconi, Guglielmo, 22
Maxwell, Gavin, 173
MI9, 74
Middlesex Hospital, 142–3
Miller, Liam, 166, 168, 172
modernism, 9, 187, 201
money, 84, 96–7, 195
Monte Carlo, 128
Moore, George, 44; *Hail and Farewell*,
    140–1
Morrell, Lady Ottoline, 53–7, 58, 61,
    151, 170, 177; correspondence with
    Sheila, 46, 54, 59–60, 195; Visitors'
    Book, 56
Moses family, *see* Beddington
Mulock, Dinah (Mrs Craik), 7–8, 22, 50
Mulock, Enid, *see* Nutting, Sir Harold
    and Lady Enid
Mulock, Ethel, *see* Beddington,
    (Frances) Ethel
Mulock, Frank Berry (Irish Grandpa),
    7, 10, 77, 79
Mulock, Mrs Frank (Irish Grandma), 7,
    10, 13, 47–8, 79–80; as widow, 67, 72, 77
Mulock family, 7–8, 178–9, 194
Murphy, Richard, 109–10, 128
Murray, Margaret, 105, 129, 138

National Library of Ireland, 195–6
Nazism, 65, 70, 179–80
New Statesman, 124, 126
Newmarket, Suffolk, 11, 28
Nicolson, Harold, 53, 99–100, 105,
    124–5; quoted 31, 96
Nicolson, Nigel, 130
Northern Ireland, 37
Nutting, Anthony, 21, 125
Nutting, Edward, 77
Nutting, Sir Harold and Lady Enid
    née Mulock, 32, 77, 136
Nutting, John, 77
Nutting, Sir John, 21, 125, 140
Nye, Robert, 169, 182, 187; letters
    from Sheila, 55–6, 101, 126–7, 138,
    169–72, 184

O'Brien, Conor Cruise, 95

O'Connor, Frank, 51, 61, 78
O'Faolain, Sean, 51, 78
O'Grady, Standish, 34
O'Nolan, Brian (Flann O'Brien), 129
O'Sullivan, Seumas (J.S. Starkey), 47,
    52; and Sheila's first publication, 61
objectivism, 18, 143
outsiders, 9, 15, 18, 177; bookish, 202;
    Jewish, 4–5, 6; untypical female
    writers, 100, 102, 151, 169

Packenham Hall, Co. Westmeath, 101
Palestine police force, 37, 42
parsimony and penny-pinching, 4, 96,
    122, 124
Parsons, Geoffrey, 85
Phi, 175, 176, 181, 183
photographs, 49, 190, 195; on book
    covers, 113, 144, 159, 186; of Sheila,
    12, 46, 49, 159
Pike, Caroline 'Sam' (Pat's companion),
    154
Plath, Sylvia 59, 68
Poetry Book Society Choice, 112–13,
    116, 170
poetry and the public, 116–17
Poetry Review, 65, 94, 185
Poetry Society, 113, 128, 129, 176
Pound, Ezra, 68
Powell, Anthony, 109; *A Dance to the
    Music of Time*, 31, 148
Powerscourt, Co. Wicklow, 35, 37, 41,
    79; and Sheila, 67, 81–2, 104, 133;
    burnt down, 160–1, 182; film set, 78,
    112; gardens, 39–40, 41, 88; heating,
    absence of, 39; history, 38–40; open to
    the public, 124, 160, 197, 201; Pat's
    funeral, 154; Pat's ventures, 123–4, 131;
    refurbishment, 81–4; sale of contents,
    81–3, 190–1; sale of house, 38, 84,
    133–4; waterfall, 40, 131, 133, 157
Powerscourt viscountcy, 38–1; *see also*
    Wingfield family
prejudice, 99; against Catholics, 120;
    against wealth and title, 119, 165, 199,
    201; in favour of wealth and title, 28,
    61, 63, 109–10

Pryce-Jones, David, 189, 195; and
    Clarissa, 189, 194
Pytchley Hunt, 11, 28

Queen's Jubilee Nurses, 45
Quorn Hunt, 32, 46

Raine, Kathleen, 85, 165, 169, 173
Rawlings, Margaret (Lady Barlow),
    128–30, 142, 145
Read, Herbert, 67, 85
Red Cross, 45
Redlich, Monica, 56
Rendall, Simon, 195–7
Reynolds, Lorna, 34
Riding, Laura, 68
Robertson, Daniel, 40
Roedean School, Sussex, 17–19
romanticism, 92–3, 102; anti-romantics,
    127
Roper, Anne, 55, 66, 91, 133, 197
Rowse, A.L. (Leslie), 101, 161, 165, 168,
    171–3, 176–8, 187, 192
Royal Dublin Society, 38, 41, 43, 134, 157
Russell, George W., *see* Æ

Sackville-West, Vita, 46, 85, 93, 98–100,
    102, 105, 119, 130–1
St John, Order of, 45
Salkeld, Blánaid and Cecil ffrench, 67
Salmon, Tom, 80, 145, 153
Sandhurst (Royal Military College), 36
Schiff, Violet, 8–9, 15, 47
Scotsman, The, 167, 169, 170–1
Senussi language, 37, 73
shooting, 4–5, 11, 27–31, 80, 89, 100
Sitwell, Sacheverell, 151
Slazenger, Gwen, 131–4, 137, 154,
    160–1, 182, 191
Slazenger, Ralph, 131, 133–4, 160–1, 182
Slazenger, Wendy, 134–6; marriage to
    Mervyn, 134–7; Mervyn divorced, she
    marries Ray Watson, 161, 162–3
Slazenger family, 131–4, 182, 191, 193
Smith, Elizabeth, of Baltiboys, 79, 81
snobbery, 99, 110, 129, 179–80; belated
    awareness of, 186

Soldiers', Sailors' and Airmen's Help
    Society, 45
Solomons, Bethel, 47, 51
Somerhill, 28, 46
Somerville, Edith and Ross, Martin, 202
Southey, Robert, 27
Spain, 137, 179
Standard, The, 38
Starkey, Estella (Solomons), 47
Starkey, James Sullivan, *see* O'Sullivan,
    Seumas
Stephens, James, 47, 55, 56, 62
Sudan, 37
Suez, 49
Sunday Independent, 169, 197
Synge, J.M., 34

Tamborine, Miss, 142, 143
Telford, Joy, 120–2
Temenos, 171
Time and Tide, 103, 116, 119, 130
Times, The, 116, 160, 169, 171, 187, 198
Times Literary Supplement (*TLS*), 85, 103,
    117, 158, 171, 176, 185–7
Toksvig, Signe, 46, 51–3, 56
Trinity College, Dublin, 86
Troubles, The, 33, 37, 133, 154
Turf Club, 120
Tynan, Katherine, 62–3

Vermeer, Jan, 83

War of Independence, 86
Watson, Ray, 161, 162–3
Weidenfeld & Nicolson, 130, 143
Wellesley, Lady Dorothy, 58, 61, 62, 63,
    66, 93–4, 100
West, Rebecca, 151, 154, 167, 176, 181,
    186, 187
Westminster, Hugh Grosvenor
    (Bendor), 2nd Duke of, 10
Westmorland and Cumberland
    Yeomanry, 4–6, 9–10, 14, 181
Whistler, Lawrence, 55
White, Terence de Vere, 158
Wilson, Patsy, 155
Wilson, T. Frederic, 24, 50, 96–7

Wingfield, Anthony, 149, 150, 173, 186, 193

Wingfield, Brian (son of Mervyn and Sybil), 43, 45

Wingfield, Deirdre (cousin), 97–8, 122

Wingfield, Grania (b. 1934, later Langrishe, daughter of Pat and Sheila), 29, 47, 56, 70, 73, 83, 102–3, 105; 154, 202; education, 89–91, 97–8, 186; marriage, 111, 119–22, 134–7; move to Ringlestown, 136–8, 147; provides for her father, 139–40; seeks to build on Camillaun, 145; stays with Sheila, 147, 159, 186, 190; and this book, 142

Wingfield, Guy (son of Pat and Sheila), 72, 73, 74, 91–2, 143, 194–5; in America 91, 96, 136, 143, 148, 178, 194; takes an interest in his ancestry 178–80

Wingfield, Julia, 149, 150, 173

Wingfield, Lewis Strange, 83, 191

Wingfield, Mervyn, 7th Viscount Powerscourt, 40, 83, 190

Wingfield, Mervyn, 8th Viscount Powerscourt (Pat's father), 36, 43, 67, 80–1, 190–1; army service , 36, 41; duty and responsibility, 41; eccentricities, 45; vews, 37, 38

Wingfield, Mervyn 'Pat', 9th Viscount Powerscourt (1905–73), 34, 36, 77–8; according to Sheila, 55–6, 89, 157–8; and Africa, 37, 73–4; appearance 35, 191; army service, 36, 69, 70, 71; prisoner of war, 73–6, 97; character, 56, 64, 74; as father, 89, 149, 194; work, 42, 45, 113; farming at Bellair, 131, 134, 137

Wingfield, Mervyn 'Murphy', 10th Viscount Powerscourt (b. 1935, son of Pat and Sheila), 48, 70, 91, 125, 162, 178; Irish Guards 111; marriage, 134–7, 154;

Wingfield, Sheila née Beddington, Viscountess Powerscourt (1906–92), 11, 23–4; accidents, 150, 163, 181, 183, 194, 197; alcohol, 89, 148, 165, 181, 192; ancestry, 4–9; appearance, 24, 42, 46–7, 191; books, 4, 26, 30, 54, 79, 90; car, 145, 146, 162; character, 124, 131, 135, death, obituaries and burial, 198–9; 138; drugs, 60, 107–8, 122, 145–6; childhood, 12–15; credibility of, 22, 196; diaries, 107–8, 142, 197; duty and responsibility, 43, 44, 154; education, 17–19, 20, 23; T. S. Eliot, 112–13; and Ethel, 157; feelings, 86, 118, 154, 169, 188, 193; generosity, 96, 121, 159; illness, 58–60, 72, 114–15, 142–3, 145, 150, 170, 172, 189, 193; Irishness, 9, 11, 141; Jewishness, 111, 178–81; leisure activities, 9, 11, 24, 27–30, 31, 143, 145–6, 148–9, 150, 155, 167, 181, 187; marriage, 43–4, 89; meanness, 122, 158; as mother, 59, 60, 89–92, 149, 194–5; men friends, 25, 67, 127, 175–6, 181, 183; obscurity, 116, 118, 125, 169, 176, 201; parents, *see* Beddington, Claude, Ethel; Pat, 55–6, 60, 67, 89, 132–4, 138, 139; reading, 4, 19, 20, 50, 59–60, 70; re-tells family history, 178–81; will, 149; wistfulness, 108, 121, 176, 189, 196; Yeats, 66, 127, 156

Works of; *Poems*; 161–2, **205–20**; 'All But Gone From Bermuda', 186; 'Alter Ego', 119; 'An Answer from Delphi', 119; 'Any Weekday in a Small Irish Town', 141, **216–17**; *Beat Drum, Beat Heart*, 69–70, 85–6, 116, **206–7**; almost universally liked, 70, 85, 92, 94, 113; but not quite, 85, 116, 163, 187, 199; read on BBC Radio, 128; 'A Bird', 201, **205**; 'Brigid', 141, **214–15**; 'Cartography', 143–4; 'Chosroe the Second', 116; 'Clonmacnois', 93, 141; 'Darkness', 129, 130, 138, 154, 198, **212–13**; 'Elegy for Certain Friends', 119; 'Epiphany in a Country Church', 106, 127; 'Epitaph', 93; 'The Fantastic Keepsake', 129; 'For My Dead Friends', 130; 'A Frightened

Creature', 175, 181, **219–20**;
'Funerals', 117–19; *God's Nature,
A Guessing Game*, 125–6, 130, 180;
'Hazards', 162, **218–19**; 'History',
93; 'The Hours', 65; 'The Hunter',
103; 'In a Dublin Museum', 141,
216; 'Ireland', 33, 137, **208**; 'The
Journey', 29; 'Keeping House',
171; 'Lazarus', 201; 'The Leaves
Darken', **214**; 'Lines for the
Margin of an Old Gospel', 119,
127; 'A Melancholy Love', 33, 146,
216; 'Names', 18; 'No Entry', 93;
'No Escape from Ireland', 141;
'No Instructions', 188, **220**; 'The
Oath', **217**; 'Odysseus Dying', 52,
65, 67, 94, 126, 137, **205**; 'On Being
of One's Time', 130, 145; 'On
Looking Down a Street', 145, **211**;
'One's Due', 188; 'Origins', 178,
208–10; 'Patriarchs', 130, 156;
'Pitchforks', 162, **215**; 'Poisoned in
Search of the Medicine of
Immortality', 115, 127, 137, **210**;
'Romantic Landscape', 93; 'Sea at
Dalkey', 144; 'Sparrow', **217**; 'A
Tuscan Farmer', 103, 113; 'Venice
Preserved', 113, **211–12**; 'View',
141, 161, **215–16**; 'Village Seasons',
192; 'Waking', 167, 169; 'We Were
Bright Beings', 188, **218**; 'When
Moore Field Was All Grazed',
213; 'Winter', 52, 93, 126, **205**;
'You Who Pass By', 144
Poems, collections; *Poems*, 62, 65,
66–8; *A Cloud Across the Sun*, 93–4;
A Kite's Dinner, 108, 115–19; *The
Leaves Darken*, 143–5; *Her Storms*,
100, 167–9; *Admissions*, 168, 169;
Cockatrice and Basilisk, 184;
Collected Poems, 66, 143, 144, 176,
182–8, 195, 196
Memoirs; *Real People*, 13–14, 24,
48–9, 54, 66, 72–3, 95, 96, 101–2,
103, 129, 149, 151; omissions, 23,
30, 45, 56, 74, 101–02, 178; quoted,

3, 58, 70, 81, 88; *Sun Too Fast*,
11–12, 20, 24, 110, 151–3, 155–7,
158–9, 181; omissions, 109, 157;
quoted, 23, 27, 35, 66, 83, 99, 107,
112, 138, 142; *Ladder to the Loft*,
140, 192, 195–7
Wingfield, Sybil, Lady Powerscourt
(wife of 8th Viscount), 41–2, 43, 45,
78, 80
Wingfield family, 38–41, 82, 99, 154,
190, 194
Wingfield homes: Bellair, Co. Offaly, 7,
10, 13, 33, 67, 77–80, 81, 106, 138;
Camillaun, Co. Galway, 145, 150; Old
School House, Godden Green, Kent,
62, 67; Stonepitts, Kent, 46, 50, 52, 55;
Powerscourt, 35, 37, 41, 44–45, 81–4,
123–4, 133–4; Ringlestown House,
Co. Meath, 136–7, 147, 160, 166; Tara
Beg, Co. Meath, 139–40, 154; Palma
au Lac, 139–40, 145, 150, 163, 170,
181; visitors 175, 186, 189, 190, 194,
197; Pink Beach, Bermuda, 146–7;
Valdemere, Paget, 70
women, 3, 33, 60; and the Big House,
88–90, 103; and careers, 33, 103, 123,
160; novelists, 8, 19, 50, 202; poets, 68,
169, 173, 202; reading secretly, 26
Woodham-Smith, Cecil, 151, 154, 164,
165, 167
Woolf, Virginia, 28, 46, 53, 55, 77, 80,
98, 177
Wright, Doreen, 'Dar' (Pat's sister),
74–5, 77, 78, 192–4;
Wright, Susan, 122
Wyndham, Francis, 176, 185

Yeats, W.B., 47, 50, 51, 54, 61–6, 94–5;
and Lady Wellesley, 93–4;
'Meditations in Time of Civil War',
86; and Sheila, 144; her stories of him,
66, 127, 156; his opinion of her, 58, 63,
65; their correspondence, 69, 195; his
opinion of Wilfred Owen, 61
yeomanry, 9–10, 14
Young, Kenneth, 116–17